Creating the Semantic Web with RDF

Professional Developer's Guide

Creating the Semantic Web with RDF

Johan Hjelm

Wiley Computer Publishing

John Wiley & Sons, Inc.

NEW YORK • CHICHESTER • WEINHEIM • BRISBANE • SINGAPORE • TORONTO

Publisher: Robert Ipsen
Editor: Carol Long
Managing Editor: Angela Smith
Text Design & Composition: D&G Limited, LLC

This book is printed on acid-free paper. 

Published by John Wiley & Sons, Inc.

Published simultaneously in Canada.

Library of Congress Cataloging-in-Publication Data:

Hjelm, Johan.
Creating the semantic Web with RDF: professional developer's guide / Johan Hjelm.
p. cm. – (Professional developer's guide series)
ISBN 0-471-40259-1 (pbk.:alk. paper)
1. Web site development. 2. Cataloging of computer network resources. 3. Metadata. 4. Artificial intelligence. I. Title. II. Series.

TK5105.888 .H55 2001
005.2 '76–dc21

2001017848

Printed in the United States of America.

10 9 8 7 6 5 4 3 2 1

Professional Developer's Guide Series

Other titles in the series:

Advanced Palm Programming by Steve Mann and Ray Rischpater, ISBN 0-471-39087-9

WAP Servlets by John L. Cook, III, ISBN 0-471-39307-X

Java 2 Micro Edition by Eric Giguere, ISBN 0-471-39065-8

Scripting XML and WMI for Microsoft® SWL Server™ 2000 by Tobias Martinsson, ISBN 0-471-39951-5

GPRS and 3G Wireless Applications by Christoffer Andersson, ISBN 0-471-41405-0

Contents

Preface

It may sound strange, but despite the billion-plus pages on the World Wide Web, there is too little information there. There is no information about the information; all Web pages are exactly alike in the eyes of a search robot. Imagine a library where all books have the same text on the cover, and the only catalogs are compiled by photocopying the books, cutting up the copies, and arranging the words in order of frequency. That is the status of the World Wide Web today.

There is a simple way of doing something about this, which is by using metadata to describe the library—creating a catalog and making the authors describe their own books. Metadata can be embedded in HTML or XML pages, it can be centrally linked, and it can be used to select the items you need. Why do you have to browse through hundreds of pages about irrelevant topics when you search on the Web? Because the computer does not have a way to identify what is relevant—neither what you consider relevant, nor what the author thinks should go on top. Using the systems, datastructures, and ideas in this book will help you fix that.

When you have a large set of data items and a way to describe their relationships, you have a database. The Resource Description Framework (RDF) promises to make the Web not just one big heap of text, but a place where it is actually possible to identify which pages are more important than others when you search, and to exchange the contexts of the metainformation (to make sure you and your neighbor mean the same thing when he says potato and you say potatoe). Levels of importance express a relation. Database management is a well-established discipline, but it cannot work with the unstructured text on the Web.

The key to this is operations on the metadata. If you remember your high school algebra, you can do about as well as intelligent agents today, although the programming of them has turned out to be fiendishly complex—mostly due to the fact that researchers, in the hunt for the ultimate solution, try to make them do everything. Anthropomorphizing computers does not make them simpler to use, actually. As I have been writing this book, I have become convinced that we do not need intelligent agents. We need stupid agents. The KISS (Keep It Simple, Stupid) principle applies to everything that involves people, and even more so to intelligent agent design. Nobody can expect a Web user to understand how an ontology is different from an orthodontist.

This book tries to explain a set of XML-based technologies that at least purport to be simpler than their predecessors. The future will decide whether it's true, but I believe so. And I also believe it is possible to design systems that make use of them, and scale the systems using pieces of the advances in artificial intelligence (AI) from the last 50 years or so.

There are two parts to the Semantic Web: The semantics, which come from structured markup and the application of AI technologies; and the Web, which is not a technology so much as a social phenomenon. The purpose of this book is to highlight the technologies that you can use to create a new Web that is more convenient for the user than the old one, and bring about the same revolution that the original Web brought.

If you add metadata to your pages, you will be able to create a more intelligent Web that does not overwhelm your users with information, but helps them select from it. This will probably not happen in the public Web first, since it is rapidly becoming its own legacy application, what the WAP Forum calls the "classic Web." Instead, the future of metadata, at least in the short run, is Intranets. I have given some examples, but it is really up to you to build the systems. Trial and error is the best experimental platform, but making your company more efficient should be an excellent motivator, at least for your manager to sign off on your buying this book.

Disclaimer

The content of this book represents the position and opinions of the author. It does not represent the position or ideas of Ericsson or any other current or previous employer, nor those of my publisher, John Wiley & Sons.

Who Is This Book For?

This book is intended for anyone who wants to understand how metadata can be used to make retrieval and management of information better. It is about the fundamentals, so if you read it, you should have more than a passing interest in using the technology or implementing applications. You may be a programmer (although it is not a programmer's book), or you may be a Webmaster looking for bells and whistles. Or you may be looking for a way to provide your users with a better experience—my favorite reader.

It is, however, not a cookbook for you to cut recipes from that will magically make your Web pages semantic. You have to think for yourself. Either way, you need to have a clear understanding about how the Web works, and you need to have been wondering how it could be improved. Well, here is the answer.

Acknowledgments

As with all books, this is not the result of the imagination of the author. The story I have to tell was based on the work of a lot of people. This book is dedicated to all of them. The most important ones are: my Chinese staff (Zhu-san, Yu-san, and Peng-san), for forcing me to explain. My former colleagues at the W3C (TimBL, Ralph, and Eric especially), who are the brains behind the ideas in this book, even if they can not explain them. My colleagues at Ericsson, especially Erik Svedmark, Rolf Leidhammar, and Peter Arnby, for their unwavering, if at times somewhat bemused, support. My friends in the CC/PP working group and the UAProf drafting committee, especially Hidetaka Ohto, Graham Klyne, Lalitha Surayanarayana, Sandeep Singhal, and Franklin Reynolds. All those others who have helped me understand, especially Greg FitzPatrick. Those who helped me with reviews, especially Elena Neira (RDF Schema *is* a context interchange format!), Mikael Nilsson, and Peter Stark. And to Carol Long, the publisher, with more excuses than usual.

CHAPTER 1

Metadata, Resources, and the Resource Description Framework

This book is about a technology that lets you tailor and filter content; create ad hoc portals; build profiles of users, information services, and objects; and generally give the user a richer, custom-fit experience. It is about how you can build metadata systems, especially systems that use profiles to create information services. Profiles, of course, are nothing but structured metadata descriptions, so they are not really remarkable in themselves. The remarkable thing happens when you start applying profiles to create services.

The Web is less than ten years old, and chat rooms are rife with complaints about the World Wide Wait. While there are some companies who deliver excellent service, most do a really bad job of it. The reason is not just that they do not understand what adds value, it is also a consequence of the enormous amount of data on the Web.

You may well wonder what this has to do with wireless. But wireless access to Web information has proven to be not just the trigger for new types of devices and presentation formats, but for new types of information services as well. There is also a theoretical foundation: The more restricted the properties of a device, the less complicated grammars it can handle. And RDF is a very simple grammar.

The way we use wireless devices is profoundly different from the way we use desktop computers, even though the information is the same. Building transactional services on top of the information requires that you know more about both the information and the user than the services geared toward passive browsing. This is something we already see on the Web, but the real catalyst has been iMode in Japan and Wireless Application Protocol (WAP) in Europe, which have set off a landslide of creativity among developers.

Metadata enables search engines to get better results with fewer hits, making searches more precise and tailored to the users' needs. Metadata enables personalization—the current silver bullet of marketing prophets. Metadata lets you filter out information you do not want (or that you do not want to reach someone). It is really simple to add to a Web site. What is missing is software and services that use it, but those are coming too.

However, this way of using metadata is scary to old-economy Chief Information Officers (CIOs) and Web designers. You are giving control to the users. You are giving information away, and it might decrease the number of hits on your pages.

If your company still measures success on the Web in number of hits, fire the Webmaster and the CIO. What matters is not how many people pass your store, but how many people enter and buy. Fewer users may get the information, but they are the right users, and the conversion rate among them will be higher. The irritation of users who get your page when they were searching for something completely different will also decrease, increasing your goodwill by default.

Metadata is about relationships. It is about descriptions of resources, which in this context are things which provide services: servers, database engines, Webcams, anything that is providing information. When you write a table in HyperText Markup Language (HTML), you have a set of relationships in mind that describes the rows and columns. If this could be formalized in a machine-readable language, the system could use those relationships, too. HTML version 0.9 was very poor in most respects, compared to HTML 4.0. Yet it contained the core of what was necessary to start off the industry. In many respects, Resource Description Framework (RDF) is the same today.

The Web today runs on HTML, but it has become an old technology that can only take you so far. You need new technology to enable new services. Indeed, the traditional Web is proving to be a legacy that is hard to overcome. The way information services are used and deployed in the new environment requires a different kind of service than that which is available on the traditional Web: a type of service that is more convenient, easier to use, and faster than the old Web. And, of course, usable and useful on the old Web as well.

RDF was developed at the intersection between the knowledge management world and the library metadata world. It is a graph system layered on top of Extensible Markup Language (XML), and thus has two roots: Directed graphs, which are probably more familiar to database programmers; and XML, which is certainly familiar to the large contingent of programmers who have learned it in the last few years.

The XML aspect is important for several reasons. XML is as close to a global, universal data format as we come today (because it uses Unicode, it is more universal than ASCII, which is restricted to the Latin alphabet). How to handle it in databases, how to transport it over the network, and how to build applications that use it are all well understood. And it has a large installed base, with plenty of applications.

RDF builds on XML to create descriptions, and descriptions are metadata: data about data. It can be very hard to understand, and there are basically two ways of explaining it: As object properties, or as profiles. Which is more useful to you depends on your background.

First, let us start with the concept of descriptions. A description of a document is a document in its own right. Documents are nothing but a sequence of fragments, elements of information, and the order and structure of the fragments constitute a metadescription of the document. Of course, there can be other descriptions as well, such as what the document is about, how it should be presented in different formats, and anything that pertains to the document but is not the document itself.

In RDF, you always identify the object you are describing by a unique address, the Universal Resource Identifier. The descriptions can be object identifiers as well (URIs). This means that in object-oriented terms, you can describe which classes an object belongs to—and then compare the listing of classes for this particular object to other objects—and so find out what they have in common.

The descriptions are also data. Data about data is data, too. And metadata is nothing but data about data. It can be embedded in the document, or exist separately from it, as a document or as headers in a protocol, for instance. But there is nothing that limits the use of metadata to documents. It is possible to describe any object using metadata. And anything can be an object, from the collection of all information in the universe down to the letters on this page.

When the metadata about the object is structured to provide a description, and the structure is common for all instances of the same type of object, it is a profile. The profile can have different values for different instances, but the structure is always the same. So, all the books in the library can be described using the same library cards, but each library card will have different content, even though they all include book title, author, and so forth.

What falls under one classification to one man, however, is something else to another. No object falls unambiguously into a single classification. Not even in physics can we find unambiguous ways to describe the objects we talk about. What is a quark? Is an electron really a wave or a particle? And it just keeps going uphill from there.

Language, from the point of view of the language philosopher, is based on a social contract between the sender and receiver. If I am speaking Japanese and you know only English, you will not receive the message I am sending. If I am speaking Japanese grammar with English vocabulary, your understanding will also be seriously impeded. There has to be agreement about the syntax (the combination of the words), the vocabulary (the mapping between symbol and concept), and the semantics (the meaning of the vocabulary). RDF is a set of rules for creating semantics, and RDF Schema is a way of creating vocabularies.

In practice, however, you rarely need to get that philosophical. You do have to recognize that classifications are necessarily arbitrary and that the names of concepts are inherently meaningless. Any knowledge representation scheme will have to take this arbitrariness into account.

Representing knowledge in a computerized format has been high fashion in the computer industry for a long time. Knowledge representation systems are an important aspect of metadata, but they have a big inherent weakness. While they are mostly geared toward the scientific domain, they assume they are general, both in vocabulary and structure. Of course, they are not, and while they have come up with a lot of valid results in the field of intelligent agents, the work still suffers from the assumptions that there are universal ways of representing knowledge within one, centrally determined framework. This is most evident in the classification schemes used in the library world. Classifying, as they do, information objects that represent anything, they do have presumptions to be general. But they are really specific, not in the least culture-specific. A library in Sweden is not classified in the same way as a library in the United States.

RDF addresses this by providing for a decentralized scheme. Using the same structure, it allows anyone to create their own vocabulary. This enables you to take the good things from the artificial intelligence community (intelligent agents and reasoning systems) and apply the good things from the Web (the transport system, the data representation, the decentralization and independence from a particular system). This intersection is the topic for this book.

What Is RDF?

RDF is a format to make assertions—statements that are intended to point something out. It has two roots: metadata and knowledge representation. The concepts do overlap, but the technologies which have been developed in the two fields, and the understanding of them, are very different.

Library communities have struggled to come up with a universal format for describing books that can be used in electronic catalogs. The result is the Dublin Core format (named after Dublin, Ohio, and not Dublin, Ireland). It is basically a set of attribute names and rules for which values they can take. The attributes are limited to those that make sense in the world of books, and not for a more general set of knowledge representation, or even for magazines.

The knowledge representation community, on the other hand, was the hot thing of the late 1980's, expected to become the next huge thing in the software industry. It fizzled for different reasons, but they came at the problem from a different direction. An expert system is a set of rules, into which you can fit knowledge as input, and get different knowledge sets as output (for instance, if the input is the symptoms of a patient, you can get a recommendation for treatment as output). But this means that you want to find a way of representing any and all knowledge that fits into the system.

This brings a different set of problems. If you just think about metadata within one single domain, it makes sense to have a table with the attribute names in one column, and the attribute values in the other. But if you want to compare the attributes to something else, how do you know what they represent? What is the unit of measurement if thickness is 1, for instance? Inches or centimeters? Or millimeters? Or meters? Or miles? This seemingly simple problem made the Mars Surveyor crash, and it can easily make someone else misunderstand what you want to present, especially if you want to present it to a computer program. A computer is stupid, and if you do not tell it exactly what you want to say, you cannot expect the receiving software to take any relevant actions.

RDF, the Resource Description Framework, was developed by the World Wide Web Consortium (W3C) to create a format for making assertions that leverage the XML format to represent and transport information. XML, however, is not a markup language; it is a set of rules for creating markup languages. I will talk more about this in Chapter 2, but suffice to say that using XML brings us as near to a universal data format as is possible nowadays.

However, XML gives only the rules for how the byte strings should be cobbled together to form a coherent whole, which can be used by a widely spread set of computer programs. How an XML data set should be interpreted is determined by the Document Type Description (DTD), which essentially creates a schema for an application of XML. But XML does not say anything about the information itself, only the way it is structured.

The level above XML determines how the information is interpreted, and this is where RDF exists. It builds to a very large extent on experiences from the knowledge representation community, creating a way of comparing different knowledge representations by making the user define them in a specific way and enabling the comparison to use a format which is defined in a branch of mathematics called graph theory. RDF is a way to express relations between objects, something XML does not allow you to do.

Describing Data: The Concept of Graphs

A relation between two objects can be described in many ways; one way is to draw on a piece of paper two circles representing the objects, and a line between them representing the relation. This is actually the beginning of a well-established analysis method for applications, using Unified Modeling Language (UML) to describe the relations. However, once you have established a description of the relationships, it is possible to do much more with them.

A description of a Web site is like the morning promenade of a German philosopher (not because "neither can whistle"). These two far-flung concepts are connected in that the same theory can be used to relate the description of one Web site to another.

First, the description of the Web site. There are a seemingly (if not actually) infinite number of ways to describe a Web site. However, they all have one thing in common: Each describes a Web site. (In case it describes an object that is not a Web site, the logic is the same.) The descriptions can be broken down into logical elements, as follows: Instead of writing "this is my really fun site that talks about lots of great stuff that I found in other places on the Web and that I really liked," you can write "site has property=fun (according to: you); property=links (to: stuff from the Web, appreciated by: you)." You are describing an object (the site) that has properties (fun, links) that have values (that you think it was fun, that the stuff is from the Web). So far, anyone familiar with object-oriented analysis will not have discovered anything remarkable.

If you draw your description on paper, you can draw it as dots connected with lines: In mathematics, this is called a graph. Since the description can be thought of as a graph, the branch of mathematics that includes graph theory—topology—can be applied to it. I will take this reasoning a little further, but I will not try to give you a real introduction into graph theory, because that would go too far.

The simplest graph you can imagine is two dots connected with a line. If the dots represent something, they can be nodes, and the line connecting them an arrow. If the line is an arrow, it has a direction. The Web is a directed graph in which the nodes are documents, and the arrows are the links between them (because a link has a single direction, at least in HTML). As a matter of fact, the entire Web is a big directed graph, because the links are unidirectional (they go from one document to another). This is changing with the introduction of bi-directional links in HTML 4.0 and Xlink/Xpointer, but the Web as you know it is a one-way street. Links go only forward, not back.

If you add attributes to the arrow—called an arc in mathematician-speak—you are creating a labeled directed graph. This is the format that RDF uses to describe resources.

A set of documents which has a set of properties can be described as nodes in a network, with arrows (properties) pointing at the values of the properties. Since each property applies to only one object, this is a directed graph, a diagram that you can follow in one direction only. The arrows do not have to go in one direction (but there has to be one arrow per direction). For a simple graph, this is not complicated. Here is what the statement, "Napoleon was emperor," looks like as a directed graph:

Napoleon → emperor

(As a matter of fact, I am cheating. What it says is "Napoleon has the property Emperor." It says nothing about the temporal aspect, that he actually is no longer emperor). If you are familiar with object-oriented programming, you will see that this is the same as the Booch methodology analysis statement that the object Napoleon has the property Emperor. And indeed, RDF is a format to describe the properties of objects, which are identified by their Uniform Resource Identifiers (URIs). You do not, however, have to subscribe to any of the mysticism often surrounding object-oriented programming. The objects here are not programming objects, they are information objects, which is different. Information objects do not follow the same rules as programming objects. For instance, they cannot do anything (they do not have methods associated with them), and the inheritance of properties between classes is not at all as clear-cut.

RDF is primarily intended to describe information objects, but it is not really restricted to that. It can be used to describe anything that has a URI, which in principle can be any object. And because objects are related to our perception ("What constitutes an object?" is a question that we will not go into here, but it is one that philosophers struggle with), anything we can perceive or imagine can be an object. And provided it can be given an identifier, it can be described mathematically. Provided that identifier can be a URI, it can be described in RDF, as it can then be a resource in the sense of RDF.

The graph above can also be formulated as a triple of values: The resource being described, the property name, and the property value. RDF describes how to take the triples into XML, and how to do this in a way that maintains the integrity of the graph.

The W3C runs an excellent validation service based on the Simple RDF Parser and Compiler (SiRPAC). Figure 1.1 is an example of what the graph would look like, as well as the RDF associated with it.

To a mathematician, the paper drawing and the mathematical formulation of the graph are the same thing, just formatted a little differently. This means that to a mathematician, an XML encoding of the graph is just another form of expressing it. You can interchange the different description formats; they are

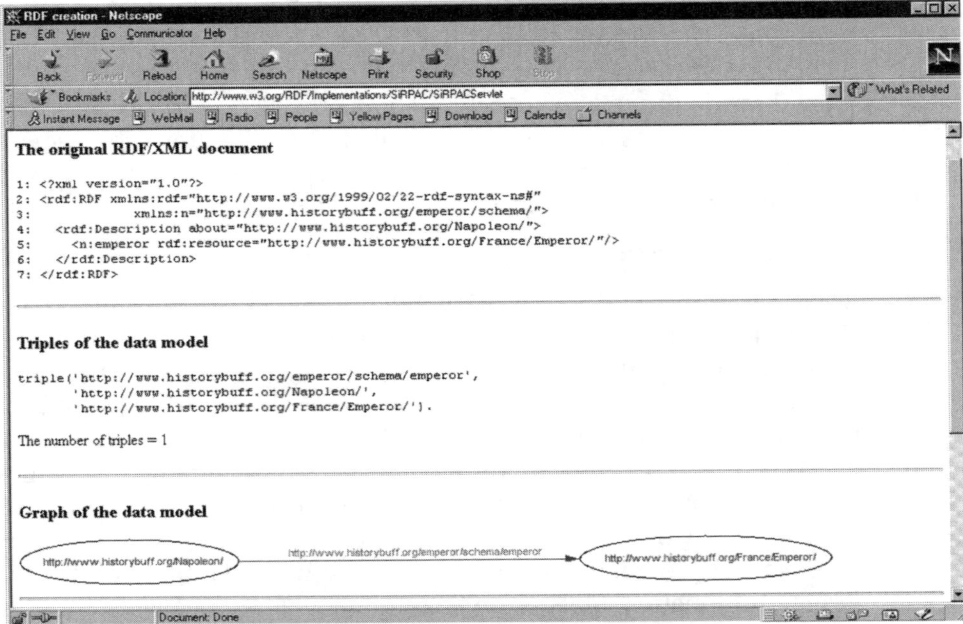

Figure 1.1 The statement, “Napoleon is emperor,” in RDF.

equivalent from a mathematical standpoint. And because programming is a way of creating mathematical models of actions, this also means that to a program, they are equivalent.

To a mathematician, graphs are very rarely unique. They can be transformed into other graphs, and operations can be conducted on them. Algebraic operations are used to model computer software. This means that there is a well-established way of going from the graph format of RDF to a way of handling it in the computer.

The more you want to say, however, the more complex it becomes. A graph does not have to be two-dimensional, either; it can have n dimensions and be arbitrarily complex. Of course, this slows down processing and decreases the readability. But it is possible to express quite complex relationships as graphs. Here is a graph of the statement that Napoleon first was a lieutenant, then a general, then a consul, and finally emperor:

Napoleon → lieutenant → general → consul → emperor

Of course, the graph could be drawn differently. This graph actually does not refer back to Napoleon, but refers from one concept to the other.

There is an entire mathematical theory associated with graphs, how they should be handled, what transformations are allowed and possible, and so on. The operations you can do on RDF descriptions are described in graph theory.

Since the XML description is just another way of expressing a graph, it is possible to do exactly the same operations on the XML description as on the graph drawn on paper. It is somewhat complicated to go back to the graph from the XML representation, however, because the same XML representation can be drawn as several different graphs (all graphs which have the same format are the same to a mathematician).

Because you are working with triples of information that contain relationships to each other, you can also filter out information with a much higher degree of precision than alternate technologies. If you have an attribute-value-table, you can filter out information based on the value of the attributes. If another site does not share the same attributes and values, you cannot use information from that site in your filtering process. However, if both your site and the other site express the information about yourself in a format that relates the statements to you, you will be able to filter out information to create a much more precise selection of information for the user. This can, for instance, be applied to a site which creates a home page from two different sites (what might be termed a personal portal) based on the user's preferences. It can be used to describe the copyright restrictions you have set on the use of the information, and it can be used to describe the relationship of your site with the site providing the personal portal.

As you can understand, whether you call the arcs *Evidence A* or *a horsetail* does not matter to the underlying graph. However, the properties of the elements can change the graph. You need to declare what elements you are going to use, and which properties they are going to have. These properties will change the way you can make statements. They will change how the terms interrelate, both in the current graph and with elements in other graphs. You need to declare the elements and their properties, and the structure in which they can occur, the schema of the graph.

Schema in the present context refers to a data structure. It has gained that use in the database industry, where it describes the structure of a database table: the columns and their headings, and what restrictions there may be on the data in the columns.

Both the properties and the RDF elements are objects in their own right, and can be the subjects of statements in themselves. This means that there can be graphs chained to the graph you look at orthogonally; or in any number of dimensions, because to a mathematician, the paper drawing is not necessarily the clearest description.

RDF Vocabularies

A schema does not define only the data structure for your graph. It also defines the terms you can use in it, the vocabulary of the description. For instance, the schema provides property names and property values, as well as constraints on them that enable their use in calculation. To a computer, a vocabulary is just a set of objects with specialized properties: one word can only be a figure, another can only be five characters long, and so on. A computer cannot have a relation to the vocabulary as such. It is silly that I have to point this out, but the anthropomorphization that follows on the use of *intelligent* for agents means that users tend to ascribe to them properties that they do not have. Large parts of this book will be devoted to demystifying the relationship between agents and data.

The artificial intelligence field is important in many aspects, not in the least because it serves to identify the problem space. There are four problems that, in translation from concept to practice, have dogged intelligent agents:

- Data encoding
- Data transport
- Resource discovery
- Drawing conclusions based on data

The artificial intelligence work has largely concentrated on the last one, and no practical systems exist that solve the first three problems in a distributed fashion. Using the technologies developed on the Web, however, all four of the problems become simple. Applying technologies from the World Wide Web to artificial intelligence systems solves problems that have dogged researchers for the last twenty-five years, at least.

There have been a number of vocabularies that attempted to describe specialized domains before RDF was invented. Most of them are specialized vocabularies defined for an area of artificial intelligence. There are a few examples of other types of vocabularies where an attempt has been made at formalizing a terminology. (There are probably as many terminologies as there are disciplines, and most specialized domains of knowledge have their own terminologies: Engineers talk about nuts and bolts in a particular way, whereas a theater director will have a precise vocabulary to describe the action on the stage.) The examples include the rules for games, which are formalized very precisely to determine which types of clubs are allowed in golf, or how you can touch the ball in soccer. These rule books contain very precise definitions of the different aspects of a game. But they are not concerned with information objects; if we were talking about a sports service, it might make sense to define the vocabulary in terms of the rule book for the game, for instance.

RDF gives you a format for describing information objects, but it does not say anything about what terms you should use to make the statements that describe the objects, and what those terms mean. It does, however give you a format for the terms and their formalized descriptions. It gives you the graph structure, but not the names and properties of the nodes.

Knowledge is always inherently based in the experiences of the user, and if it is expressed in a formal structure, it is important to describe it in such a way that one instance of a term does not have a completely different meaning than another. Here, we come back to the ambiguity of descriptions. For instance, the term *suit* means *a set of clothing* in one case, and *a set of playing cards bearing the same symbol* in another; it is very hard to know which suit I am talking about if I do not declare which domain it is in. In conversation, I usually do so implicitly. But if the word occurs without any supporting information, there has to be a declaration about what it is supposed to mean. Once I have explained to you that a suit is a piece of clothing, you will go happily to court to receive your suit. You, however, know that in a courtroom, a suit is not a piece of clothing, but a lawsuit. A computer does not. It will assume that they are the same thing, if you do not tell it otherwise. Remember, computers are really stupid, and one of the biggest mistakes of the artificial intelligence movement was to overestimate the intelligence potential of computers and to underestimate the enormous amount of learning required to think like a person.

Because computers are stupid, you have to be very careful to define terms in a totally unambiguous way. In RDF, the declaration of the terms you will use in the assertions (the statements about the objects) is done in a separate document called a RDF Schema, and in a specific language (the RDF Schema language). The schema also has to be accessible at the URI you use to declare the namespace for the elements you are using.

One of the interesting things about RDF is that a central repository is not needed, because every time an unknown term is encountered, the RDF processor has to download the schema in order to make sense of the term. However, if there is an agreement among several actors to use a specific set of terms for a given domain of knowledge, the RDF processor will not need to look up a new schema every time, decreasing traffic in the network and speeding up processing. This is the case in the User Agent Profile (UAProf) vocabulary for CC/PP, for instance (a vocabulary describing client devices in the Composite Capability/Preferences Profile format).

Scenarios for Metadata

Metadata-based profiles can be used to change the services a Web site provides, enable new types of services, and allow developers to program presentation and tailoring of data. Metadata in libraries (the most common example) is used to find books; for example, you can search for the books in the card catalog by author or by classification (according to the Dewey decimal system, or some other system). But metadata does not have to be limited to one type of description. You can also find out which books are oversize and are placed on a separate shelf. Knowing which metadata will become the most useful is impossible to say in advance. To the librarian, the book classification is the most important. To the historian of the printing industry, the size of the book, its age, and the number of pages will be the points of interest. It is also hard to say what is data and what is metadata. The distinction may depend on how the data is used.

Now, regard the book as an object, and the information about it as an information object. A book has a number of properties, such as whether the book is available or not, which language it is in, where it is in the library, who has recently borrowed it, and so on. Those properties—the attributes of the book (what determines its *bookness*) and the values of those attributes—are all part of the information object.

Metadata applications are similar even when used in different ways. The underlying information structures are the same, irrespective of what is done with them when they are presented to the user. This means that there are potentially an infinite number of applications, which can cover any area in the universe. Of course, it is not possible to describe all of them in one book, but it is possible to describe the general principles behind them. And so, let us look at a few scenarios.

The Library Visit

The library community already uses metadata to a large extent; indeed, the library community has been driving the development of metadata technologies. The library card catalog is probably the best-known example of metadata in existence, and also the one with the best-established pedigree.

Lisa Simms, for instance, is studying at the University of Hawaii to be a teacher. Today, she needs to find a book by the French pedagogue Cèlestin Freinet, famous in Europe for his development of a participatory school system. She switches on her computer and looks up Freinet in the library search engine.

It turns out that there are no books by him in the library, so she turns to the university search engine, and at the same time types in her query into her regular search engine.

The regular search engine found a number of hits on phrenology, the “science” of divining people’s characteristics by the bumps on their heads.

The university search engine, which classifies the sites by their content, does not list the phrenology sites; it does list a number of sites in French, which she cannot read. She curses herself that she did not think to turn on the language preference in her browser, so that it could match her language preference with the language of the Web site.

It turns out that the Graduate School of Education at the University of California, Berkeley, had a class on Freinet last year. Not only does the system tell her that one of his books is available in French from UC Berkeley and in English from UC Irvine, it also provides a link to a site set up by a student in the Berkeley class last year as part of a project to use computers in a Freinet school. The student's site was not even listed by Lisa's regular search engine, but she found all the information she needed because it was classified in such a way that the university search engine could find it.

Along with her search results, she gets to see an advertisement from the French bookstore chain FNAC to buy a Freinet book and have it shipped tomorrow, with the chance to win a trip to Paris for two. Tempted as she is, she would not be able to read it, so instead she borrows it from UC Irvine.

Dynamic Yellow Pages

Lara Mann is looking for a grooming service for her poodles. As a Los Angeles stylist, she realizes the importance of her dogs' image for her own image. She does not have the time to take care of them herself, however, so she needs to find a dog stylist close to her home. She takes a look in the yellow pages.

Under "Dog Care" there are a number of stylists, including three on the street where Lara lives. It does not say when they are open, however, nor whether they are any good. Two of them have very nice advertisements, but Lara had a horrendous experience with a hairdresser once, and she knows better than to trust advertisements. She is a member of the Poodle Owners Club of San Joaquin Valley, so she sends out an e-mail to her friends and asks whether they have any experience with the stylists near her.

While she is online, she also finds a couple of Web sites with poodle information, featuring consumer reviews of stylists. After reading a few of them (although they are all anonymous), she gets a really bad feeling about one of the stylists (who had the biggest advertisement). But when she gets the answers to her e-mails, the other ladies are overwhelmingly positive.

Poor Lara does not know what she should think. How is that stylist really? Whom should she trust? She ends up taking her poodles to one of the others, who colors them bright red instead of cool pink, and cuts Soviet flags into their coats as well as Stalin mustaches. She regrets not choosing the stylist she was doubtful about, who meanwhile has given her neighbors' poodle an incredibly tasteful treatment.

Of course, she can do all this today, but there is no standardized and simple way to link all the pieces together. How do you determine which e-mail talk to trust about which stylist? There is no way to way to link annotations to objects to get the opinions of others attached to the Web site.

Position-Dependent Information

Charles Rowland is lost in a foreign city. It's his first visit to the fascinating city of Yokohama, but he must have gotten turned around on his way from the gigantic Ferris wheel in the harbor to Izeyake Mall. In Japan, houses are numbered in the order that they are built, and there are no street names. Not much help. Looking at the signs on the street, he still cannot figure out where he is, because he cannot read a word of Japanese.

Luckily, he brought his PDA with a GSM receiver. Not only does it have a map with a big red dot in the middle showing where he is when he switches it on; he can also type in the name of the hotel, and the PDA shows him which direction it is. As he walks toward the hotel, the PDA continuously searches for sites on the Internet, compares their positional relevance with his position, and about lunchtime points him to a very nice little restaurant.

If there had not been any such descriptions, he would have been lost. And of course, he doesn't know that the map is generated from a description of the city and presented to him as a vector graphic, which makes it easy to zoom in, double-click on a famous place, and get a video clip.

Corporate Knowledge Representation

You have probably wondered who in your company is the great expert on a certain subject, or where on the intranet the configuration files for the video projector are. An intranet suffers from the same problems as the Internet: It is hard to find information, and when you do, you do not know what is relevant. Since business success is about getting an information advantage, finding information fast is critical to getting ahead of your competitors. And not just finding information, but finding the right information. Selecting the most relevant pieces in the enormous cloud of information that enters your company every day is critical to keeping it competitive.

On the other hand, in a company, this is easier to fix. There are no standard formats for data on the Internet, but you can easily enforce them inside your firewall. Or, as is likely to be more popular, you can enforce a specific metadata structure for certain types of information. This will enable your company to make sense of its own information faster, and relate it to external information better. Not only can it lead to enormous savings because you will not have to reinvent the wheel several times; it can also help you relate your information to that of your competitors, and discover how your company should develop to do a better job of servicing your customers.

Take Helen Farnsworth, who is a salesperson at historybuff.org, a company that publishes interactive games based on historical battles and other events. In reality, it is a division of major games maker Arcaditopia, and this is exactly why Helen is in trouble. She has a customer who is interested in their new game for a nationwide chain, but she cannot answer his questions, especially not about Elba. She can't answer mainly because the questions are about the historical accuracy of the game, and while she can tell the customer everything about the shelf space the game will take, and how much memory it will use, she does not know who beat Napoleon at Waterloo.

So she does a quick intranet search. The regular search engine gives her several hundred answers, among them Napoleon Jones in the accounting department. She searches for individuals with knowledge about Napoleon the historic person, and throws in Elba to make sure. Her meta-search engine helps her to find Herbert Wollmeyer III, the resident expert on the Napoleonic wars. And his "100 quick questions about Napoleon" tells her everything the customer asks about Elba (like, it's a part of Italy). And the customer buys 100,000 games.

The systems ribed in these quick scenarios get information that is customized in some sense. They get you an information set adapted not just to your personal profile (such as your credit rating), but also to the device—mobile phone, PDA, or PC—that you are using. Everything I describe above, you can get from the Web today. But you can get it only from isolated systems, and you can only use it for your PC, as a rule.

The implementation of these systems is very different from the traditional computer systems you are used to, however. They are generating information based on profiles, and creating optimized profiles based on the different profiles that are being received from the client, describing it and its situation. Using RDF, of course.

What Do You Need to Do?

As a site owner, there are a few things you need to do to create metadata for your site. As of today, there are few tools that let you insert the data automatically, especially if you are using XHTML. However, a summer intern and some clever programming will give you a metadata system that can be used in automating the insertion of metadata in your site. Meanwhile, there are a few things you can do:

Analyze your information. Analysis of information is a special discipline within knowledge management, with well-established methods and models. You do not need to go that far, however. It is enough if you do a quick and dirty subjective analysis (i.e., what do you think your site is?)

Determine what you want to say. Is your goal that people who download your pages should be aware of who created it, or is it that they should find you easier with a search engine? Or both? Is your target group other companies in your business, or do you want to reach anyone and everyone on the Web?

Classify your information. Remarkably few sites (even the do-gooders of the Web, the W3C) distinguish between officially published documents, e-mail lists that are archived, and temporary pages that are work items. Classifying your documents according to a pre-established vocabulary will let users find the documents on your site that are most relevant. *Determine which vocabulary suits you.* Once you have an understanding of you want to say, you can determine which formal vocabulary you should use to describe your site.

Create the statements. Having determined that, you can create the statements that describe your site. This can be done using any one of a number of different tools.

Insert the statements in your documents. Once you have created the statements, you can insert them into your documents (or templates, if you run a database-driven site). And then, users will be able to work with your information in a way that is much more satisfying to them than today.

CHAPTER 2

Using RDF to Annotate Text and Photos

RDF can be used to describe anything. This makes it hard to demonstrate, because you cannot point to a specific use case. However, the W3C has developed two different applications that demonstrate how it works: annotation of text, and annotation of photographs. Syndication of data is also demonstrated by the O'Reilly Meerkat channel, which uses RDF Site Summary (RSS).

Annotations are a natural fit for RDF. Not only do they create a statement (the annotation itself) which is about a document, they also enable you to relate the statement to the author, the time, the purpose, and other information. In the case of photographs, the annotations can relate to camera quality, for instance. This also means that the information can be presented in different ways, depending on the author, the authors affiliation, and so on. This can be particularly useful in an intranet, in which you can create different annotation views on depending on who the viewer is—given that he has the right affiliation, of course.

The only tools available today for creating annotations (using an open format) are the Amaya browser/editor from the W3C and the PhotoRDF client. The first is actually a full-fledged client, doing everything that Tim Berners-Lee intended the Web to do, and demonstrating the standards of the W3C. The second is a set of Java classes that basically works like a form. Amaya uses HTTP PUT to deliver the annotations to the Web server (which is also a piece of demonstration software, the Jigsaw server from the W3C, with an RDF database module for it).

If you do not want to use these specialized tools (and like all demonstration applications, they sometimes do not work well, even if Amaya seems to have stopped crashing), but instead want your users to use standard software, it becomes a little more problematic. You could create a window that pops up and holds a form set that is used for annotations, tied to a servlet or CGI script that does the parsing, validation, and storing in the database, file, or whatever medium you have selected.

We will also look at a third product in this chapter: The Protégé-2000 system from Stanford University. This is annotations cubed, a real tool for knowledge representation. It is relatively simple to use, but it points to the complexities of knowledge management, in that it is never possible to achieve total knowledge for a domain (if that domain is not very small). If the target is moving, such as in the mobile industry, it is better to create unstructured annotations, just to have said something. And this could be done with Amaya, although a good idea might be to lift out the annotation component and create a separate system.

To annotate a document, you have to have an editor and someplace to store the information. If you do not configure a server, things are stored on your own hard disk, but it becomes harder to share them with others that way (in the W3C world, it does become impossible, if you do not have a server running on your computer. HTTP is not a peer-to-peer system, and only allows servers to serve up information). This means that you first have to configure a server, and install two special libraries for the software. In the W3C system, those consist of a database management system (MySQL), and the Practical Extraction and Report Language (PERL) parser/interpreter. MySQL is actually not special: It is a standard database management system, and the RDF database manager is layered on top of it (more on how this works in Chapter 3). The annotations system has been set up to work with a standard Common Gateway Interface (CGI), so there should be no problem for you as an administrator. The system also has an HTML interface, so it is possible to read annotations (if not write them) using a regular web browser, by pointing it at http://<server>/CGI/annotate.

Using Amaya, however, you have to configure which server to use. Annotations are reached by selecting the Annotations menu.

As you can see in Figure 2.1, the document I am working with has a little pen in the top left corner. This is the way Amaya indicates that I have annotated the document.

Next, select the menu. You can see in Figure 2.2 that the number of functions is actually quite limited: Annotate selection, Annotate document, Post annotation, Delete annotation, Load annotations, Local filter . . . , and Configure . . . . For a system in which you are allowed to make unstructured annotations, no more is needed (if, however, you were supposed to categorize the document, the layout would be different).

Figure 2.1 The top menu bar in Amaya, with the pen icon to the left.

Amaya allows you to select a section of a document for annotation, or to annotate the entire document. This can be useful in cases in which you are collaborating with someone and want their comments, but not inline inside the document. It also avoids using proprietary formats. If you have multiple reviewers and set up a server that only they have access to, their comments will be private to that group. There is no inherent security in the W3C annotation system and no server-side filters (e.g., the engineering department is working on a specification, but does not want the marketing people to know what they really think). RDF can be a solution to this, too, as we will see in Chapter 7, "Device Descriptions and User Profiles."

If you select the Annotate Document function, the window shown in Figure 2.3 will open. This is the editor window for Amaya, and it is the workbench to create annotations.

When you create an annotation, Amaya automatically includes some base facts. These are the name of the user (or rather, the user's identity), the source

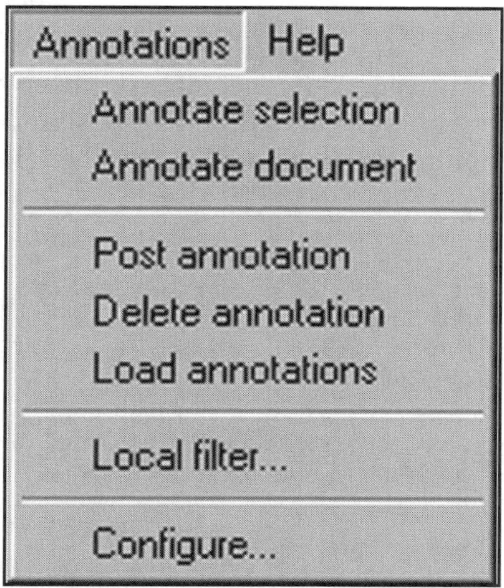

Figure 2.2 The menu choices for annotations in Amaya.

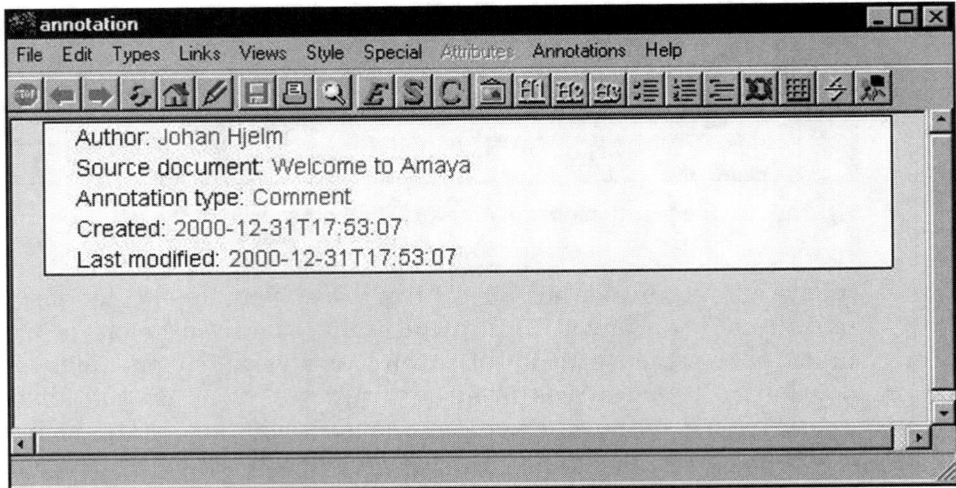

Figure 2.3 The Annotations window in Amaya.

document, the type of annotation, the date of creation, and the time it was modified. The actual annotation looks like this:

```
<?xml version="1.0"?>
<html xmlns="http://www.w3.org/1999/xhtml">
<head>
  <title>Annotation of Welcome to Amaya</title>
</head>
<body>
<p>This is an annotation. </p>
</body>
</html>
```

It does not look very interesting. However, all the metadata has been stored in a separate file, which is associated with the annotation (as a description of it), so the file contains both the description of the annotation and the reference to the document that is being annotated.

```
<?xml version="1.0" ?>
<r:RDF xmlns:r="http://www.w3.org/1999/02/22-rdf-syntax-ns#"
xmlns:a="http://www.w3.org/2000/10/annotation-ns#"
xmlns:http="http://www.w3.org/1999/xx/http#"
xmlns:d="http://purl.org/dc/elements/1.0/">
<r:Description>
<r:type resource="http://www.w3.org/2000/10/annotation-ns#Annotation" />
<r:type resource="http://www.w3.org/2000/10/annotationType#Comment" />
<a:annotates r:resource="file://C:\PROGRAM
FILES\AMAYA\amaya\AmayaPage.html" />
<a:context>#xpointer(/html[1])</a:context>
```

```
<d:creator>Johan Hjelm</d:creator>
<a:created>2000-12-31T18:00:29</a:created>
<d:date>2000-12-31T18:03:22</d:date>
<a:body r:resource="file://C:\PROGRAM
FILES\AMAYA\users\default\annotations\annots3vufm4p.56.html" />
</r:Description>
</r:RDF>
```

We will look further at what all these things really mean in Chapter 3, "RDF and XML." For now, it is sufficient to note that these things have been stored with the actual annotation. Quite logically, too, because they are metainformation about the annotation. The object is the annotation, the metadata is all the rest. Incidentally, the metadata became much larger than the annotation itself in this case.

To create the annotation, just write in the bottom of the window, below the facts box, as shown in Figure 2.4.

Amaya does not store all this information for archival purposes (something that might be very useful for future historians), but it provides ways of doing things with the information. There are also a couple of other information items you can provide.

You do not have to be restricted to working with one server only. It is quite possible to set up several servers. As shown in Figure 2.5, I have set up only localhost (the default), which means that annotations are stored only on my hard disk. If I had been using an annotation server, there would have been several servers in the annotation server window. There can be only one annotation post server, however, because the post function does not allow you to post to more than one server at a time. You can also set up autoloading of annotations (as you can see,

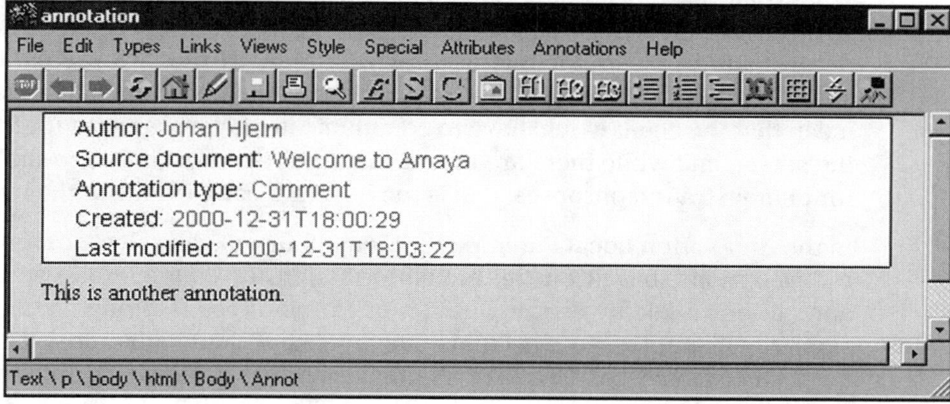

Figure 2.4 Writing an annotation is done below the box containing the facts describing the annotation.

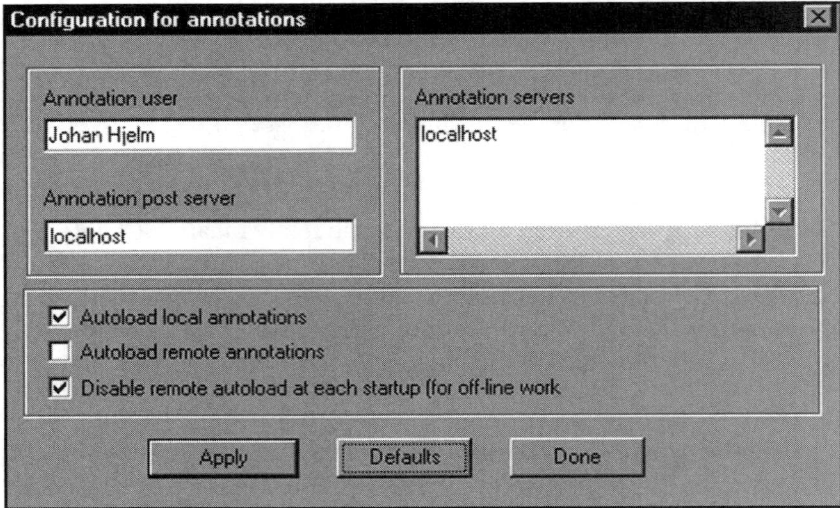

Figure 2.5 The Amaya annotations configurations menu.

it enables offline work, which is what I am doing at the moment). The automated loading of remote annotations allows you to avoid thinking about loading.

This is an instance in which the benefits of using RDF immediately become apparent. If there had been several annotation servers, and they had all been using different formats for the annotations, it is doubtful that any programmer would have bothered to create a tool that would allow you to read from them all. As it is, by using a generalized format, you can read from any server that presents its annotations in RDF.

What is more, you can filter out annotations. Filtering is done locally, however, so you have to import all the annotations before you can filter them. This is unfortunate because it is one of the weaknesses of the new system that consumes a lot of unnecessary bandwidth. However, doing it any other way would mean that the client would have to communicate the preferences for filtering to the server, and while there are efforts in that direction, it is not possible yet. So for demonstration purposes, this is the best that can be done at the moment.

In the Annotation Local Filter Menu (Figure 2.6) you can select some simple filtering options, based on the metainformation, of course. You can filter out annotations made by certain authors of certain types (although in the present version, all annotations are comments, by default), and annotations that come from a certain server. The servers are selected in the lower window with the scroll bars. You can show or hide them. (The partially hidden option could occur if you could select to filter out annotations of certain types and on certain servers, but this is not implemented yet.) If you filter out annotations made

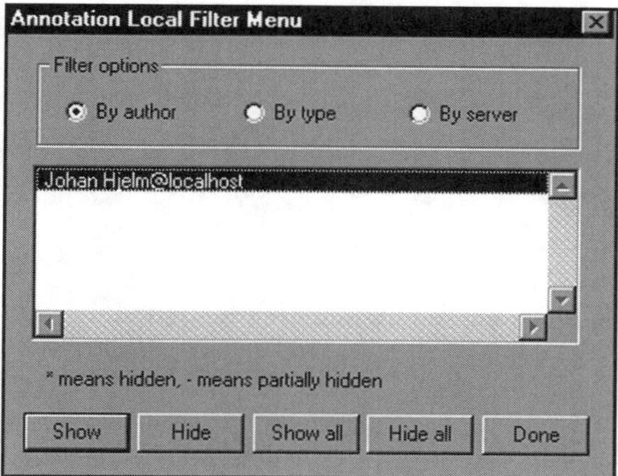

Figure 2.6 The Annotation Local Filter.

by someone or on a certain server, you will not see the little pen icon in the place where the annotation would have occurred.

When you are done with your annotation, you can select to post it to the annotation server. You can also choose to save it and post it later. As the user who created the annotation, you can also select to delete it. Clicking on the pen icon takes you to the annotation. You have to click on all of them to see what the annotations are about because there is currently no support for indicating the type, user identity, or server by the icons. (You could imagine having a little photo of the person annotating, for instance.) As yet, this is as good as it gets, and it is good enough for demonstration purposes.

rdfpic: Annotation of Photographs

The W3C has also developed another demonstration application, rdfpic. It is really an annotation system, as well, but the subject of the annotation is not a traditional document but a photograph. (Of course, you could use the Amaya annotation system to annotate photos as well.) The developer, Bert Bos, created it because he wanted to annotate his own holiday photos.

The rdfpic application is a Java applet consisting of a form (see Figure 2.7) where you can annotate the JPEG file you are storing. You can also use it to edit annotations made by others, as well as to import schemas (but it does not work like a self-adapting editor).

You can create annotations without a photo, but that would not be very much fun. Instead, load a photo first. Select the Image menu, and choose Load new

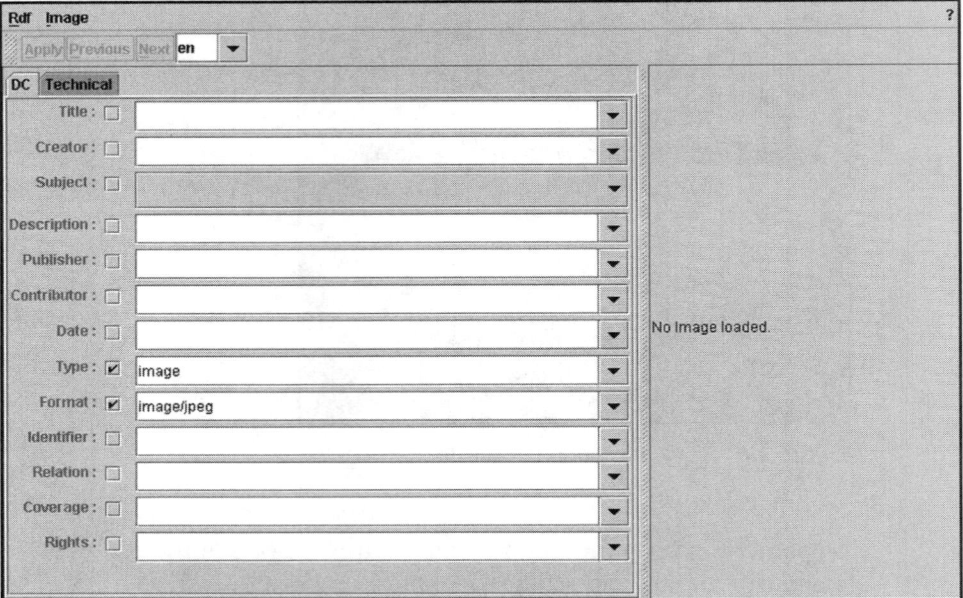

Figure 2.7 The rdfpic menu.

image. You can have several photos loaded at once (e.g., if you have been on holiday and want to annotate all your holiday photos at once).

To load an image, use a file system browser to select the file, and it will appear to the right, as in Figure 2.8. You are then ready to start annotating. The rdfpic system uses two schemas at once: the Dublin Core schema for document information, and a separate technical schema for technical information (see Figure 2.9).

The technical information does not include all the technical metainformation that is actually available for a JPEG photo, but only that which relates to the photographer. This means the camera, the lens, the film used, and the development date (assuming, of course, that you are not using a digital camera, because there would not be any film or development dates in that case).

It is, however, the Dublin Core part of the information that is interesting. Dublin Core data are supposed to describe documents, and here we have a prime example of a document. You can fill in a number of information items, some of which are free text, some of which you select from a menu, as shown in Figure 2.10. In order from the top, they include the title of the photograph, the name of the photographer, and the subject of the photo. The subject has to be selected from a menu, because this is one of the Dublin Core instances that is qualified with a separate schema.

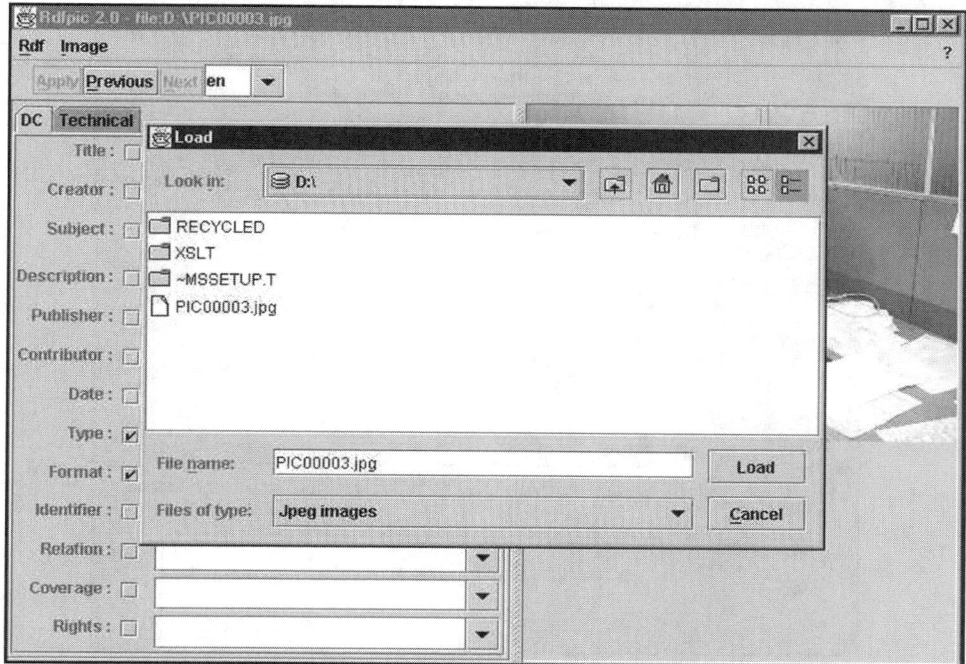

Figure 2.8 The file system menu in the rdfpic system.

The categories you can select from are fairly limited. They are Portrait, Group-Portrait, Landscape, Baby, Architecture, Wedding, Macro, Graphic, Panorama, and Animal. Somebody will have had an interesting vacation.

To extend this set, you will have to create a schema of your own and import it into the application. The description can be anything, as long as it describes the document.

We will go through all the Dublin Core elements more in depth in Chapter 6, "More Metadata Vocabularies," so there is no need to describe them further here. But here is what the result looks like with some information filled in:

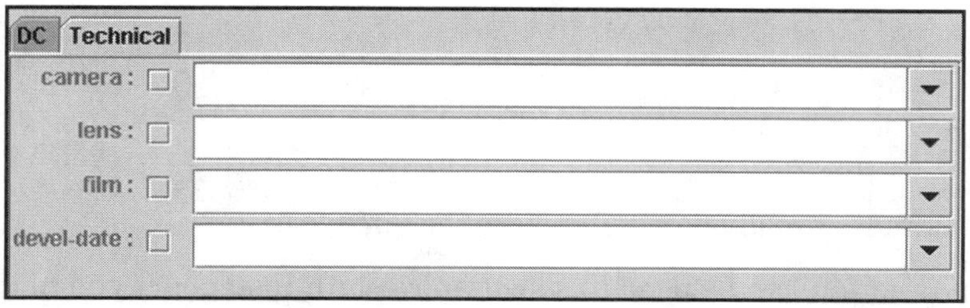

Figure 2.9 The technical schema menu in rdfpic.

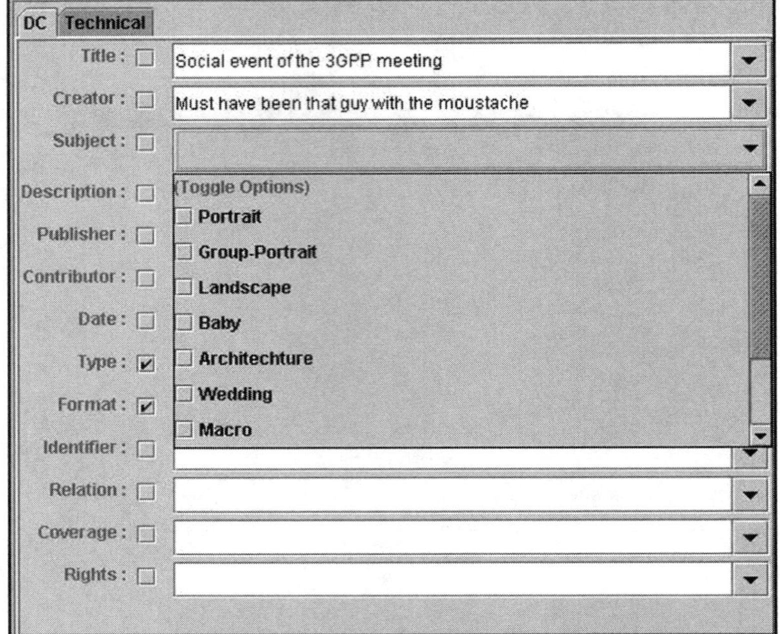

Figure 2.10 The Subject toggle options in rdfpic.

```
<?xml version='1.0' encoding='ISO-8859-1'?>
  <rdf:RDF xmlns:rdf="http://www.w3.org/1999/02/22-rdf-syntax-ns#"
      xmlns:rdfs="http://www.w3.org/TR/1999/PR-rdf-schema-19990303#"
      xmlns:s0="http://purl.oclc.org/dc/documents/rec-dces-199809.htm#"
      xmlns:s1="http://sophia.inria.fr/~enerbonn/rdfpiclang#">
    <rdf:Description rdf:about="">
      <s1:xmllang>en</s1:xmllang>
    </rdf:Description>
    <rdf:Description rdf:about="#image">
      <s0:Coverage>New York</s0:Coverage>
      <s0:Description>Fun and games after dinner</s0:Description>
      <s0:Creator>Must have been that guy with the
moustache</s0:Creator>
      <s0:Title>Social event of the 3GPP meeting</s0:Title>
      <s0:Type>image</s0:Type>
      <s0:Publisher>Johan Hjelm</s0:Publisher>
      <s0:Format>image/jpeg</s0:Format>
    </rdf:Description>
  </rdf:RDF>
```

There should normally be a URI where the #image is.

This information can be used to select images, for instance if you only want to show the pictures you took in Nice, and not those that were taken in Cannes or

Menton. If there were a filtering function, you would use it the same way that you used the filtering in the Amaya annotations system.

Protégé-2000

When you annotate a document, you are making a statement about the knowledge it contains. You are also, probably without knowing it, making a statement about your knowledge of the domain of the document.

Protégé-2000 works in terms of projects, and each project represents the knowledge base in a domain.

In the project menu shown in Figure 2.11, you can choose to open an existing project, import one, or create an entirely new project. If we do that, we get the menu in Figure 2.12, in which we can select whether we want to save the data in text format, RDF, or directly as a JDBC database. While this may be more efficient if you want to optimize the performance of your project, saving it in RDF allows you to interchange data with other applications, as we have noted previously, and even draw conclusions about data from different domains.

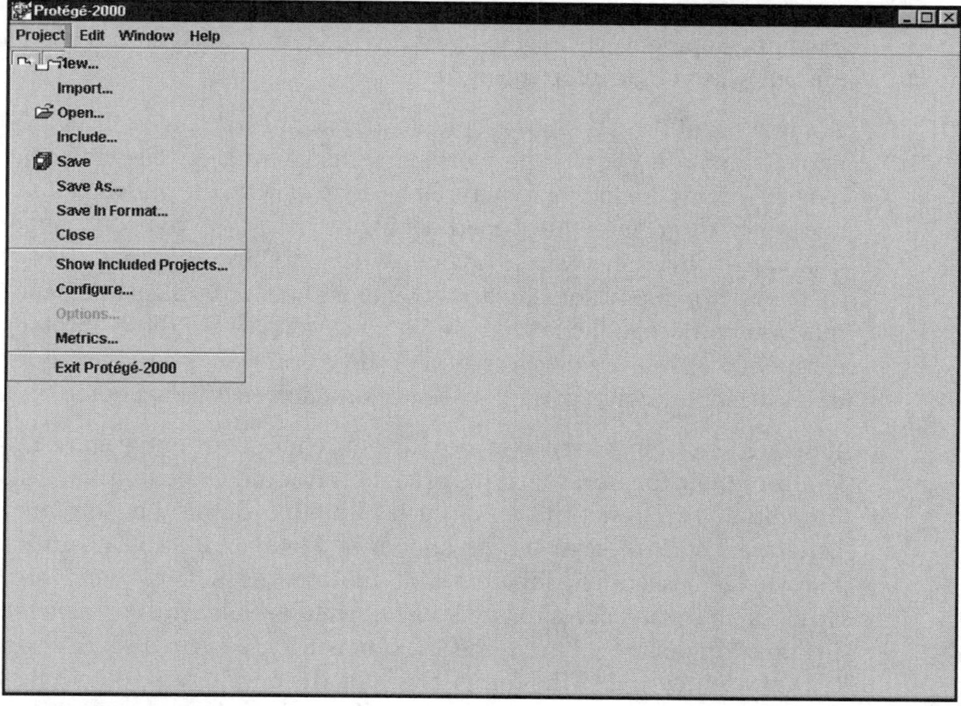

Figure 2.11 The project menu in Protégé-2000.

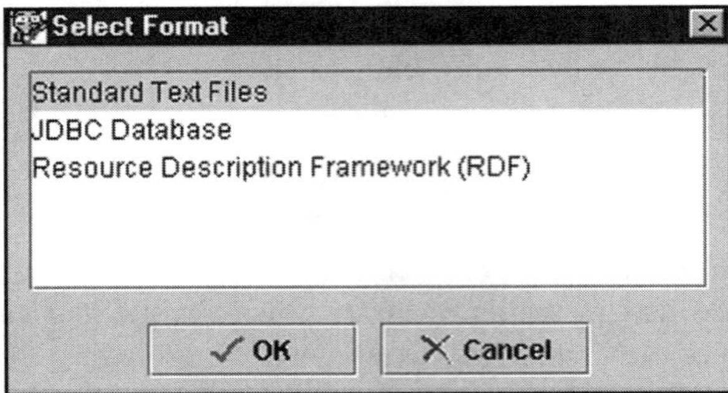

Figure 2.12 The format menu in Protégé-2000.

When you want to create a series of statements about a domain of knowledge, you create a project. The project is both the domain of knowledge and the framework in which you operate during the analysis of the domain. In traditional AI, you always analyze the entire domain of knowledge before you start creating the system. This usually means that either the domain is very small, or you will spend a long time on your analysis and planning. Protégé-2000 is a step away from this, indeed, in the first sentence of the manual; the claim is as follows: "The development of a successful knowledge-based system built with Protégé-2000 is more of an art than a science." However, it is designed for iterative development, with which you revise your ontologies (and schemas) continuously as you develop the system.

The makers of Protégé-2000 recommend that you start out with an analysis of the knowledge base you will be working with. There are well-established methodologies for this, including structured interviews with the domain experts. It is not necessary to go into those methodologies here (we will touch upon them in Chapter 9, "Implementation Advice: When Intelligent Agents Meet RDF"), but there are two important facts to remember about it: It takes time, and it requires that you work together with the domain experts to build the ontology, which in essence is a formalized description of the words you use to talk about a domain of knowledge. (Don't worry if it seems complicated; this is a complex discipline.)

It makes sense not to try to create the entire model from the start. Protégé-2000 is a tool built for iterative development, after all. Once you have started with the initial ontology, you can enter information directly in the forms that are generated by Protégé-2000. As shown in Figure 2.13, you fill in instances of knowledge, essentially objects that fit into the schema, and continue this process until you have a reasonable knowledge base. You can also let users test the development you have done, which usually leads to a set of revisions, both to the ontology and to the forms. Revising the ontology is something you would rather avoid, especially after the knowledge base has grown a bit, because to revise the ontology might mean revising the entire knowledge base.

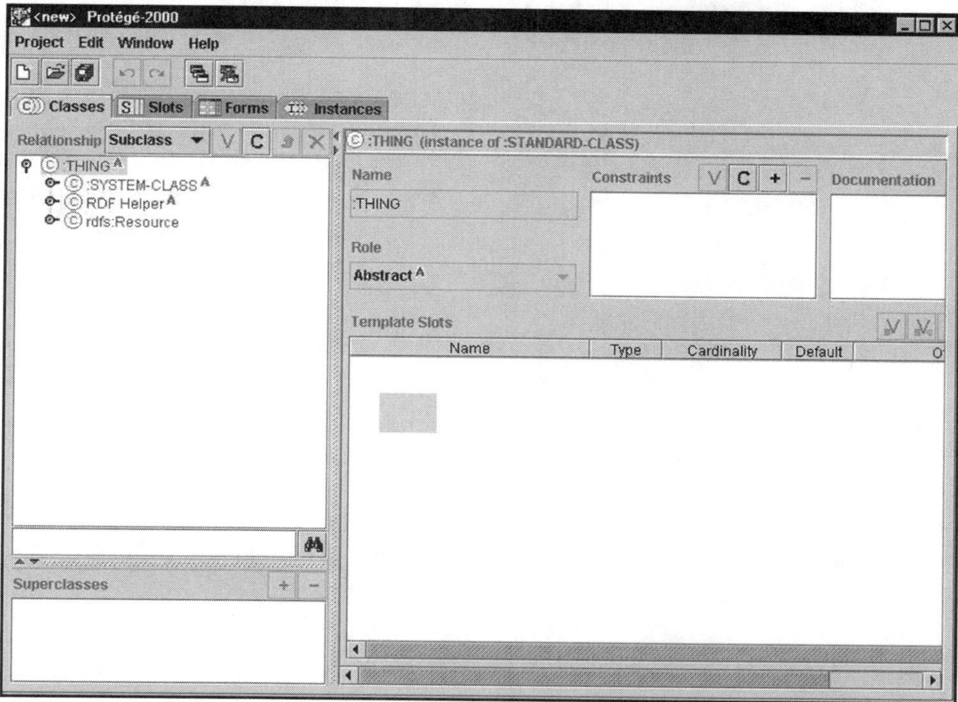

Figure 2.13 The ontology definition screen of Protégé-2000.

When you are creating applications using Protégé-2000, it is important that your model of the knowledge (that you have been using in designing the ontology) balances the needs of the domain expert in building the knowledge base (i.e., creating the instances). That need must, in turn, be balanced against the requirements of the system used for problem solving (inference engine or matching system). This implies that the domain ontology design in terms of class and slot structure should be modeled with a set of problems and a problem-solving method in mind, as well as being designed to allow for a feedback tool for a specific set of users.

This is not something you can sit down and do in five minutes, like it is to get up and running with Amaya annotations. This also demonstrates that the problem is bigger than just using a new data format. What you are being asked to do is actually create a model in RDF. Protégé-2000 uses RDF as a storage format, but it also has its own schema and vocabulary. We do not need to go into it more here, because the goal of this chapter is to demonstrate a few user interfaces to RDF. But we will come back later to the role and use of RDF Schema, if not Protégé-2000.

CHAPTER 3

RDF and XML

Modeling statements as graphs is one of the foundations of RDF. But RDF data can be viewed in three representations: as a graph, as triples, and as the XML representation. For humans, the graph representation is far easier to understand. The triples are accessible to application software, which will use them as input into their operations. And the XML version is suited for transporting between computers. Mathematically, they are equal.

The triples of RDF consist of the three parts of the graph: the resource, the property, and the property value. Constants (String values) may be included; they are called literals. A relationship between a resource and a literal is expressed by a statement, which connects a subject with an object via a predicate (e.g., the statement with *this book* as subject, *author* as predicate, and *Johan Hjelm* as object expresses that the author of this book is Johan Hjelm). RDF data consists of triples, not just attribute-value pairs. A triple consists of a node, a property, and a property value. Graphs look similar to entity-relationship diagrams, but they have more dimensions (direction, for one). It is possible to map entity-relationship diagrams into RDF graphs, but not the other way around.

RDF is a very simple format for predicate logic, as well. In a predicate logic statement, like "Aristotle is mortal," the predicate (or property) of the subject "Aristotle" is "mortal." Like all logic statements, it is possible to draw conclusions by generalizing from the assertions (such as "Aristotle is mortal"). The RDF graph is a way of connecting a property and its value with a uniquely identified object. Conclusions can be drawn from combining several assertions (a simplification, of course, as I will describe more in Chapter 8, "Reasoning about Metadata: Rules and Ontologies"). The difference from traditional predicate logic is that the syntax of RDF is declared in the RDF Schema, which means it is specific to the application instead of general, like predicate logic. The RDF schema is used to define the set of resources that may be used by a model, including constraints for resource and literal values. It creates the structure which you later fill with your description.

RDF is based on mathematical graph theory. Each information object—resource—is a node, and the property connecting it to another node (what is being described by the resource) is an arc. To borrow a metaphor from Greg Fitzpatrick, musician and RDF guru, think of it as a road, with gas stations, exits, and turnoffs. A graph consists of a minimum of a node (the resource) and an arc (the properties of the resource). So the road is the arc, and the gas station is the node—and the property value is the number of kilometers to the node.

Nodes can be any Web resources (pages, servers, basically anything for which you can give a Uniform Resource Identifier (URI)), even other instances of metadata. The arcs—the connections between the nodes—are attributes on the nodes. The arc always starts at the resource and points to the value. Attributes are named properties of the nodes, and their values are either atomic (text strings, numbers, and so on) or other resources or metadata instances. That property values can be resources means that they can be nodes in their own right, which is the same as saying that a leaf node can also be a branch.

This configuration allows you to build a labeled directed graph to create structured statements about a resource (think of it as choosing the way you will go, and which gas stations you will stop at). The graph has a direction, because the resource (which is a node) points to the node through the arc. RDF properties may be thought of as attributes of resources and in this sense correspond to traditional attribute-value pairs. RDF properties also represent relationships between resources.

Graphs are hard to handle in a computer, even though they are easily read and understood by us humans. RDF was developed by the World Wide Web Consortium (W3C) to serve as a general-purpose format for all statements about objects and serialize them in XML. So XML is the other parent of RDF, with graph theory. The encoding of RDF in XML is described in the RDF model and syntax specification.

To serialize a graph is relatively simple. Think of a simple graph, like

```
Napoleon → Emperor → France
 |
 → Corsican
```

which expresses the statement that Napoleon was a Corsican and Emperor of France. This can be written like

```
Napoleon
 Emperor
  France
 Corsican
```

which looks, as you can see, very similar to a table of contents of a document. Structure is as simple as that. Let us see how the XML encoding works.

Here is another simple RDF graph:

http://www.wireless-information.net → Creator → Johan Hjelm

This is a fairly simple statement. It says that Johan Hjelm is the author of the resource http://www.wireless-information.net. If we wanted to make sure that it was clear that it was this Johan Hjelm, and not another Johan Hjelm who had written the book (there are actually several Johan Hjelms in Sweden), we could use the URI http://johanhjelm.com instead, because a URI is a unique identifier. We might also want to make clear that we meant creator in some special, well-defined sense, by using a special element, `dc:Creator` (as opposed to `biblical:Creator`, for instance). Of course, then we would have to declare where the definition of that special element came from. This is done using XML namespaces in the XML encoding of the RDF graph. So here is what an XML document serializing the statement in the graph will look like:

```
<?xml version="1.0"?>
 <rdf:RDF xmlns:rdf="http://www.w3.org/1999/02/22-rdf-syntax-ns#"
             xmlns:dc="http://purl.org/dc/elements/1.1/">
   <rdf:Description about="http://www.wireless-information.net/">
     <dc:creator rdf:resource="http://johanhjelm.com/whois/"/>
   </rdf:Description>
 </rdf:RDF>
```

The actual statement in the graph looks like it was just a small part in the middle. Let us deconstruct it to see what parts it consists of.

```
<?xml version="1.0"?>
```

The XML declaration shows that this is XML, and declares which version it is.

```
<rdf:RDF xmlns:rdf="http://www.w3.org/1999/02/22-rdf-syntax-ns#"
```

The `rdf` element begins here: It encapsulates the actual statement and is followed by the namespace declaration. It also declares the RDF namespace (i.e., where to find out what all tags prefixed with `rdf:` mean) and gives it a unique identity.

```
xmlns:dc="http://purl.org/dc/elements/1.1/">
```

The second namespace declaration declares the Dublin Core namespace, here prefixed with `dc:`. Both namespace declarations are attributes on the `rdf` element.

```
<rdf:Description about="http://www.wireless-information.net/">
```

The `rdf:Description` element declares which resource the statement is about. Here, we use about (as opposed to id) because the resource is external to the description.

```
<dc:creator rdf:resource="http://johanhjelm.com/whois/"/>
```

The `dc:Creator` element contains the value of the `dc:Creator` property. This could, as noted, be another resource (e.g., http://johanhjelm.com). There can be more properties for the same resource.

```
</rdf:Description>
```

Here, the `Description` element ends

```
</rdf:RDF>
```

and the `rdf` element ends. If we run this through a parser with a graph generation function, we will get the result that is pictured in Figure 3.1.

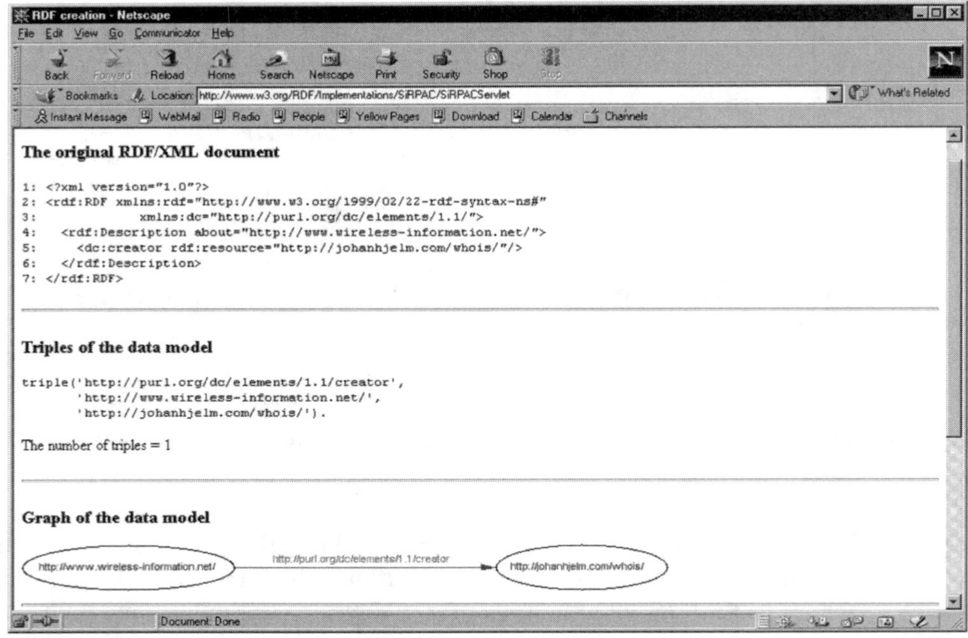

Figure 3.1 The analyzed RDF statement in SiRPAC.

A document (at least one of the type we are used to thinking of) has an inherent structure, and in this case it is a tree. All XML documents can be modeled as trees, since there is a top-level element in which all the other elements nest, and the elements which nest in each other can be modeled as branches on the tree. Web sites are often visualized with a tree structure (and if they are written in XML, they do have a tree structure in the markup of the document). But there is more than one structure in the information.

An application, especially a browser-based application, consists of three parts: The first is the semantic layer, which holds the content. The second is the syntax layer, which concerns the structure of the information. The syntax layer is what creates the user's sequence of interaction with the information, and holds the events that can take place when the user interacts with the application. It is by following the rules the designer lays down in the syntax of the application that the user can fulfill the task he set out to accomplish when he accessed your site.

RDF works at the semantic layer (there is some debate about this, though, because the RDF syntax, of course, works at the syntactical layer). It is at the syntactical layer that you have to follow certain rules to enable consistent and robust behavior. These rules establish the grammar of the language for the interaction with the site. In RDF, the words of the language are defined by you using RDF Schema, the grammar is defined in the RDF Syntax specification (and partly by XML), and XML defines the shape and function of letters to form words. The third layer is the lexical layer, where the semantic and syntactic information are further refined to concrete data types that are required for human interaction (audio, visual, spatial, and so on).

In a Web site, there is an inherent structure of the tasks, the syntax layer; parallel with this, there is also a structure of objects, the semantic structure of the information. It is the semantic objects that you work with when you design the presentation and the content of the information. In a tree diagram, the objects are leaves of the tree, and the arcs are the branches connecting them. This can be used as a hierarchy constituting the modality abstracting user interface. You can also reverse the process. Using this structure, you can identify the information objects you should use to structure your source representation, before it is encoded in XML. The encoding will then match your model.

To create structured data, it is sufficient to use XML. Using HTML is not good enough, because HTML data is not structured; that is, there is no formal structure that a computer can understand, even if you make it conform to a specific pattern, for instance by applying a template. Because computers are stupid, you must tell them exactly what you are doing. This means that if you describe a resource, you must do it in a way that makes it clear that it is a resource and the following description refers to it. And of course, before you do that, you must declare that what you are doing is describing a resource. This is where the use of XML comes in handy, because it lets you define the structure of what you are doing in a relatively simple way. The RDF encoding is an attempt at making this machine-understandable, by adding the references to the objects being described and creating relations between the elements of the description.

Of course, using a standardized procedure for the consistent encoding of the method makes it possible to interchange metadata between different applications. Using one where the vocabulary can be defined by anyone also enables the definition of vocabularies by different organizations and communities. The mechanism to handle this in RDF is based on XML. RDF imposes structural constraints on XML, creating an unambiguous method to express semantics.

The XML serialization is not the canonical version of the RDF statement, however. All representations of a graph are in theory equivalent, but several different graphs can be serialized to the same XML representation. This can cause problems when you want to reconstruct your graphs, although more so for modeling than for processing, as it turns out. In practice, it is easier to regard the graph as the canonical version. But RDF does not have to be expressed in XML, even if that is the most convenient way of encoding the information. A drawing of the graph or an expression in a LISP-like language is as valid as an encoding of the assertion. It is the method that is important, not the particular way it is expressed.

The History of RDF

The architecture of RDF was designed by the members and staff of the W3C. A lot of the original ideas came from Tim Berners-Lee, the inventor of the Web, who actually had intended much of it to go in the Web as we know it—but he released it early, and it did not have all the functionality that he intended. Most of his time since then has been spent trying to make people catch up with his original intentions. The way he has communicated the ideas has not been simple to understand, however, making acceptance in the Web community less than stellar.

The history of RDF began in 1995, when the W3C defined the Platform for Internet Content Selection (PICS) in an effort to calm the vocally expressed fears of several organizations, mostly those representing the Christian Right in the United States, about the possibilities of children and youngsters downloading inappropriate material. As it turned out, PICS was never used to solve that particular problem to any large extent, because users instead turned to programs that gave them direct control of the content being downloaded (although some of those programs do use PICS).

PICS is a mechanism for communicating the ratings of Web pages from a server to a client, and so is a prime example of a metadata application. The ratings are communicated as labels that contain information about the content of the pages. PICS does not contain a fixed set of criteria for appropriateness, nudity, violence, things deemed to be against the Qu´ran, or anything else. The labels are neutral, and their meanings are determined in the database at the server end. Actually, this is similar to how cookies work, even though they were intended to allow users to control which information is given out to a service provider.

The idea behind PICS was for different organizations to come up with their own ratings, and users could then set their browsers to filter out content which they regarded as inappropriate (i.e., anything that did not fit their preferences). Because the labels were neutral, the label "Fu3XHGOHjlk*Y*#$R%" could mean "sexually explicit content" if interpreted by one service provider, and "tantric sutras" if interpreted by another. As long as the labeling is consistent, this works.

PICS had several weaknesses, however (for instance, the dependency on the active rating by an agency), and in the course of working on the next generation of the system, it became clear that the infrastructure which was being defined would apply to a number of other metadata communities as well.

As a result, the W3C created a working group and brought together the requirements of several different metadata communities into a coherent system. Nobody invented it; the specifications are the result of the work of the people in the working group, as is often the case in the W3C. The RDF Syntax became a W3C Recommendation in 1998, and the RDF Schema is currently a Candidate Recommendation in the W3C. W3C Recommendations are not formal standards, however, but exactly what they say they are: Recommendations to the members of the W3C.

The URI: Universal Resource Identifier

RDF has a number of important properties that were designed into it from the start. It describes resources (which can be anything that has a URI) in terms of properties and property values. The property types are interchangeable because they can be encoded in XML. RDF is also inherently scalable, because it uses the mechanisms of the Web (which if anything have proven to be scalable). The value of a property can also be a resource, with its own corresponding properties and values. RDF is independent of any central organization, because anyone can invent a property type. As long as the definition is done in an RDF schema and the file containing the schema is accessible by an HTTP client (or a server acting as a client), you can download it and your own RDF processor can resolve what the creator of the RDF description meant with the elements he had created. This means that it will be possible to do searches based on assertions made by others: If you can just walk the graph, you can determine its semantics and hence the resource it describes.

The ideas of Tim Berners-Lee that are at the basis of the World Wide Web hinge on the use of Universal Resource Identifiers to address objects. What is more, his idea is that, in principle, not only is a URI a unique address, the resource it points to is also unique—and it is referenced, rather than copied, whenever needed. He has borrowed this particular thought from Ted Nelson, the visionary who invented hypertext; in essence, what it means is that there will be no degradation through copying and that the resource will always be under the control of the originator. It is not how the Web is used in practice. But it is the way RDF works.

The URI is crucial for RDF, because it determines what the object is that is being described (the subject of the statement) and it gives each resource a unique identity.

URIs are not restricted to referencing information objects, but can also be proxies for a physical entity that in itself does not have a URI. This is how a physical device description can be created in CC/PP, the Composite Capabilities/Preferences Profile format. In CC/PP, the statements relate to the URI where the device description is found, and by splitting it up into components (which are fragments of the RDF description), CC/PP can handle the different aspects of the device's capabilities. If the URI in the resource identifier contains a fragment identifier (the hash mark, #), it is only a subcomponent (a fragment) that is identified by the anchor id for the fragment of the resource that the URI refers to.

The URI itself is a string of characters that identifies an abstract or physical resource, according to the specification that describes URIs, RFC 2396. This is not strictly true anymore, because RFC 2396 was based on the versions of the Domain Name Service (DNS) that handled characters only (and only 7-bit ASCII at that). A URI today is really a bitstring, but because the standards are not quite set yet, I will assume that the old standard still applies and refer to URIs as if they are composed of characters. However, by the time you read this, it is very likely that there will be a new version of the DNS that handles Chinese characters (which strictly speaking are not characters, but ideograms), as well as other alphabets and writing systems. This would mean that you could have a proper Chinese or Thai name for your site, for instance.

The three parts of the Uniform Resource Identifier name represents the three important parts of the concept: URIs are uniform, they identify resources, and the resources are resources. OK, that sounds like a tautology if there ever was one. But here is how it works.

A resource can be anything that has an identity. And because any object can have an identity, any object can be a resource. This is circular reasoning, and there have so far not been any real attempts to resolve it. Nor are they needed, since in practice the identity is being regulated by the scheme describing the resource.

Because the URI is an identifier, it should not be used for parameterization unless the parameters are part of the unique identity of the object. If you create a URI for each step you take, the coordinates are part of the identity of the footsteps. But when you request an object, you should not put your position in the URI: It has nothing to do with the object, because it comes from you. This is often misused (you have probably seen URIs 254 characters long, generated by lazy database programmers); but while it may look like a quick fix that takes care of an immediate problem, it creates more problems in the long run.

Because a URI can address anything, you could create RDF descriptions for anything—such as the direction of your steps or (more practically, perhaps, and a real use case) the books in a library. What most often happens is that the identifier points to an information object that in turn describes the object you are actually making statements about. When you talk about a library book, you most often point to the card catalog of the library (actually, the computerized version of it), not the library book itself (which will cause a problem if the location of the book is a part of the URI: What if it has been checked out? Will its URI change second by second as you carry it home? As you can see, parameterization does not belong in the URI).

Another aspect of the URI is its recognizabilty. In theory, a URI can be 255 characters (256 minus one, the root dot) long, but in practice, nobody could remember a URI like that. This matters, even though Tim Berners-Lee intended that URIs should not be visible to humans (in particular, the protocol part should be something you should never have to care about); as it happens, URIs have become as well-known as zip codes. Now, those of us old enough to remember when we started using zip codes will recognize how complicated it seemed to add a string of numbers to the address. Today, nobody even thinks about it. In the seven or so years since the Web was released upon humanity, URIs have become a fact of life, very much like zip codes. First being a fashion item (this author had a laughing attack the first time he heard an announcer on the radio try to read out a URI, in 1995), they have become an indispensable part of an organization's address. Like brochures, business cards, and the sign on the door, it is an indispensable part of a company's identity. And indeed, it is not just an identifier, it is a part of both the identity and identification of the object.

A URI consists of a scheme and a scheme-specific part. (The scheme depends on the protocol being used to access the object. There is one scheme for http, one for FTP, one for the file system in Windows, and so on. "Scheme" is not the same as a "schema"; a scheme is a way of writing things, whereas a schema is a way of describing things. For instance, an RDF schema.) The URI scheme defines the name space of the URI. In the URI http://www.historybuff.org/Napoleon, the scheme part is http, the :// differentiates the scheme from the scheme-specific part, and www.historybuff.org/Napoleon is scheme-specific.

If you have been using the Web for a while, you probably wonder what happened to the URL, the Uniform Resource Locator. The answer is that a URI can be a URL, but it does not have to be. In the URI file://my_documents/RDF_book/ch03.doc, the location of the file ch03 of the type doc is in the subdirectory RDF_book of the directory my_documents. The operating system maps the file name to a location on the hard disk of the computer.

In the *file* scheme, the identification of an object is synonymous with its location. The URI is a URL. However, if you use a Web server to access the same file, the scheme for it could be http://www.historybuff.org, since there will be a mapping between the file system and the Web server in your computer. Actually, it will be between the http scheme and the file scheme. Because an object can be anything (for instance, a library book, which is in the wrong format for the hard disk of your computer), the identifier does not have to be related to the location. (What if somebody checked the book out? Is its location in the home of the borrower, or in his bag as he takes the bus from the library, or forgotten at a café?) The scheme determines whether the location is a part of the identity of the object or not. In the file scheme, it is. In the http scheme, it is not.

The uniformity implies that the same type of identifier can be used for many different types of objects, irrespective of the access method and how they are handled. Both ftp://www.historybuff.org/Napoleon and http://www.historybuff.org/Napoleon are valid resource identifiers, even though the access protocols are different (whether they refer to the same resource is a different question). Of course, the way this is structured is also dependent on the Internet way of doing things. Conceivably, you could have had different systems, depending on whether you dialed in or had a fixed connection. But now, the separation of transport and application means that because the physical access method is translated into IP, and the application protocol only works with the IP layer, the method you use to access the Internet is transparent to the system. It really is a question about which application protocol you use. Each application protocol contains systems to translate addresses to IP addresses (using the DNS).

You might have noted that the URI is the same for both FTP and HTTP. This is no coincidence, but the very *uniformity* from the first part of the *URI* abbreviation. It may look like it refers to a file system, but there is nothing that says that it has to. Indeed, there can be local mappings to whatever underlying identifier is used internally in the system. When you access a database-driven site like the CNN Web site (http://www.cnn.com), for instance, the file does not exist previous to your requesting it. It is generated from a database using a set of rules that are tied to the URI.

URIs are not tied to a specific protocol, which means that they can be used in different access protocols. This means that when a new protocol is invented, it can use the same URI (except for the scheme, the protocol part) to address the resource (or resources) that can be handled using that protocol.

Not all resources are network-retrievable, however, because the access method may not be network-connected (for instance, you or I can be considered resources—my employer does, as I hope yours do—but we are not downloadable). This has meant that there has been some contention about what you address when you dial a phone number (Is it the call or the terminal at the other end of the line that is being addressed?), and conceivably, you could have a URI for each memory you have, or each step you take (just three-dimensional coordinates plus time and your personal identity should do it). These are marginal aspects, and while the mechanism strictly speaking works for these edge cases as well, it is not really something you want to use it for. It works best when referring to a network-accessible resource, and that is plenty enough.

The third part of the URI is the identifier part. An identifier is "an object that can act as a reference to something which has an identity," and because that can be anything, anything can be identified. At least anything in a space of possible addresses that is as large as the number of the characters allowed with 256 as the exponent. However, in the URI, the identifying object is a sequence of characters with a restricted syntax (given that DNS only handles 7-bit ASCII, and only in a certain way, at least currently).

How XML Namespaces Work

XML namespaces identify a set of element names by using prefixes in the RDF code and declaring the namespace in the head of the document. Now, it is time to explain how XML namespaces work, and why they are important. For instance, how do you create your own namespace?

If you are a programmer, you are probably familiar with the use of namespaces in programming languages. However, namespaces in XML are not quite the same thing as namespaces in programming languages. They are not sets of names, but a mechanism to identify names and to make them unique. This uniqueness avoids collisions due to markup intended for some other software package using the same element type or attribute name.

XML namespaces depend on URIs. The identification of the namespace is a URI, but that is the only function of the URI in this context. Namespaces are usually declared in the beginning of a document, in the namespace declaration. However, it is quite possible to have a namespace declaration anywhere in the document; in that case, the namespace declaration is considered to apply to the element where it is specified and to all elements within the content of that element (that are nested within it), unless overridden by another namespace declaration with the same identifier part. Note that default namespaces do not apply directly to attributes. Namespace declarations in RDF can be associated with an individual `Description` element or even an individual `propertyElt` element (i.e., any property name).

A namespace is declared using a family of reserved attributes. Such an attribute's name must either be `xmlns` or have `xmlns:` as a prefix (these two are reserved, but you can use any other prefix for your namespaces). These attributes, like any other XML attributes, may be provided directly or by default. The attribute's value, a URI reference, is the namespace name identifying the namespace. There can actually be several names that have the same functionality but are identified by different URIs.

Because URI references can contain characters that are not allowed in names, they cannot be used directly as namespace prefixes. The namespace prefix serves as a proxy for a URI reference. It is the prefix, mapped to a URI reference, which selects a namespace. The combination of the universally managed URI namespace and the document's own namespace produces identifiers that are universally unique.

There can be several different namespaces in the same XML document. Namespace names are arbitrary, and depend on the URI used, not on the prefix. Prefixes for the same namespace can vary between documents, because the scope of the declaration is only the current document. The default namespace can be set to the empty string. This has the same effect, within the scope of the declaration, of there being no default namespace.

Here is a simple example (from the name space specification) of two namespaces used in a document: `bk` and `isbn`. Both are declared using the xmlns prefix, and are then available throughout the document.

```
<?xml version="1.0"?>
  <!-- both namespace prefixes are available throughout -->
```

```
<bk:book xmlns:bk='urn:loc.gov:books'
        xmlns:isbn='urn:ISBN:0-395-36341-6'>
    <bk:title>Cheaper by the Dozen</bk:title>
    <isbn:number>1568491379</isbn:number>
</bk:book>
```

Using this mechanism, you can essentially expand any XML document with the elements and attributes from any other XML document. Because the XML processor has to resolve them, this might mean a delay in processing, but it does not mean that the processing slows down.

RDF as XML

I have been using RDF a great deal up to now, and you have probably figured out at least some of the elements and attributes yourself. Table 3.1 lists the element set and Table 3.2 lists the attribute set of the RDF syntax. The names of RDF elements and attributes follow the interCap convention, which means that they start with small caps, and large caps are used to distinguish different parts of the name. Since XML is sensitive to whether large or small caps are used (in which it is different from HTML), this will mean that About and about are two different names.

The Abbreviated RDF Syntax

RDF is normally written as we have written it up to now, with the property value as the element content. There is, however, also a second method to write RDF in XML, with the property value in the attribute value of the element. The long syntax looks like this:

```
<rdf:description about="http://www.wireless-information.net">
<dc:creator>johanhjelm.com</dc:creator>
</rdf:description>
```

And the abbreviated syntax looks like this:

```
<description about=http://www.wireless-information.net dc:creator
="johanhjelm.com"/>
```

In other words, you are using the same elements, but you are collapsing them into attributes. This is useful when no human has to read the RDF code, but it can become quite messy if you try to write it yourself. It is also rather easy to transform between the forms using Extensible Style Language Transformations (XSLT), which is a transformation language for XML applications. So if you generate RDF, it is easier to do it this way, but if the RDF has to be

Table 3.1 RDF Elements in XML

ELEMENT	EXPLANATION	NAME	MEANING
`<rdf:RDF>description</rdf:RDF>`		RDF	This element is a wrapper in XML that marks the start and end points for the content that can be mapped into the RDF data model. The RDF element is optional if the content can be known to be RDF from the application context.
`<rdf:Description idAboutAttr attribute> propertyElt element </rdf:Description>`	`idAboutAttr` is either the `About` or `ID` attribute, and `propertyElt` is the name of the property in question	Description	`Description` contains the elements that cause the creation of statements. For purposes of the basic RDF syntax, the `Description` element may be thought of as a placeholder for the identification of the resource being described. `Description` provides a way to give the resource name just once for several statements.
`<propName>value</propName>` or `<propName resourceAttr/>`	`propName` is the name of the property, and `value` is the value	`PropertyElt`	A single Description may contain more than one `propertyElt` element with the same property name. Each such `propertyElt` adds one arc to the graph. The schema designer defines how to interpret this. The element is of course not called `propertyElt`, but the property name, in your document.
`<rdf:Seq idAttr >member(s)</rdf:Seq>`		`sequence`	A Sequence is an ordered list of resources (URIs) or literals (strings). `sequence` is used to declare that a property has multiple values, and that the orders of those values are significant. There can be duplicate values in the sequence. One use of `sequence` is to preserve an ordering of values, for instance Japanese Kana ordering.

continues

Table 3.1 RDF Elements in XML (Continued)

ELEMENT	EXPLANATION	NAME	MEANING
`<rdf:Bag idAttr>member(s)</rdf:Bag>`		`Bag`	A Bag in RDF is an unordered list of resources (URIs) or literals (strings). There is no significance in the order of the values. There can be duplicate values. The use of a `Bag` container does not mean there are repeated properties of the same type. You will need to decide on a case-by-case basis which one (repeated property statement or `Bag`) is more appropriate to use.
`<rdf:Alt idAttr>member(s)</rdf:Alt>`	`Alternative` is a list of resources or literals that represent alternatives for the (single) value of a property that is to be used.	`Alternative`	`Alternative` might be used to provide alternative language translations for the title of a work (a use inspired by content negotiation using alternative variants in HTTP), or to provide a list of Internet mirror sites at which a resource might be found. An application using a property whose value is an Alternative collection is aware that it can choose any one of the items in the list as appropriate. An `Alt` container is required to have at least one member. This member will be identified by the property `_1` and is the default or preferred value.
`<rdf:li resourceAttr/>` or `<rdf:li>value</rdf:li>`	`resourceAttr` is the attribute of the list instance, value is the value of the item (group member)	`referencedItem` and `inlineItem`	The container objects in RDF use `li` as a convenience element to avoid explicitly numbering each object in the container. The `li` element assigns the properties `_1`, `_2`, and so on as necessary. The name `li` was chosen for its similarity to the `li` element in HTML, but unfortunately it is now confusing, as its function is quite different.

Table 3.2 The Attributes in RDF

<table>
<tr><th>ATTRIBUTE</th><th>WRITTEN AS</th><th>MEANING</th></tr>
<tr><td>aboutAttr</td><td>about=URI, where URI is the URI that identifies the resource</td><td>This attribute is the identity of the resource that is being described. A Description element without an About attribute represents a new resource. This may be a surrogate, or proxy, for some other physical resource that does not have a recognizable URI. The value of the ID attribute of the Description element, if present, is the anchor id of this inline resource. The About attribute refers to an existing resource, the ID attribute to a new resource.</td></tr>
<tr><td>idAttr</td><td>ID=IDsymbol, where IDsymbol is an XML fragment identifier</td><td>If another Description or property value needs to refer to the inline resource it will use the value of the ID of that resource in its own About attribute. Either ID or About may be used in the Description but both cannot be used together in the same element. It can be a fragment identifier, in which case the description only refers to that particular fragment.</td></tr>
<tr><td>aboutEachAttr</td><td>aboutEach=URI or aboutEachPrefix=string</td><td></td></tr>
<tr><td>propName</td><td>Qname</td><td>A property name has to be a qualified name in the XML sense.</td></tr>
<tr><td>value</td><td>description | string</td><td>The value of the property attribute can be either a description or a string that is a piece of XML.</td></tr>
<tr><td>resourceAttr</td><td>resource=URI-reference</td><td>Within a propertyElt, the resource attribute specifies that the statement refers to a resource identified by a URI (rather than a piece of literal text). The resource identifier of the object is obtained by resolving the resource attribute URI-reference in the same way as for the About attribute.</td></tr>
</table>

Table 3.2 The Attributes in RDF (Continued)

ATTRIBUTE	WRITTEN AS	MEANING
`Qname`	`NSprefix:name`	A qualified name must be written as a namespace prefix (see namespace declarations in the previous section) and a name. The name is arbitrary.
`URI-reference`	a URI, interpreted according to RFC 2396	This is simply the identifier of the resource or property.
`IDsymbol`	any legal XML name symbol	The ID of an XML fragment can be any legal XML name symbol, i.e., anything within the Unicode character set.
`name`	any legal XML name symbol	The same as `IDsymbol`.
`NSprefix`	any legal XML namespace prefix	Property names must be associated with an RDF schema. Qualifying the element names with a namespace prefix can do this.
`string`	any XML text, with <, >, and & escaped	Strings must be well-formed XML. This means that the usual XML content quoting and escaping mechanisms should be used.
`aboutEachAttr`	`aboutEach=URI` or `string`	The value of an `aboutEach` attribute must be a container (`bag`, `alternative`, or `sequence`). Using this attribute with a container as the value is the same as making statements about each of the members separately. The reason is that you often want to refer to the group as a group, not having to enumerate the members. The `aboutEachPrefix` attribute is a shorthand syntax that declares that there is a Bag whose members are all the resources whose fully resolved resource identifiers begin with the character string given as the value of the attribute. The statements in a Description that has the `aboutEachPrefix` attribute apply individually to each of the members of this Bag.

continues

Table 3.2 The Attributes in RDF (Continued)

ATTRIBUTE	WRITTEN AS	MEANING
`bagIDAttr`	`bagID=IDsymbol`	This attribute specifies the resource ID of the container resource. `BagID` and the `XML` ID should not be confused. The ID here specifies the identification of an inline resource whose properties are further detailed in the Description. A Description may have both an `ID` attribute and a `bagID` attribute. `BagID` also specifies the identification of the container resource whose members are the reified statements about another resource.
`member`	`referencedItem` or `inlineItem`	The member property is used with containers to show the identities of the objects in the `Bag`.
`typedNode`	`<typeName idAboutAttr` or `bagIdAttr` or `propAttr/>` or `<typeName>propertyElt</typeName>` `where typeName=Qname`	This attribute determines that a node is of a type that has been declared in the RDF schema. It is essentially a shortcut mechanism. Resources may be instances of one or more classes; this is indicated with the `rdf:type` property.
`parseLiteral`	`parseType="Literal"` or `"Resource"`	The `parseType` attribute changes the interpretation of the element content. The parseType attribute should have either the value `"Literal"` or `"Resource"`. This value is used when the system determines how an RDF parser should interpret a value. If it is literal, the RDF processor should not interpret it. It is a minimum-level solution to express RDF statements with a value that has XML markup.

human-readable, the compact form is too complicated. So we will use the long form for the examples in this book.

The RDF Data Model

For a system that is meant to be able to describe anything, RDF has surprisingly few elements. The RDF element is the top-level element that encloses the RDF statement, so that the XML processor knows where to start handing information over to the RDF processor. It is possible to exclude it if it is obvious that this is a RDF statement, for instance, if this is a document with only RDF in it.

The `Description` element contains the elements that make up the assertion itself. There can be multiple assertions inside a Description, but they all relate to the same object, because the URI being described is an attribute of the Description.

`Description` can have two types of attributes which contain the URI, and which are treated somewhat differently. The `about` attribute is a URI and resolved as such; if there is a fragment identifier attached to the URI (an anchor following a #), the resource being described is only that fragment. Otherwise, the entire resource is the object of the description.

`about` refers to an existing resource. If the Description or a property value needs to refer to the resource that is the object of the Description itself (self-reference), it will have to use the `ID` attribute in the statement that is self-referencing. This will mean that another URI will be created, as a resource from which an arc can point at the original URI as a property of the new resource. `ID` or `about` can be specified as attributes to the Description, but they cannot be used together. The values for the ID cannot be used more than once in a single document (i.e., everything that is inside the `rdf` element).

Resources are all Web objects described by RDF expressions. A resource can be any information object, for instance a Web page. A resource may also be a collection of objects, for instance a Web site or a section of a site. Resources are always named by a URI reference, and as anything can have a URI reference, anything can be a resource. (URIs can be extended to include any new object or object type imaginable, even if it has taken some time to create a URI for telephones.)

The resource is identified by the `<description>` element. Typically there will be more than one property listed for the resource; `<description>` provides a way to give the resource name just once for several properties. Each element may contain more than one property element of the same property type, each of which adds one arc to the graph. How to interpret this graph is defined in the schema. When the about attribute is specified with <description>, the properties in the <description> refer to the resource whose URI reference is given in the about.

RDF Resource Collections

RDF containers are a way to handle collections of objects, most often resources, in RDF (note that they explicitly do not refer to sets in the mathematical sense). To represent a collection of resources, RDF uses an additional resource that identifies the specific collection (an instance of a collection, in object modeling terminology). This resource must be declared to be an instance of one of the container object types using the type property.

Container structures give rise to an issue about statements: when a statement is made referring to a collection, what *thing* is the statement describing, or in other words, what is the object? Is the statement describing the container itself or is the statement describing the members of the container? The object being described (in the XML syntax indicated by the about attribute) is called the referent in RDF. The referent of the Description is the container (the Bag), not its members.

One would sometimes like to write a statement about each of the contained objects individually, instead of about the container itself. In order to express that *Ora Lassila* is the creator of each of the pages, a different kind of referent is called for, one that distributes over the members of the container. This referent in RDF is expressed using the aboutEach attribute. This new referent type is called a distributive referent. Distributive referents allow us to *share structure* in an RDF Description. For example, when writing several descriptions that all have a number of common statement parts (predicates and objects), the common parts can be shared among all the Descriptions, possibly resulting in space savings and more maintainable metadata. Distributive referents are expanded into the individual statements about the individual container members (internally, implementations are free to retain information about the distributive referents—in order to save space, for example—as long as any querying functions work as if all of the statements were made individually). Using a distributive referent on a container is the same as making the statements about each of the members separately.

In the RDF statement, the description will often need to refer to a collection of resources. This may be the properties of a device, or the works that a person has created, or the students in a course, or the software modules in a package. These values are atomic, because they are not references to other resources. Lists of atomic values are handled using RDF containers, and there are three types of those.

Bag is an unordered list of resources (URIs) or atomic values (*literals*, i.e., strings). It is used to declare that a property has multiple values; the order of the values does not matter, and there can be duplicates of resources and duplicate values in literals. It is just what it sounds like: a bag full of stuff. There is no significance to the order in which the values are given. The Bag might, for instance, be used for a list of part numbers where the order in which the parts are processed does not matter.

`Sequence` is an ordered list of resources or atomic values (literals). It works just like any numbered list: the order is significant. It is intended to hold a listing of values, for instance, in alphabetical order. It is still possible to have duplicates of the same value, however. The Sequence is used to declare that a property has multiple values. `Sequence` might be used, for example, to preserve an alphabetical ordering of values. Duplicate values are permitted.

`Alternative` is a list of resources or values that represent possible alternatives for the (single) value of a property. Any of the items in the list can be selected, depending on the circumstances in which it is used (for instance, if the list of alternatives is used for the selection of document variants for content negotiation, the language variant which the user requests can be selected—irrespective of its place in the list of alternatives). `Alternative` might be used to provide alternative language translations for the title of a work, or to provide a list of Internet mirror sites at which a resource might be found. An application using a property whose value is an Alternative collection is aware that it can choose any one of the items in the list as appropriate. There must be at least one member in the list (otherwise, there would be nothing to choose from).

A single node can be the value of more than one property; that is, it can be pointed to by more than one arc. For example, a single Web page might be shared between several documents and might then be referenced more than once in a *sitemap*. Or two different (ordered) sequences of the same resources may be given. The `xml:lang` attribute can be used to associate a language with the property value. The language of a string value is considered by RDF to be a part of the atomic value, so it does not add to the data model for RDF. RDF does not contain any mechanism for sets, which in principle could be a Bag without duplicates (so other works based on RDF can define set mechanisms). An RDF statement does not say anything about the individual pages, the members of the Bag. When a statement is made referring to a collection, the object that in the XML syntax is indicated by the `About` attribute is called the referent in RDF. The referent of a `<description>` is the container (the Bag) itself, not its members. This also means that there is no way of expressing that there is a union or intersection between two Bags, for instance. They are simply nodes in the graph, and whether they share the same values or not depends on the direction of the arcs. They will, however, remain parts of the same graph, and there is no way of stating that the arc pointing to them is also being pointed to by another arc (except as a qualified property value).

When the container contains a collection of resources (URIs), RDF uses an additional resource (a URI that points to that specific container). If this URI did not previously exist, it can be created and assigned an ID. To declare which of the three container types this resource belongs to, the type property is used (as an arc pointing to the value from the resource, in parallel with the arc pointing to the contents of the container). The resources belonging to the collection are identified by a simple name (_1, _2, _3, etc.). All three container types use the `<li>` markup so that users familiar with HTML can identify it as a container, but the semantics are not the same as those of HTML (where `<li>` is used to mark up an unordered list). The membership property names are assumed to be present, and need not be written out explicitly, when `<li>` is used. Note, however, that the way `<li>` is used here is quite different from the way it is used in HTML. It is, actually, not even the same attribute (it is in a different namespace). To create a collection of resources in RDF, you must declare an additional resource to be an instance of one of the container object types defined above, which is done using the `instanceOf` property type.

When the container object is used to hold multiple values of a property, the resource is the property and it points back to the resource that the property refers to. All the values in the container refer to the same property of the resource. It is also possible to repeat properties of the same type, which means that you do not have to use a container object if you do not want to. If there is no other relation between the values, other than belonging to the same property, they can be multiple instances of the same value. If, however, they have a relation, they will need to be in a container object (a Bag, Sequence, or Alternative). As an example, consider a shelf of novels in the library. They all have the property of being on the same shelf, but some of them may also have the property of being written by the same author. In the first case, their only relationship is that they happen to be there; in the other, they belong in the Bag (or List, if ordered by publication date) of novels by that author.

The contents of a container object may have something more in common than being grouped in the container object. There may be a property they all have in common, for instance (in the case of the novels), being written by the same author. In that case, the RDF aboutEach attribute refers to a property value of all members of a container object. A distributive referent allows one single description to relate to all the elements in a container object. It can be used to point to a number of values common to the members of the container object; in the case of the novels on the bookshelf, not just that they have the same author, but that they have the same publisher, same printer, and the same color on the cover as well. In principle, however, the `aboutEach` is equivalent to having the same attributes on all members of the container objects. There is a way in the RDF Model and Syntax specification to make an `aboutSome` statement (referring to the first six members, say), if this would even be useful. It can possibly be added as an additional mechanism, however.

It is possible to do this for objects that are URIs. The `aboutEachPrefix` attribute lets you declare that all members of a Bag which are URIs and begin with the URI defined in the `aboutEachPrefix` have a common value. This means that all files or Web pages that are part of the structure can have the same attribute. If the `aboutEachPrefix` contains the URI http://www.knigi.ru/ and has the value Fyodor Dostoyevsky, this will apply to both http://www.knigi.ru/theidiot/ and http://www.knigi.ru/thebrotherskaramazov/. But again, it would have been possible to write this as one attribute for each of the members of the Bag (and if it is a mixed bag of Russian novels, that may be easier).

Reified Statements

RDF would be of little value if it were only possible to make statements that were simple facts. There is, however, a mechanism in RDF to make statements about statements ("he said that she said"). In philosophy, this is called a *reified* statement. The reason for this is that it does not refer directly to the original statement (in which case you would need a recording of what she said), but to a model of the statement, in essence what he said that she said. If you wanted to refer to the original statement, you could just point to its URI and make a statement about that, but it would not be the same as the statement about the statement that you wanted to make (instead of saying "I hear he said that she said that Dostoyevsky was boring"), you would say "he said that she made the following statement (a recording of her saying that Dostoyevsky was boring)." And the resource you wanted to refer to was not her statement, but his statement about her statement, which means that your statement must contain a model of both. Essentially, the model is a subgraph of the higher-order statement. That a graph contains a model of a statement does not preclude it from containing the original statement (as in the case when what she said is contained in the same graph as what he said she said, as well as what she said he said she said).

The model of the statement has a subject, which identifies the resource that the original statement talked about. The predicate is the property of the original statement. The object is the value of the predicate. Finally, higher-order statements can have a type, which is the same as the types used for containers in RDF. This actually becomes a lot clearer if we refer to the underlying graphs.

RDF uses a new resource to represent the original statement. A statement that is reified as a new resource X will contain the type as well, so that the statement "The policy for the intranet can be found at http://www.metadata-information.net" can be broken down into a statement of the form {location, {http://www.metadata-information.net"}, "intranet policy"}, and reified (essentially, modeled, as you see) as

```
{type, [X], [RDF:Statement]}
{predicate, [X], [location]}
{subject, [X], [http://www.metadata-information.net]}
{object, [X], "intranet policy"}
```

The types in the `type` property are described in the RDF Schema specification.

All RDF statements consist of triples, as we saw above. This is the key to implementing RDF parsers and browsers. Triples consist of the predicate, subject, and object. This means they have a formal relationship (in the mathematical sense) as well as being ordered. And because the subject of an RDF statement is always a resource, identified by a URI, and they always appear as subject-object-predicate, this should be easy to translate into software even if you are used to thinking in attribute-value pairs. Here, you have a subject, which has an object, which has a predicate, instead of having an attribute, which has a value.

Statements about statements are higher-order statements, in the RDF terminology. But they still consist of triples. And because the object of a subject can be a resource in its own right, the statement about the statement can continue the graph. This also means that the relationship will be clear when you draw the graph, as well as when you parse it as a sequence of triples.

You can also collect statements, as implied by the `Description` element, in a Bag. The Description in that case has an attribute, `bagID`, which is not the same as `ID` but only identifies a container resource whose members are higher-order statements about another resource. It is possible to have both a `bagID` and an `ID` attribute on a Description.

The `Description` element itself is an instance of a Bag resource. The members of this Bag are the resources that correspond to the reification of each of the statements in the description. If a `bagID` attribute is specified, its value is the identifier of the Bag; otherwise, the Bag is anonymous.

In the RDF specification, the XML encoding of RDF is described as a number of XML elements. When you create a metadata description, this is the syntax you use. Here is an example of a Dublin Core Web page classification represented as RDF encoded in XML:

```
<RDF
  xmlns="http://www.w3.org/1999/02/22-rdf-syntax-ns#"
  xmlns:rdf="http://www.w3.org/1999/02/22-rdf-syntax-ns#"
  xmlns:dc="http://purl.org/metadata/dublin_core#"
  xmlns:l="http://mycorp.com/schemas/my-schema#">
  <Description about="http://www.Webnuts.net/Jan97.html">
    <dcsubject
      rdf:value="020--Library Science"
      l:Classification="Dewey Decimal Code"/>
  </Description>
  </RDF>
```

What this says is that the page Jan97.html in the site www.Webnuts.net has a Dublin Core subject that is Library Science, 020 according to the Dewey Decimal code.

The different namespaces make the elements unique, using the namespace mechanism. Each set of elements—the vocabulary—has to be described by a schema, which contains more information than what is available in the DTD. The RDF Schema language describes the parameters of the elements, but the formal description of data types has to be done in the XML Schema language, if you want to do it at the same level as data types in programming languages. That would bring us too far from describing the data in RDF, though, so you will have to read about it in the specifications if you want to find out how it works.

To further illustrate how to use aggregates, consider an example of a document with two authors specified alphabetically, a title specified in two different languages, and having two equivalent locations on the Web:

```
<rdf:RDF
  xmlns:rdf="http://www.w3.org/TR/WD-rdf-syntax#"
  xmlns:dc="http://purl.org/metadata/dublin_core#">
  <rdf:Description about="http://www.foo.com/cool.html">
    <dc:Creator>
      <rdf:Seq ID="CreatorsAlphabeticalBySurname">
        <rdf:li>Mary Andrew</rdf:li>
        <rdf:li>Jacky Crystal</rdf:li>
      </rdf:Seq>
    </dc:Creator>

    <dc:Identifier>
      <rdf:Bag ID="MirroredSites">
        <rdf:li rdf:resource="http://www.foo.com.au/cool.html"/>
        <rdf:li rdf:resource="http://www.foo.com.it/cool.html"/>
      </rdf:bag>
    </dc:Identifier>

    <dc:Title>
      <rdf:Alt>
        <rdf:li xml:lang="en">The Coolest Web Page</rdf:li>
        <rdf:li xml:lang="it">Il Pagio di Web Fuba</rdf:li>
      </rdf:Alt>
    </dc:Title>
  </rdf:Description>
</rdf:RDF>
```

This example illustrates the use of all three types of collection. The order of the creators is significant, so the Sequence container is used to hold them. The locations on the Web are equivalent, and their order is not significant, so a Bag is used. The document has only a single title but that title has two variants, so the Alternatives container is used.

An XML Primer

XML is a metalanguage, a specification for how you should create new markup languages for documents containing structured information. It has superficial similarities to HTML, but because XML mandates the use of < to start a tag and > to end it makes it no more similar to HTML than a bus is similar to a train because both have wheels. HTML has a different set of roots, and HTML is a single application of SGML. XML can have many applications, for instance XHTML (the successor to HTML), RDF (as we have seen), SVG (a vector graphics format), and so on. XML is not really a markup language; it is a rule set for creating markup languages.

When you create an XML application, you create an information model that accurately describes your information set, instead of using an all-purpose model or one developed for some other purpose (the problem that has plagued the AI industry). This model is expressed in the Document Type Description (DTD) or the XML Schema, a document which describes the elements in an XML language. In the DTD or the XML schema you specify a set of elements that will contain your information, declare which rules they have to follow, and give them names that are globally unique (which is possible because you are using the global URI naming system). XML makes sure all new languages follow the same basic rules (if this sounds confusing, you can play football, rugby, and soccer on the same field, but the rules for how and when you may use the field are the same, and you have teams that use a ball and score goals in all the games). Belonging to a family of common rules allows you to transform one XML language into another (using XSLT, which is another standard in the XML family), and it allows you to write software that can work with the markup without having to be rewritten for each new markup language you want to work with. It is impossible to say how many different types of XML applications there are because there is no central registry (indeed, one of the central ideas for XML is that there should not be a central registry, even though several organizations have undertaken to register XML applications in their domain).

XML is a way of making sure that all data follows the same rules. You declare which elements (the start- and end-tags) you are going to use in the DTD or the schema, and you declare what types of data the elements will contain, which attributes they can have, as well as other constraints on them, for instance, how often they can occur in the document, what attributes they can have, if there are size restrictions on the content they can contain, and so on. If the document follows the rules you have defined in the DTD (and the XML 1.0 specification), it is valid XML. If it just follows the specification, it is just well-formed. A document cannot be called XML if it is not well-formed; that is one of the rules of the language.

Henrik Frystyk-Nielsen, then on the staff of the W3C, once jokingly described XML as "you just put angle brackets around everything." There is a great deal of truth in that statement. XML is a metalanguage for applications that express structured information sets. Structured information is really very simple: The information is ordered according to a predetermined pattern. The information in this book is not really structured: It uses typographical elements to make semantic points, and it does not have any regularity in the way information is ordered. But because the text has chapter headings, subheadings, and subsubheadings under the subheadings, it is structured to some extent. The headings can be used to construct a tree structure that describes the book. But the structure does not say anything about the meaning of the content. A table is also structured. It always has rows and columns. Different instances of the same table also follow the same rules, even if the content of the cells is different. The columns always occur in the same order, and the rows are always the same length. If there were a markup for the table, it would reflect the way the table was ordered. Creating XML applications is like creating tables without being confined to the format of rows and columns.

A design goal for XML was that it should be human-readable and machine-understandable. HTML is human-readable, but not machine-understandable: there is no way for a computer to make sense of the tag sets (how do you know whether the ASCII characters inside an <H1> tag are text or figures, for instance? And where does a <P> end?). In XML, you can declare the data types of the elements, so the computer can process the content. It is still possible for a person to understand text that is full of markup. XML, however, by allowing you to define the datatypes of the elements, also allows you to define what the computer should do with the content within the elements. One application of XML that has gained fairly widespread use is as a universal format for exchanging information between computers, for instance, translating a database in a proprietary format to an XML-based format and then importing it into another proprietary database format. There is nothing that says that XML documents have to be displayed at all. They can also be input for another computer program. Strictly speaking, though, XML is not machine-understandable, because the logic is not declared in the content. For that, you have to use RDF.

The advantage of XML is that you can make up your own elements, which you can use to process the information. Let us say we want to describe a seminar I held a couple of years ago:

```
<seminar>XML for content management</seminar>
<venue>Ericsson Cyberlab NY</venue>
<time_of_day_24>18:30</time_of_day_24>
<day>27</day>
<month>May</month>
<year>1999</year>
```

I just made these elements up, and this could be an XML fragment. It does not have to be harder than this. However, if you define new elements every time you want to describe something, it becomes impossible to process—how do you know if `<venue>` in the example above is the same as `<location>` in some other example? If you use a predefined application of XML, it becomes much easier for anyone who wants to write an application processing the information.

XML itself is defined in a family of related specifications. The XML specification defines the syntax of XML, that is, how elements (the combinations of start- and end-tags) and attributes should be defined. The XSLT specification describes a standardized way of transforming content formatted in one XML markup to other formats, for instance, HTML and ASCII. XSLT is interesting because it is possible to transform documents into RDF. It is also possible to transform documents into other formats conditional on RDF embedded in the document structures, which means that you can build your own heuristics into the transformations. XML namespaces define how different tag sets are handled together. Several more specifications describe, for instance, how to handle linking and pointing into an XML document from the outside (creating a link for which there is no anchor, in essence), how to handle pieces of an XML document (fragments), and so on. Because they are not central to the encoding of RDF in XML, however, we will not go into them here.

Because XML is a metalanguage that defines semantic markup, a large number of applications are being defined to use XML, for instance, for data exchange between applications. These include e-commerce applications, vector graphics, mathematical equations, server APIs, musical notation, and a huge number of other types of information structures. One XML application is the Wireless Markup Language (WML) used in the Wireless Application Protocol (WAP) environment, which is produced by the WAP Forum. WAP is the standard for representing information on cellular phones and other handheld devices.

XML is a markup language for documents containing structured information. Structured information contains both content (words, pictures, etc.) and markup, in essence indicators to show the role of the content piece (a fragment, in the correct terminology). Content can have different roles in different places in a document: the same word in a heading has a different meaning from when it occurs in a footnote. Almost all documents have some structure.

A document is really nothing but a container object, containing a collection of other objects, ordered in some way and connected through relations and inheritances (parent-child relationships). A picture can be an object, an old idea to anyone who has been designing HTML pages. The fact that text and other elements in a page can be objects in themselves is probably not as clear. But in XML, you can reference these objects using URIs, something called an inline reference. An XML document can be composed of nothing but inline references, which are resolved by the XML processor when the document is received at your computer; the XML processor looks up and retrieves the content behind the URIs.

A markup language is a mechanism to identify structures in a document. The word *document* refers not only to traditional documents, but also to data contained in other XML *data formats*. These include vector graphics, e-commerce transactions, mathematical equations, object metadata, server APIs, and a thousand other kinds of structured information.

XML, SGML, and HTML

Like HTML, XML makes use of tags (words bracketed by < and ' ') and attributes (of the form `name="value"`), but while HTML specifies what each tag and attribute means (and often how the text between them will look in a browser), XML uses the tags only to delimit pieces of data, and leaves the interpretation of the data completely to the application that reads it. The XML specification specifies neither semantics nor a tag set. In other words, if you see `<p>` in an XML file, don't assume it is a paragraph. In fact, XML is really a meta-language for describing markup languages. In other words, XML provides a facility to define tags and the structural relationships between them. This is the information that goes into the DTD or the XML schema. Because there's no predefined tag set, there can't be any preconceived semantics. All of the semantics of an XML document will either be defined by the applications that process them or by stylesheets. RDF is an application adding semantics to XML (actually, RDF Schema adds the semantics).

Development of XML started in 1996 and it has been a W3C Recommendation since February 1998. SGML was developed in the early 1980s and has been an ISO standard since 1986. XML is defined as an application profile of the Standard Generalized Markup Language (SGML) defined by ISO 8879—but it is also defined as an application of itself. DTDs express the XML application as an application of SGML, XML schemas as an application of XML. XML is, roughly speaking, a restricted form of SGML. The designers of XML simply took the best parts of SGML, guided by the experience with HTML, and produced something that is no less powerful than SGML.

XML is different from HTML in many more ways than being an application profile of SGML. It uses Unicode, which is a 16-bit format for representing almost all characters that are being used all over the world (it was really intended to be used for all characters, but there are some that are not mapped into the character set, mostly in Japanese and traditional Chinese writing, even though the most frequently used characters are covered). HTML up to version 4.0, on the other hand, used 7-bit ASCII as its least common denominator. The reason HTML used

7-bit ASCII is the same as for mail systems, where some older mail servers are not equipped to handle modern character sets. However, 7-bit ASCII misses many characters that are important to people outside the United States, such as inflections, accents, and umlauts, and it is also very complicated to represent Chinese and Japanese characters. This is one reason for using Unicode: it is possible to parse all XML content using the same parsers, irrespective of the language in which the content is written. URIs, however, which identify the resources, still have to be 7-bit ASCII on the insistence of the Internet Engineering Task Force (IETF). And the URI encoding excludes some characters, as well.

Writing XML is also different from HTML in that it requires that the elements—the combination of start and end markup tags—be closed. Open-ended tags like `<P>` are not allowed; they have to be closed, like `<p>...</p>` (and element names must be in lowercase, according to the XML convention, although technically, they could be uppercase as well). Elements can either be structured with a start- and end-tag (`<tag> content </tag>`), or as an empty element with the end-tag included in the start-tag (`<tag/>`). The first type is elements with content, the second is elements with no content (used for elements with attributes only).

In XML, as in HTML 4.0, it is possible to have attributes on markup. Attributes are placed inside the start-tag, so `<start beginning="now">` means that the element start has an attribute name beginning, and an attribute value that is now. The attribute value must be in quotes. Attributes, though, have a much larger role to play in XML than in HTML. They also play a very large role in RDF.

Element names describe what the element is about, while attributes provide further information (which can be used in the processing of the content, or the application). Attribute values give you control over the element, but the element drives the application. You can, for instance, define an alternate representation, when it should be used, and in what ways (you recognize the "alt" element from HTML). This can be used to facilitate transformations, control how the content is applied, and do many other things. Note, however, that in applications such as WML, the interpretation in the device is very restricted, and you may not use attributes as you like.

XML is case-sensitive, so `Creator`, `creator`, `CREATOR`, and `cREATOR` are interpreted as four totally different elements. Element names in lower case is the best existing practice (so `creator`, not `Creator`), but the practice that has developed is also to use capitalization in elements where it increases readability (`documentCreator`, not `documentcreator`, for instance), something called the interCap convention. The important thing is to watch this very carefully, because you cannot take uppercase element names and render them in lowercase automatically.

HTML browsers normally render a document line by line as it is received at the client. The XML model is different. When a document arrives at a client, it is processed through a number of steps. First, the character data is decoded from the binary encoding used over the network, creating a stream of Unicode characters. The document is then parsed, that is, the XML processor steps through the document and identifies the elements it contains and how they should be handled.

Unlike HTML documents, XML documents do not have to be structured in the order they should be displayed or processed (you may not want them to be displayed at all). That they are ordered as they should be processed, instead of as they should be rendered, results in a tree structure that can be manipulated by programs and scripts via the Document Object Model (DOM) of the W3C, which essentially is an application programming interface (API) to the data in the document. There have been discussions about APIs for RDF, but so far, there do not seem to be any winners.

To further confuse things, an XML document actually has two different object structures. Each XML document has both a logical and a physical structure. Physically, the document is composed of units called entities. An entity may refer to other entities to cause their inclusion in the document (an *inline reference*). A document begins in a *root* or document entity. Logically, the document is composed of declarations, elements, comments, character references, and processing instructions, all of which are indicated in the document by explicit markup. The logical and physical structures must nest properly within each other.

A document has to contain one or more elements. There must be one element, called the root, or document element, which does not appear in the content of any other element. The document entity serves as the root of the entity tree and a starting-point for an XML processor. For all other elements, if the start-tag is in the content of another element, the end-tag is in the content of the same element. More simply stated, the elements, delimited by start- and end-tags, nest properly within each other.

XML APIs

One of the basic ideas of XML is that the document is structured. One other idea, just to confuse things, is that there is no document, but a collection of objects which is ordered, something that is not quite the same. These are two different and complementary views of the same information set, using the same technique, and a prime example of how a technology can be different depending on who is talking about it. One idea is essentially the view of the database programmer, the other is the view of the XML programmer.

To the database programmer, the document is a series of text fragments, and the XML specification actually refers to XML documents as consisting of several entities containing either parsed or unparsed data. Parsed data is made up of characters, some of which form character data, and some of which form markup. Markup encodes a description of the document's storage layout and logical structure. XML provides a mechanism to impose constraints on the storage layout and logical structure, which we will explore further in Chapter 5, "RDF Schemas." But to the XML programmer, the document is the thing, and to manipulate the document you need an API.

APIs map program code to function calls so that a programmer can use the functions without having to do everything from scratch. APIs often become standards, usually by being accepted throughout an industry. For XML, there are two standard APIs: DOM and the Simple API for XML (SAX).

DOM is a W3C recommendation resulting from several years of study by a working group of industry representatives. The W3C DOM specifies interfaces that may be used to manage XML or HTML documents. In the DOM specification, the term *document* is used in the broad sense, meaning any file produced by an application. The DOM identifies the interfaces and objects used to represent and manipulate a document, the semantics of these interfaces and objects (including both behavior and attributes), and the relationships and collaborations among these interfaces and objects. This is the same model as in object-oriented programming languages, in which the data itself is encapsulated in objects that hide it, protecting it from direct external manipulation. The functions associated with these objects determine how the objects may be manipulated, and they are part of the object model.

With the DOM, programmers can build documents, navigate their structure, and add, modify, or delete elements and content. Anything found in an HTML or XML document can be accessed, changed, deleted, or added using the DOM, with a few exceptions. In particular, the DOM interfaces for the XML internal and external subsets have not yet been specified.

The name *Document Object Model* was chosen because it is an *object model* in the traditional object-oriented design sense. The documents are modeled using objects. The model discusses not only the structure of a document, but also the behavior of a document and the objects of which it is composed. Documents have a logical structure much like a tree, or rather, several parallel trees (created by the structure imposed by the nesting of elements within the XML root element). The root element serves as the root of the element tree for the document. In other words, the nodes in the tree do not represent a data structure, they represent objects, which have functions and identity.

The DOM is a programming API for documents. It is not a competitor to the Component Object Model (COM), which, like CORBA, is a language-independent way to specify interfaces and objects. The DOM may be implemented using language-independent systems like COM or CORBA; it may also be implemented using language-specific bindings like the Java or ECMAScript bindings, which have been specified by the W3C working group. DOM is not dependent on any particular programming language. It is specified in IDL, the OMG Interface Definition Language. It is based on an object structure that closely resembles the structure of the documents it models. However, the DOM does not specify that documents must be implemented as a tree, nor does it specify how the relationships among objects should be implemented. It is a purely logical model that may be implemented in any convenient manner.

The DOM Level 2 specification consists of several modules: Core, HTML, Views, StyleSheets, CSS, Events, Traversal, and Range. The DOM Core represents the functionality used for XML documents, and also serves as the basis for DOM HTML. A compliant implementation of the DOM must implement all of the fundamental interfaces in the Core chapter with the semantics as defined. Further, it must implement at least one of the HTML DOM and the extended (XML) interfaces with the semantics as defined. The other modules are optional.

The DOM originated as a specification to allow JavaScript scripts and Java programs to be portable among Web browsers. *Dynamic HTML* was the immediate ancestor of the DOM, and it was originally thought of largely in terms of browsers. However, when the DOM Working Group was formed at W3C, it was also joined by vendors in other domains, including HTML or XML editors and document repositories.

Several of these vendors had worked with SGML before XML was developed; as a result, the DOM has been influenced by the SGML Groves and HyTime standards. Some of these vendors had also developed their own object models for documents in order to provide an API for SGML/XML editors or document repositories, and these object models have also influenced the DOM.

The interfaces defined in the DOM are abstractions. In essence, they allow you as a programmer to specify ways to access and manipulate applications' internal representations of documents. As with all properly designed APIs, the abstract interfaces do not imply or rely on a particular implementation. Each DOM application is free to maintain documents in any convenient representation, as long as the interfaces in the DOM specification are supported. Some DOM implementations are foreseen to be existing programs that use the DOM interfaces to access software written long before the DOM specification existed.

When a DOM representation of a document is serialized as XML or HTML text, applications will need to check each character in text data to see whether it needs to be escaped using a numeric or pre-defined entity. Failing to do so could result in invalid HTML or XML.

Knowing that you need a parser to make sense of an XML document, you could implement it on top of DOM, since it has to work with the XML serialization of RDF in XML. (The XML document must be run through a piece of software called the XML processor before it can be handled by other applications.) Of course, the object orientation of the DOM allows for a direct connection between the triples in the serialization of the graph and the objects in the tree.

DOM constructs an object tree and contains event handlers that are related to user and system events (e.g., `OnMouseOver`) to trip actions. Essentially, you write in your program that an action should be taken on a certain part of a tree when an event occurs. This works well if you have the tree in the computer memory and will work with it as a static document. An alternative approach to getting at the data in the document is to use the parser, and when the document is read, call the application directly when a parsing event (such as the start and end of elements) occurs. The application has to implement the event handlers to deal with the different events. This is similar to handling events in Windows, or any other graphical user interface. Note that neither excludes the other.

In some ways, the SAX approach is the total inverse of the DOM approach. While DOM is batch-oriented, SAX is stream-oriented. In practice, however, they can be exchanged. It is possible to construct a parse tree using an event-based API, and it is possible to use an event-based API to traverse a tree in memory. To the programmer, this means that which API you use for your application (the document remains the same, because the events are independent of the application) depends on what you want to achieve. If you are doing machine-to-machine communication, you may want to use SAX, because it enables you to process the documents in a fashion that is easier to integrate with other software. (Remember, though, that you cannot process an XML document line by line, as you would an HTML document: An XML document has to be processed in its entirety.) SAX may also be more economical with computer memory, which very likely is more critical in a server-based application than in your PC. On the other hand, if your application involves user events, it makes more sense to go the DOM route. Both work with the standard libxml library, and both come with bindings to the most common programming languages, so you do not have to consider them in terms of platform dependency (e.g., one only works for Windows).

To the information designer, it does not matter greatly which API your programmers have selected to use. Speed and other user characteristics of the application may be influenced by this, but are more dependent on implementation than API selection. And over the Internet, bottlenecks in the network are likely to have far larger influence than server performance. At least during busy hours.

RDF APIs

As yet, there are no standard APIs for RDF as there is for XML. Because the actual deductions and inferences take place at a level above XML (which is only usedto transport and encode the RDF, remember), you cannot apply standard calls in your application to address the RDF. The easiest way is probably to use a parser and extract the triples, and work with them in your application.

There have been several ideas discussed for an RDF API, all of which would work with the information in different ways. There is a proposal for an RDF Schema API that would access, but not be able to work with, the information. No standard proposal has yet been developed, and discussion is still ongoing in the RDF interest group, but what has been proposed so far is an API with the calls shown in Table 3.3.

Peter Hannapel, in his summary of the discussions, gives an example of a short script demonstrating the usage of the RDF Core interface. The script creates a small RDF model and performs a query on it.

```
#Creating the model
Model Example;
Example=Example.create;
Example.setSourceURI("http://example_server.de/rdf/models/example");

#Creating Resources and Literals
Resource paper =Example.createResource("http://paperServer/paperURL");
Resource author =Example.createResource(""); #noname resource
Resource author_predicate =Example.createResource("author");
Resource firstname_predicate =Example.createResource("firstname");
Resource lastname_predicate =Example.createResource("lastname");
Literal author_firstname = Example.createLiteral ("Peter");
Literal author_lastname = Example.createLiteral ("Hannappel");

#Creating Statements
Statement paper_attr_1= Example.createStatement (paper,
author_predicate, author);
Statement author_attr_1= Example.createStatement (author,
firstname_predicate, author_firstname);
Statement author_attr_2= Example.createStatement (author,
lastname_predicate, author_lastname);

#adding the Statements to the model
Example.add (paper_attr_1);
Example.add (author_attr_1);
Example.add (author_attr_2);

#Use of the find method
Model authorInfo=Example.find(author,0,0);
```

Table 3.3 RDF API Function Calls and Return Values

FUNCTION CALL	RETURN VALUE
`String getLabel()`	The URI, if the RDFNode is of type `Resource`. The Content, if the RDFNode is of type `Literal`.
`String getURI()`	Returns the URI of the Resource.
`Resource subject()`	Returns the subject of the statement.
`Resource predicate()`	Returns the predicate of the statement.
`RDFNode object()`	Returns the object of the statement.
`Model create()`	The method returns an empty model.
`Model duplicate()`	The method returns a copy of the model calling it.
`Literal createLiteral(In String str)`	The method returns a new literal with content str.
`Resource createResource(In String str)`	The method returns a new resource with URI str.
`Statement createStatement(In Resource subject, Resource predicate, RDFNode object)`	The method returns a new triple with Subject, Predicate, Object as given.
`void add(In Statement t)`	The method adds the given statement to the statements of the model.
`void remove(In statement t)`	The method removes the given statement from the statements of the model.
`void setSourceURI(In String URI)`	The method sets the base URI for the model, which has the following effects: At the creation of new resources, the URI may be modified. The URI is used at serialization. When set, the method getURI returns the sourceURI.
`String getSourceURI()`	The method returns the base URI of the model, if previously set.
`int size()`	The method returns a count of the statements in the model.
`Enumeration elements()`	The method returns an enumeration containing each statement in the model.
`boolean contains(In Statement t)`	The method returns true if the model contains the statement, false otherwise.

Table 3.3 RDF API Function Calls and Return Values (Continued)

FUNCTION CALL	RETURN VALUE
`Model find(In Resource subject, Resource predicate, RDFNode object)`	The method returns a *sub-model* containing all statements matching the query parameters. Null values for parameters match anything. `find (a,0,0)` returns a model containing all statements with subject a. `find (a,0,c)` returns a model containing all statements with subject a and object c. `find (a,b,c)` returns a model containing all statements with subject a, predicate b, and object c (i.e., the statement `{a,b,c}` if existing in the model queried).
`SetModel intersect(In Model m)`	The method returns the intersection of the calling model with another model.
`SetModel difference(In Model m)`	The method returns the difference of the calling model with another model.
`SetModel unite(In Model m)`	The method returns the union of the calling model with another model.
`Model getGroundModel()`	Returns the "standard" model the calling virtual model is based on. Virtual Model is intended to be used to add functionality to the normal model interface (e.g., active models).

There is also an example implementation by Sergey Melnik of Stanford that contains several other functions, as well as additional function calls.

The RDF and XML Processors

A graph must be walked, if the RDF is to be interpreted. Walking through a graph is done by a piece of software called the RDF processor; specifically, walking a graph is a type of parsing. A parser is a program that goes through the data and tries to make sense of it (given, of course, the terms it can use to make "sense," this being a computer and as such inherently stupid). In practice, it will translate the information into another format as it goes through it. These definitions are, of course, not the formal definitions from the dictionary.

The resolution of the RDF statements is handled by the RDF processor (it does not necessarily have to be separate in practice, but it has to be conceptually). There are very few implementation notes in the W3C documentation describing the expected functionality of the RDF processor, but there are a few things that have crystallized about its behavior, and some things that are stated in the specifications.

Before it will get the data, however, a software module called an XML processor is used to read the XML document and provide access to data content and structure. It is working on behalf of the RDF processor, here called the application. The XML specification describes the required behavior of an XML processor in terms of how it must read XML data and the information it must provide to the application.

XML documents have to be well-formed to be processed at all (indeed, to be able to call themselves XML documents). A textual object is a well-formed XML document if it fits the definition of a "document" in the XML specification, meets all the wellformedness constraints in this specification, and each of the parsed entities which is referenced directly or indirectly within the document is well-formed.

A parsed entity contains text, a sequence of characters that may represent markup or character data. The mechanism for encoding character code points into bit patterns may vary from entity to entity. All XML processors must accept the UTF-8 and UTF-16 encodings of 10646. XML files are text files. They are not meant to be read directly, but rendered or interpreted. The text format allows them to be opened in an emergency. URIs cannot contain non-ASCII characters, but XML fragment ID:s can. To avoid incompatibilities implementers are asked in the specification to use the XML convention for system identifiers, representing non-ASCII characters in a URI as one or more bytes in the UTF-8 encoding and escaping them using the URI escape mechanism (converting them to %HH, where HH is the hex notation of the byte value).

The rules for XML files are much stricter than for HTML. If the markup does not follow the specification, the XML processor will stop and issue an error message. An HTML browser does not have to do this; the reason—other than consistency —is that an HTML document can only be rendered on the screen, but an XML document can be the automated input to a corporate purchasing system from a software agent, an alarm message from a radio tower, or basically anything.

Table 3.4 summarizes the contexts in which character references, entity references, and invocations of unparsed entities might appear and the required behavior of an XML processor in each case. The labels in the leftmost column describe the recognition context.

Validity and WellFormedness

All XML documents must be well-formed, which implies they must follow the rules in the XML specification. The XML processor must report violations of the specification's wellformedness constraints, which are collected in the content of the document entity and any other parsed entities that they read.

Table 3.4 XML Processor Handling of References

TYPE OF REFERENCE	XML PROCESSOR MANAGEMENT OF PARAMETER ENTITIES	XML PROCESSOR MANAGEMENT OF INTERNAL PARAMETERS	XML PROCESSOR EXTERNAL PARAMETERS MANAGEMENT	XML PROCESSOR UNPARSED PARAMETERS MANAGEMENT	XML PROCESSOR CHARACTER ENTITY MANAGEMENT	EXPLANATION
Reference in Content	Not recognized	Included	Included if validating	Forbidden	Included	As a reference anywhere after the start-tag and before the end-tag of an element; corresponds to the nonterminal content
Reference in Attribute Value	Not recognized	Included in literal	Forbidden	Forbidden	Included	As a reference within either the value of an attribute in a start-tag, or a default value in an attribute declaration; corresponds to the nonterminal AttValue
Occurs as Attribute Value	Not recognized	Forbidden	Forbidden	Notify	Not recognized	As a Name, not a reference, appearing either as the value of an attribute, which has been declared as type ENTITY, or as one of the space-separated tokens in the value of an attribute, which has been declared as type ENTITIES.

continues

Table 3.4 XML Processor Handling of References (Continued)

TYPE OF REFERENCE	XML PROCESSOR MANAGEMENT OF PARAMETER ENTITIES	XML PROCESSOR MANAGEMENT OF INTERNAL PARAMETERS	XML PROCESSOR EXTERNAL PARAMETERS MANAGEMENT	XML PROCESSOR UNPARSED PARAMETERS MANAGEMENT	XML PROCESSOR CHARACTER ENTITY MANAGEMENT	EXPLANATION
Reference in EntityValue	Included in literal	Bypassed	Bypassed	Forbidden	Included	As a reference within a parameter or internal entity's literal entity value in the entity's declaration; corresponds to the nonterminal EntityValue
Reference in DTD	Included as PE	Forbidden	Forbidden	Forbidden	Forbidden	As a reference within either the internal or external subsets of the DTD, but outside of an EntityValue or AttValue

Beyond that, conforming XML processors fall into two classes: validating and non-validating. A validating XML processor must read every piece of a document and report all wellformedness and validity violations. A non-validating processor needs to read only the document entity.

Validating processors must report violations of the constraints expressed by the declarations in the DTD or the XML Schema, as well as failures to fulfill the validity constraints given in this specification. In order to do this, validating XML processors must read and process the entire DTD or the XML Schema, and all external parsed entities referenced in the document.

Non-validating processors are required to check only the document entity, including the entire internal DTD subset, for wellformedness. While they are not required to check the document for validity, they are required to process all the declarations they read in the internal DTD subset and in any parameter entity that they read, up to the first reference to a parameter entity that they do not read. That is to say, they must use the information in those declarations to normalize attribute values, include the replacement text of internal entities, and supply default attribute values. They must not process entity declarations or attribute-list declarations encountered after a reference to a parameter entity that is not read, because the entity may have contained overriding declarations.

This means that a non-validating processor may not detect certain wellformedness errors, specifically those that require reading external entities. It also means that the information passed from the processor to the application may vary, depending on whether the processor reads parameter and external entities. To make different XML processors interoperable, applications that use non-validating processors should not rely on any behaviors not required of such processors. Applications that require facilities such as the use of default attributes (internal entities that are declared in external entities) should use validating XML processors. For the RDF processor, this means that it still is good enough with the wellformedness check, but the validation would, of course, serve to find any troubles in the document.

For compatibility, content models in element type declarations are required to be deterministic. SGML requires deterministic content models (it calls them "unambiguous"); XML processors built using SGML systems may flag non-deterministic content models as errors.

For example, the content model `((b,c)|(b,d))` is non-deterministic, because given an initial `b` the parser cannot know which `b` in the model is being matched without looking ahead to see which element follows the `b`. In this case, the two references to `b` can be collapsed into a single reference, making the model read `(b,(c|d))`. An initial b now clearly matches only a single name in the content model. The parser doesn't need to look ahead to see what follows; either `c` or `d` would be accepted.

There are two categories of XML documents: well-formed and valid. A document that does not follow the syntax of XML cannot be well-formed. Markup character sequences in a document that cannot be parsed or are invalid mean the document cannot be well-formed. In addition, the document must conform to the grammar of XML documents. In particular, some markup constructs (like parameter entity references) are allowed only in specific places (i.e., in the DTD). The document is not well-formed if they occur elsewhere, even if the document is well-formed in all other ways. Moreover, a number of criteria that the document must conform to for wellformedness are stated in the XML specification. Some of these conditions are actually inherited from SGML, as follows:

- The replacement text for all parameter entities referenced inside a markup declaration consists of zero or more complete markup declarations. (No parameter entity used in the document may consist of only part of a markup declaration.)
- No attribute may appear more than once on the same start-tag.
- String attribute values cannot contain references to external entities. Non-empty tags must be properly nested.
- Parameter entities must be declared before they are used.
- All entities must be declared except the following: amp, lt, gt, apos, and quot.
- A binary entity cannot be referenced in the flow of content, it can only be used in an attribute declared as ENTITY or ENTITIES.
- Neither text nor parameter entities are allowed to be recursive, directly or indirectly.

According to the XML specification, a document has to be well-formed to be XML. There simply cannot be something like malformed XML. However, there can be documents that are malformed RDF but well-formed XML, for instance. If confronted with a document that is not well-formed, the XML processor is not required to do anything.

The step above wellformedness is validity. A well-formed document is valid only if it contains a proper document type declaration and if the document obeys the constraints of that declaration (element sequence and nesting is valid, required attributes are provided, attribute values are of the correct type, etc.). The XML specification identifies all of the criteria in detail. Note that a document does not have to have a DTD or XML schema to be well-formed.

When the document has passed the XML processor, the result is a document with all entity references resolved and ready to be processed by the next application layer, which in this case means the RDF processor. If it encounters a name whose semantics it does not recognize, it has to leave it unrecognized.

Transporting and Referencing RDF

If the metadata describing an object is to be of any use, it has to get from where it is stored to where it will be read, either by a human or a computer. In the case of a card catalog of a library, it is easy: You have to come to the data, by going to the card catalog and reading it. But in the case of RDF, it is different. The data will come to you (or to the application which will process the data).

Transporting RDF in HTTP

An RDF document is an XML document and, as such, is like any other document: It references the resource it is describing, and so identifies it. But the other way around is not so easy. How does a document describe that it has a metadata description associated with it?

There are four ways in the XML and HTML standards in which a description can be associated with the resource it describes.

1. It can be external to the resource but supplied by the transfer mechanism in the same transaction (inside an HTTP HEAD or GET).
2. It can be embedded in the resource itself, for instance inside an HTML document using the META element.
3. It can be retrieved independently from the resource, for instance when it is linked using the LINK element.
4. The description can contain (*wrap*) the resource, that is, the raw RDF just being poured into the document. When embedding RDF in a document, it should be embedded inline in the head of the document. This may cause problems with some older versions of browsers.

There are now ways to create an external pointer into the resource (which in some ways crosses the embedding with the wrapping and the retrieval from an external source: a true RDF triple). It is of course also possible to apply content negotiation and enable the retrieving agent to determine whether it wants a human-readable or machine-readable version of the data.

In an HTML document, however, the description can be made external to the document using the Link element in HTML 4.0 or higher. Link elements can have a number of different relation types describing the link, and the one that is recommended is the *meta* link type.

This is also tied up with the transport of the description. Today, there are basically two ways of transporting metadata: In the body of the message (the *body* of an

HTTP message includes both the *head* and *body* sections of an HTML document, just to confuse the issue). *message body* refers to anything that is sent in the message body of the protocol-that is, anything which is not specifically designated as a header. Most protocols have specified headers, and the other way is to transport the data in them. Specifically, HTTP, the protocol that is used on the Web, has only four methods (GET, PUT, HEAD, and POST), and only POST allows the client to send a document to the server, but it cannot ask for a resource at the same time. If you want to do that, you have to send the data along with the request for the resource in the GET. This is not so bad, as there are a number of headers in HTTP, and it is possible to create a new header specifically for this purpose. When you are just retrieving a piece of RDF from a server (e.g., as part of resolving the inline references in your document), you will of course use the standard GET method.

In HTTP, there is no header to describe the feature set of a terminal when making a request (even though some, e.g., the User-agent header, describe certain features). The request-header fields allow the client to pass additional information about the request, and about the client itself, to the server. Several headers can be used to provide information about some aspects of the terminal, but none is intended to provide a full description. These fields act as request modifiers, with semantics equivalent to the parameters on a programming language method invocation.

RFC 2616 lists the following relevant headers:

- Accept
- Accept-Charset
- Accept-Encoding
- Accept-Language
- Pragma
- User-Agent

It is also true that the headers available are not limited to these, because RFC 2616 (the formal specification of HTTP) states that "an origin server is not limited to these dimensions and MAY vary the response based on any aspect of the request, including information outside the request-header fields or within extension header fields not defined by this specification."

There are, however, inherent limitations to these headers in the context discussed here. The Accept request-header field can be used to specify certain media types that are acceptable for the response. There is no way of specifying anything else but media types, however. This means that there is no way of handling variations within media types using the Accept field. Nor does the User-agent header field solve the particular problem at hand. Its semantics are, after all, limited to product name and comment.

The method discussed is a special case of server-driven content negotiation, as discussed in RFC 2616. Several disadvantages of the method are presented. For instance, the RFC states that "it is impossible for the server to accurately determine what might be 'best' for any given user, since that would require complete knowledge of both the capabilities of the user agent and the intended use for the response (e.g., does the user want to view it on screen or print it on paper?)."

While it is true that an absolutely optimal representation would require more information than can be made available, it is still quite possible to achieve an optimized presentation for the current transaction, given an incomplete information set, provided the salient parameters are present. Presentation of the current Web is frequently designed for users with large screens and high-end computers. With device types proliferating, there is an emerging need for content to be formatted for rendering on different devices and different modalities such as text, sound, or a combination of the two. Hardware and layout characteristics (for example, the display or input capabilities), as well as the software environments, are as heterogeneous as the devices and device types themselves. In addition, presentation preferences vary between individual users. For content on the current World Wide Web to then be usable, the application server needs to be aware of the context or situation in which the information is being presented.

The RFC also states that "Having the user agent describe its capabilities in every request can be both very inefficient (given that only a small percentage of responses have multiple representations) and a potential violation of the user's privacy."

The question of the inefficiency has turned out to be different from what was expected when the RFC was written. Given that the majority of requests are directed at a small number of sites, and they already use database-driven content generation techniques, often with cookies and other, nonstandard methods to describe the user and the device, it is unlikely that this would introduce any additional load on the system. Given that file sizes of responses have tended to increase in the last few years, it is also unlikely that even the most comprehensive description would affect the asymmetry of the Web.

One of the few applications of RDF to date that attempts to address this is CC/PP, the Composite Capabilities/Preference Profile, that is used to describe devices, like WAP telephones. It uses an HTTP header field set—the CC/PP Exchange Protocol—defined as an application of the HTTP extension framework, which, however, seems not to have progressed beyond its current status as an Experimental RFC. What is now being discussed in the CC/PP working group is to introduce a new HTTP header, which would be capable of containing a full description of the terminal and the user preferences for its use, as requested. It is provisionally referred to as the `accept-profile` header. A profile in this context is simply a collection of properties that describe the capabilities of the client and its environment.

In the case of HTTP, a user agent generates, encodes, and appends a profile onto an outgoing HTTP request at the requesting end. Intermediate proxies along the path of the request can append additional descriptions of their capabilities or services. At the origin server, the profile can be dynamically composed from fragments of capability assertions collected from various sources (e.g., CC/PP repositories) indicated by a default URI, then parsed and interpreted to determine the features of the presentation environment.

The content can be generated either by using filtering techniques specific to a device or user's preferences (the method being out of the scope of this discussion), or by selecting an appropriate presentation format with the content intact (e.g., variants of a style sheet). Depending upon the application, a suitable variant of the content itself may also be selected (from a set) or dynamically generated (from a database).

The adapted content is returned in the HTTP response, possibly further transformed by the intermediate network elements, and finally rendered to the client.

It is possible to send a request with as little profile information as possible, using references (URIs) to enable the dynamic composition of a profile. Overrides can then be sent attached to these references. This is, strictly speaking, not a matter for the protocol (but rather the data format; the resolution of inline references is not a problem for the protocol but rather, in the case of CC/PP, the RDF processor), except for one thing: caching of profiles, which can be done using the cache management mechanisms in HTTP.

As an example of overrides, a user agent issues a request with URIs which address the profile information, and if the user agent changes the value of an attribute, such as turning sound off, only that change is sent together with the URIs. When an origin server receives the request, the origin server inquires of CC/PP repositories the CC/PP descriptions using the list of URIs. Then the origin server creates a tailored content using the fully enumerated CC/PP descriptions.

The origin server might not obtain the fully enumerated CC/PP descriptions if any one of the CC/PP repositories is not available. In this case, the implementation determines whether the origin server should respond to the request with a tailored content, a non-tailored content, or an error. In any case, the origin server should inform the user agent of the fact.

Many proxies do not support additional headers, even if the origin server and the client do so. This is due to faulty implementations as well as to the age of the systems being deployed. It can also not be expected that proxies will be upgraded just because another specification has been published. Older proxies can be expected to strip out unknown headers. One patch—which is not intended to solve the problem—is to include the user agent of the type CC/PP in the user agent field. The value of this user agent is the URI of the profile, which will then have to be requested by the server using a normal GET operation.

The `Profile` header field in the CC/PP Exchange Protocol is a `request-header` field, which conveys a list of references addressing CC/PP descriptions. The `accept-profile` header can use a similar, but simplified, format.

One way of achieving this is to use the `accept-profile` header to encapsulate a format defined elsewhere. This means that the receiving server will need a method to return an error message if it cannot parse the format of the content. One solution is to include a field that designates the format of the description. If this were not parsable, the server would return an error message ("HTTP status code 415 Unsupported Media Type"). This implies that the server is refusing to service the request because the entity of the request is in a format not supported by the requested resource for the requested method.

The header should contain a field in which the content type of the format is given (as registered by IANA). See Section 4 for a listing of some possible device description formats. If the content type is not registered, it will either result in an error message or the semantics will have to be built into the server (this would be the case when using a non-standardized format).

In case the header can be parsed, but appropriate action cannot be taken on the content, a field similar to the `Profile` warning field in the CCPP-ex protocol is useful. The `Profile` warning header field is a response-header field used to carry warning information. When a client issues a request to a server with the `accept-profile` header field, the server inquires of CC/PP repositories the CC/PP descriptions using the absolute URIs in the accept-profile header field. If any one of the CC/PP repositories is not available, the server might not obtain the fully enumerated CC/PP descriptions, or the server might not obtain first-hand or fresh CC/PP descriptions. In the CCPP-exchange protocol, the server responds to the client with the `Profile` warning header field if any one of the CC/PP descriptions could not be obtained, or any one of the CC/PP descriptions is stale. This mechanism can be used outside the CCPP-ex protocol as well, for instance when a profile is claimed to be in one format, but cannot be parsed; or when a header has been cached but cannot be retrieved, which would be equivalent to the previous case of a repository not being resolvable.

To make sure the cache is not stale, a warn-code could be used. The warn-code assigns three digits. The `1xx` indicates the status of the profile (e.g., if it is fresh or stale). The `2xx` indicates the type of content adaptation applied to the message (e.g., content selection, content transformation, or content generation). The warn-target indicates either the absolute URI or the host corresponding to the type of warn-code. The warn-target indicates the absolute URI when the warn-code is of the form "1xx". The warn-target indicates the host when the warn-code is of the form "2xx".

What follows is a list of the currently defined warn-codes in the CCPP-exchange protocol, each with a recommended warn-text in English, and a description of its meaning.

100 OK *May* be included if the cache or repository replies with first-hand or fresh information. The warn-target indicates the absolute URI, which addresses the descriptions in the repository, or the URI for the cached profile.

101 Used stale profile *Must* be included if the CC/PP repository replies with stale information. Whether the description is stale or not is decided by analyzing the HTTP header information with which the repository or cache responds (i.e., when the HTTP/1.1 header includes the `Warning` header field whose warn-code is 110 or 111). The warn-target indicates the absolute URI, which addresses the description in the repository or cache.

102 Not used profile *Must* be included if the description could not be obtained (e.g., the repository or cache is not available). The warn-target indicates the absolute URI, which addresses the description in the repository or cache.

200 Not applied *Must* be included if the server replies with the non-tailored content, which is the only representation in the server. The warn-target indicates the host, which addresses the server.

201 Content selection applied *Must* be included if the server replies with the content selected from one of the representations in the server. The warn-target indicates the host, which addresses the server.

202 Content generation applied *Must* be included if the server replies with the tailored content generated by the server. The warn-target indicates the host, which addresses the server.

203 Transformation applied *Must* be added by an intermediate proxy if it applies any transformation changing the content-coding (as specified in the `Content-Encoding` header) or media-type (as specified in the `Content-Type` header) of the response, or the entity-body of the response. The warn-target indicates the host, which addresses the proxy.

Because the architecture discussed above essentially consists of an additional header in HTTP, the security threats and problems are foreseen to be the same as for HTTP in general.

Privacy aspects, that is, the user information being accessed by an unauthorized party, are a possible security threat. This becomes more pertinent in the case of accept-profile than with other headers, because the aggregated information gives more detail about the user agent (depending on capability information encoding), and can be used to draw conclusions about the user.

In the time since its writing, there have been various attempts at solving this. The most promising to date is P3P, which enables the selection of information elements to be sent to the server. However, the last word has not been written on this topic, and until a fully secure solution has been fleshed out, users should be presented with the option of switching off the use of the `accept-profile` header.

Another possible security threat is response spoofing. In the traditional use of HTTP, this would not be a large problem, because it would just mean that a request or a response document got redirected.

However, if the information contained in the request or response is sensitive (e.g., contains personal information or configuration information), this will lead to privacy problems. The solution of these problems is beyond the scope of HTTP (being the use of secure transports, for instance).

A special case would be when the profile contains attached information about intermediaries, such as proxies (as is possible in CC/PP). This could lead to the involuntary disclosure of firewall configuration information to a third party. No solution for this is known, and the solution is most likely out of the scope of HTTP. Secure transport is one option, the encryption of the header information another. Keeping parts of profiles private is another option (actually addressed by P3P), but the solution is beyond the scope of the `accept-profile` header, because this would determine the content of the profile, and not affect the transport as such.

Other Protocols: SOAP

HTTP may be the transport protocol for the majority of all the data traffic on the Internet today, but it is not the only protocol there is. There has also been some debate about its suitability for classes of applications other than the standard browsing of documents, especially in the context of e-commerce (which, by the way, does not in any way constitute a magical world unto itself, but which easily maps onto the transactional format of HTTP). One result of these discussions is the creation of alternative protocols, some layered on top of HTTP. The most famous of these is the Simple Object Access Protocol (SOAP), developed by a consortium of companies and initiated by Microsoft. It is the foundation for the W3C work on XML protocols, but it is not the only contender on the market. Other initiatives, in the IETF as well as in other places, aim to create a protocol that is better than HTTP at interchanging semantic information, and better suited to the type of applications that are current now.

SOAP is layered on top of HTTP and uses HTTP POST to send data to a server. This is a clumsy solution that is likely to be fixed by the XML Protocols group. It is sometimes touted as an advantage, because it means that data can pass through firewalls at TCP port 80 (the port which is reserved for HTTP). That could as well be classified as a disadvantage, though, because it means that the firewall will let through application data that does not consist of documents, and may perform actions that the system administrator did not wish to allow (a nice way of saying that it may be more than viruses). Above all, SOAP is designed for Remote Procedure Call (RPC) handling, and having a remote procedure initiated from outside the firewall is precisely what most system administrators do not want.

SOAP is a message-based protocol, and message-based protocols are fairly easy to layer on top of transactional protocols such as HTTP. It uses XML to encode the messages (meaning, of course, that you can embed other markup in a SOAP message, for instance RDF). The messages are encapsulated in an envelope, which is part of the SOAP specification. The other parts are a set of encoding rules and an RPC representation. The SOAP envelope defines a framework for expressing what a message contains. It is the root element of the SOAP message, which means that all the other parts are nested within it. The envelope can contain two things besides the header and the body: the serialization rules for the particular message, and the envelope version.

The envelope contains three parts: The envelope itself, the header, and the body. The header is the first element in the envelope, if a header exists. It can contain a number of elements that control the message. The body contains the actual message.

The attributes on the header element determine how the recipient should process a message. Only two attributes are defined in the specification: `actor` and `mustUnderstand`.

The `actor` attribute is intended to declare to SOAP machines in the path of the message that should process it. Different parts of a SOAP message may be intended for different entities along the way. If an `actor` is addressed in the attribute (the address being a URI), he must process the message. Of course, actors can insert messages of their own, thus creating a chain of control messages. For instance, if the client is a WML client, but the origin of the message is in XHTML, and there are two transcoding proxies—the first can transcode from XHTML to HTML, the second from HTML to WML—the first proxy may address the message to the second (although if it is that capable, it would probably be able to transform XHTML to WML on its own). `mustUnderstand` is an attribute that is used to determine if an entry is mandatory or optional; it has a binary value where 1 means that the recipient of the header must obey the semantics or send an error message.

The SOAP body is intended for the recipient of the message, and contains the marshalling of the RPC and other messaging information. The SOAP RPC representation defines a convention that can be used to represent remote procedure calls and responses. The body of the message can also contain error messages (called "faults" in SOAP).

SOAP contains its own type system for encoding messages. It is built on the XML Schema system, but has more types and more detail. They apply only to the SOAP encoding of messages, although given that you could use name spaces to include them in any other document, it would be quite possible to reuse the type system in, for instance, RDF.

CHAPTER 4

Using RDF

As you have gathered by now, the information about your site is only as good as you make it. The quality of the inferences the system can make is determined by the profile information the user and the network provide, the rules that have been set by you or some other policy maker, and the information about your site. As a provider of a site in the semantic Web, you are responsible for two of those things: the information about the site, and the rule set that determines the way your system is going to act.

If you already have a Web site, you will most likely feel that all this is confusing: You do not have any intention of providing any rules, nor do you want to create a profile for your information. But likely as not, you have already done so without thinking about it; what we are talking about here is nothing more than formalizing something you have already done. It is not a big step from providing some information in the HTML Meta tag. Describing the heuristics for filtering is really no more difficult than describing how to use selectors for style sheets.

Despite appearances, using RDF does not drastically increase the level of complication. It is likely that you will never have to write your own RDF Schema. Just as with XML DTDs, there are ready-made schemas available for most needs. There are also tools—existing and emerging—that will help you analyze your document according to a schema, and automatically create a profile for you.

To understand how they work, think about what happens when you run a document through a search engine like Google, AltaVista, or Lycos. It generates an index of the words in the document. This is a description of the document: It describes how many times, and where, the different words in the document occur. Such an index is one example of metadata: data about the data in the document.

The index generated by the search engine is, of course, just one way of describing the document, and it is specific to the search engine, at that. But there are a number of other properties that a document has: Who wrote it, who has read it before, which software was used to write it, who owns the copyright, and so on. All of these can be generated by a computer, including the index of the words. None of them has an inherent meaning; they are just expressions of patterns that are associated with properties of the document.

But there is a limit to what can be machine-generated. The description of the document can also be a description of what it contains. This can cover the types of elements, their ranges, and other information about them. If you are a programmer, you will recognize that there are lots of other things you want to know about the object in order to build good software. If you use XML, you will have a lot of these things free, built into the object management system that XML really is.

The description can also cover aspects that depend on human interpretation, such as whether this is a love story or a tragedy, a play or a detective story. A computer cannot determine that. This is part of what metadata traditionally has been, but it is only one aspect of it.

A description of a document is a document in its own right: Data about data is data, too. And metadata is nothing but data about data. It can be embedded in the document or exist separately from it, as a document or as headers in a protocol, for instance. But there is nothing that limits the use of metadata to documents. A document is a compound object, a collection of (text) fragments that are connected in a certain order (they can be multimedia fragments, as well). However, because profiles can apply to any object, it is possible to describe anything using metadata. Anything can be an object, from the collection of all information in the universe down to the single letters on this page.

Objects have properties; indeed, this is what makes them objects. An object does not exist in and of itself, it is defined in terms of its properties; in a sense, the object is defined by its surroundings. You define it by specifying its interfaces to other objects. The names and values of the properties constitute the description of the object, its metadata.

When the metadata about the object is structured in a way that is repeatable, it is a profile of the object. Profiles are repeatable, and the structure of the profile is common for all instances of the same type of object. The profile can have different values for different instances, but the structure is always the same. So, all the books in the library can be described using the same library cards, but each library card will have different content, even though all cards refer to book titles, authors, and so forth.

Interestingly enough, this organizing principle can be used for software development as well. But before you start designing software, you have to understand what metadata assertions are, and how they are designed.

If you describe something (that is, create metadata), you are making an assertion, a statement about something (all these terms have specific philosophical meaning, and if you are schooled in formal logic, you may find me lacking in their correct use).

If the information about the document is structured properly, what could be more natural than to express it in the primary structured data format we have available, XML? And because we will need to talk about the relationship between the elements as well, we would probably like to use the premier method we have for describing relations between elements in a document: RDF.

Writing RDF

As you have probably gathered by now, there are several different ways you can write RDF: Using a dedicated editor, using a tool which generates it automatically, using a knowledge management tool, or writing it in the plain old Notepad. Using Notepad is not something I recommend, because a statement very quickly gets complicated. If you want to write XML by hand, it is generally better to use a dedicated XML editor such as XML Writer, which I have used in the examples in this chapter. The easiest way, of course, is to write it using a tool of some kind (even easier is to generate it automatically).

After you have written your RDF, you have to validate it. You can't just publish it and hope it works. After all, RDF is intended to be read by a computer, and as we noted in Chapter 1, computers are stupid, and you should not expect them to understand anything but the most literal instructions. If you send something to it and say it is RDF, it has to be RDF in all aspects—otherwise it will fail. This means that if you are writing RDF by hand, you had better ensure that it is correct before you include it in an application, if you expect it to work.

Luckily, there are simple RDF validators available. The W3C has developed one written in PERL that lets you import and visualize a piece of RDF. That is what I have used in the following examples to validate the RDF that I have written, and also to visualize it as graphs. Of course, this is entirely the wrong way

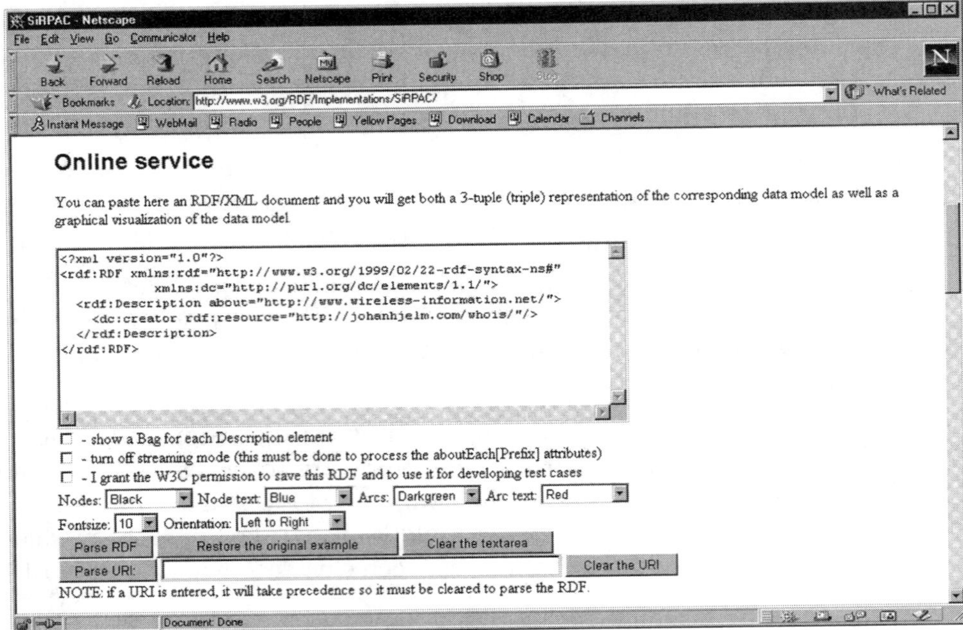

Figure 4.1 The SiRPAC validator window.

around: I should be able to first draw a graph, and then have it encoded as RDF. But nobody has written an editor like that yet (as of the writing of this book; there may be one by the time you read this. Check the Web site).

SiRPAC, the W3C RDF parser, is also available in an online version, as shown in Figure 4.1. It is extremely helpful, although the error messages can sometimes be obscure. It is available at the URI www.w3.org/RDF/Implementations/SiRPAC/, and you can simply type (or rather, copy and paste) your RDF into the document window. You can also give it a URI for a RDF file you have stored on your Web site (see Figure 4.2). It can be set to show you each description element as a Bag of its own, and it is easy to configure according to your own parameters.

SiRPAC returns results as XML, as triples, and as a visualization of the graph. There is unfortunately no way to go the opposite direction. But it is very useful to be able to check your XML against the graph you drew when you started developing.

Of course, complex graphs can be extremely hard to visualize. Not only can they be three-dimensional, they can actually be n-dimensional, where n is an arbitrary number. We humans have problems visualizing anything that has more than three dimensions so the graph you get could be an unreadable tangle. It can also be an extremely large tangle: There is, in principle, no limit

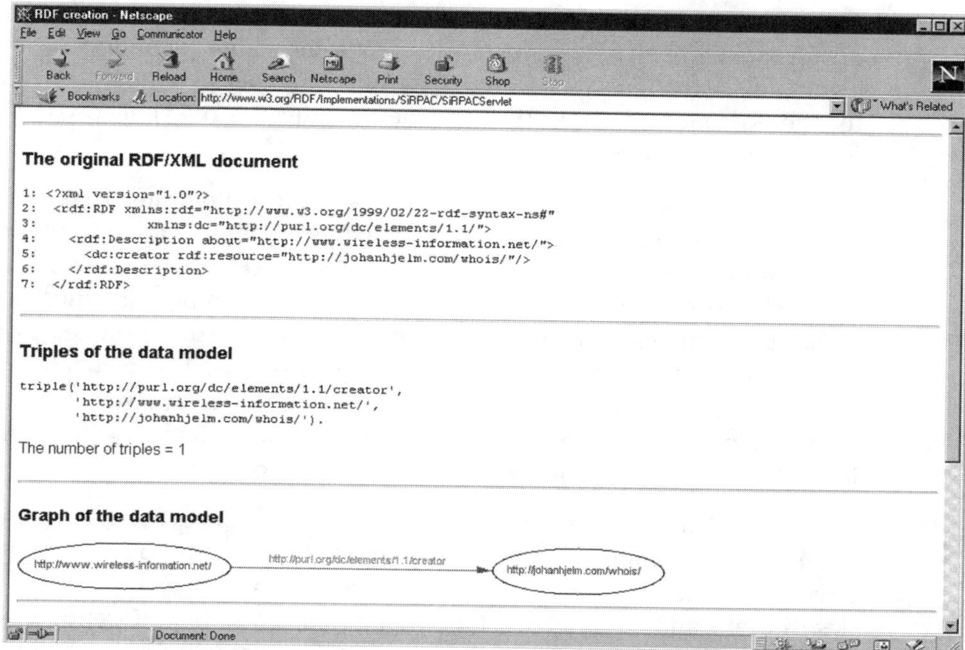

Figure 4.2 The results from SiRPAC.

to the dimensionality of the properties and resources you can include in a graph, and this can make the graph enormous (even larger than the screen you are using). There are limits in computer file systems and other, similar restrictions imposed by computers and networks, but they have nothing to do with the size of the graph, at least not in principle. In practice, they make it easier to create graphs that are interlinked, and that also makes it easier to visualize them, because you can spin off a dimension into a separate two-dimensional graph.

The description can be in a different vocabulary than the content. This may seem trivial, but it could be significant to an application using the metadata. If the description vocabulary is a UN statistics format, it may not be obvious to you what the codes are or what they mean; but to a search engine, they make it easier to create a more precise search than using the AltaVista listing of thousands of hits that are not really what you are looking for, even though they contain the word you gave as input.

This also lets you abstract the content from the document itself. It makes it much easier to apply filtering, and also enables a proxy or the origin server to filter away documents—or parts of documents—by author, by location, or by any of several other parameters. As a matter of fact, the parameters are not important. A computer cannot understand what a name in a vocabulary means.

The important thing is that it is unique, because it comes from its own unique namespace; and that the computer knows the datatype and/or the matching algorithm. In that case, it can see that if the value of the temperature parameter for the document is larger than 20, the document is relevant to you if the rain parameter is set to no.

Yes, that weather item was a silly example. But it illustrates that this filtering can be taken much further than is possible today. If you can first filter out most of the information you will not need, then the search using a search engine will be much more precise than what was possible by simply indexing. If you also declare parameters on the request, you can match the parameters with the description of the document, and so create a response that is a better match to what you are looking for. This technology does not currently exist outside the research labs, but it is not hard to use or implement; as you will see in the following chapters, the technology is being standardized.

The distinction between data and metadata is an interesting problem that you will encounter when you try to make statements about your information. You have to decide what in the content is really the information object, and the descriptions and parameters of that object. This may be different depending on what you want to describe at the moment. The same information in one view can be the object, and in another view the description of that object. They are both resources, and depending on what you want to do with them, you have to describe them differently.

Profiles, of course, are nothing in themselves but structured metadata descriptions. But the implementation of these systems is very different from traditional computer systems. Transporting profiles brings new problems, as does their creation and management. How the system acts on information is also different. You have to provide specialized reasoning and query engines to enable it. This may seem like taking down the moon right now, but the technology is no more difficult than existing computer systems, just different.

Writing small statements in RDF by hand (or writing a program that writes RDF) is relatively easy (but it rapidly becomes more complex and unmanageable using simple tools). The biggest problem is actually getting everything you need together to start.

First, you need to make sure that all the elements you need actually exist. If you cannot use elements from existing namespaces, this means you must create the namespace and the elements. This, in turn, means creating an RDF Schema, as we discussed in Chapter 3. It is very likely that you do not have to, but because one of the features of XML is that there is no central registry, you have no way of knowing which schemas already exist. You may of course be the member of a well-defined community, such as the WAP Forum, which has developed a schema of its own (in this case, UAProf for device description); or you may have an existing vocabulary which you can map into RDF, such as Dublin Core (which can be used to make assertions about information objects, like books and journals).

The fact that no schema registry exists is both good and bad. It is very likely that someone will step up and create such a registry (probably several different, actually). It is also very likely that there will be a large number of schemas that will not be registered, and which you will come to know about totally by chance. But the most likely explanation is that something will happen in the same vein as what has been happening on the Web in general: a Darwinian evolution toward the fittest. This does not always mean the most technically accomplished, nor the ones with the strongest backing, but those that fit best into their niches. If you think you have a better idea than one of the established parties, you can create your own schema. I will give you some hints about how to do it here. In Chapter 10 of this book, you will also find a listing of all the schemas I have found so far, which is by no means comprehensive, but at least can make a start.

An RDF document is, as I have described in the previous chapters, a representation of a graph. Let us write a simple example of a RDF description. Let us describe Johan Hjelm, who is identified by the URI http://johanhjelm.com, as the author of the Web site http://www.wireless-information.net, which contains information about the book he had written, called "Designing Wireless Information Services."

A graph for that statement would look something like this:

```
http://www.wireless-information.net→dc:creator →http://johanhjelm.com
                |
                dc:subject → "Designing Wireless Information Services"
```

Like all XML documents, RDF has to have some formal elements. First, you have to include the XML declaration, which, among other things, states which XML version the document uses.

```
<?xml version="1.0"?>
```

Then, you have to include the namespace declaration. This is required for the XML processor to find the other namespaces you are using in the document and download them so they can be used. Here, the namespaces used are the RDF namespace and the Dublin Core namespace.

```
rdf:RDF xmlns:rdf="http://www.w3.org/1999/02/22-rdf-syntax-ns#"
    xmlns:dc="http://purl.org/dc/elements/1.0/">
```

Then the actual RDF description starts. First, you have to declare what the description is about. Note the difference between `description about` and `description id`, which represent different things in RDF, as we pointed out in Chapter 3.

```
<rdf:Description rdf:about="http://www.wireless-information.net">
```

After this comes the Dublin Core `Creator` element, which declares who is the creator of the resource.

```
<dc:Creator>http://johanhjelm.com</dc:Creator>
```

Then you declare the subject, which in this case is my last book.

```
<dc:Subject>Designing Wireless Information Services</dc:Subject>
```

And finally, you have to wrap it up with the description end tag and the RDF end tag.

```
  </rdf:Description>
</rdf:RDF>
```

So, in its entirety this simple description looks like this (and it does not have to be more complicated):

```
<?xml version="1.0"?>
<rdf:RDF xmlns:rdf="http://www.w3.org/1999/02/22-rdf-syntax-ns#"
       xmlns:dc="http://purl.org/dc/elements/1.0/">
    <rdf:Description rdf:about="http://www.wireless-information.net">
         <dc:creator>http://johanhjelm.com</dc:creator>
         <dc:subject>Designing Wireless Information
Services</dc:subject>
    </rdf:Description>
</rdf:RDF>
```

This means that when you are defining the metadata you will use to describe your site, it makes sense not to start writing RDF and then see what happens. It is smarter to start by identifying what you want to say about the site, and then automate the creation of those descriptions.

Help is at hand, however. You do not have to do the work yourself. The UK Office for Library and Information Networking (UKOLN) at the University of Bath in England has developed a metadata generator, which analyzes your pages and creates Dublin Core metadata. This can be output as RDF, and you can use it in combination with other information (for instance, RSS). You can use it at http://www.ukoln.ac.uk/metadata/dcdot/ (see Figure 4.3).

The result is output as Dublin Core in the RDF encoding. For www.wireless-information.net, the Web site describing my previous book, it will look like this:

```
<?xml version="1.0"?>
<!DOCTYPE rdf:RDF SYSTEM "http://purl.org/dc/schemas/dcmes-xml-
20000714.dtd">

<rdf:RDF
  xmlns:rdf="http://www.w3.org/1999/02/22-rdf-syntax-ns#"
```

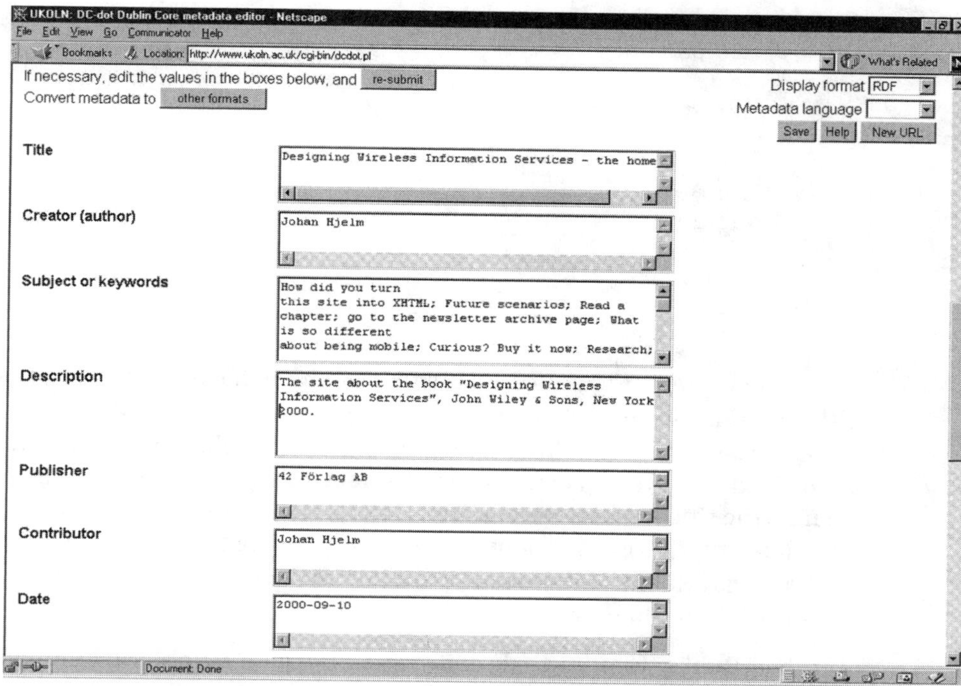

Figure 4.3 The input field in the dc.dot metadata analyzer.

```
xmlns:dc="http://purl.org/dc/elements/1.1/">
<rdf:Description about="http://www.wireless-information.net">
  <dc:title>
    Designing Wireless Information Services - the home page
  </dc:title>
  <dc:subject>
    How did you turn this site into XHTML; Future scenarios;
    Read a chapter; go to the newsletter archive page; What is
    so different about being mobile; Curious? Buy it now;
    Research; Object orientation; Maintenance policy,
    copyright, etc; Help me fix the book; Designing Wireless
    Information Services; What's in the book; A simple WAP
    tutorial; Other information; Links for the book; User
    interface design; send me an email; Software development;
    Do you want to read more about me, Johan Hjelm; some talks
    and presentations; Content design; Having problems with the
    CD? Download the files here
  </dc:subject>
  <dc:publisher>
    European Regional Internet Registry/RIPE NCC
  </dc:publisher>
  <dc:date>
    2000-09-10
```

```
      </dc:date>
      <dc:type>
        Text
      </dc:type>
      <dc:format>
        text/html
      </dc:format>
      <dc:format>
        4076 bytes
      </dc:format>
    </rdf:Description>
  </rdf:RDF>
```

As you can see in Figure 4.4, you will, of course, have to correct some errors. RIPE NCC is not the publisher, it is the registry for the IP address. Luckily, that is very easy. If you scroll down below the output file, you will see a series of input fields, where you can correct the values that were not quite right. You can change the title, creator (i.e., author), subject, description, publisher, contributor, date, type, format, identifier, source, language, relation, coverage, and rights management. All these are parameters of Dublin Core, which we will discuss further in Chapter 5.

Another Dublin Core-to-RDF analyzer is Reggie, which is maintained by the Australian research organization Distributed Systems Technology Centre. It is a Java applet (the UKOLN editor is a set of forms), and it is available at http://metadata.net/dstc/. Type in the URI of the Web page you want to analyze, and click on Go. It then opens the window you see in Figure 4.5 where you can select from among a number of metadata formats under the Select a Syntax button. Fill in the values in the form. You can then choose to get the result in the browser, or get it e-mailed to you (something that some firewalls will block).

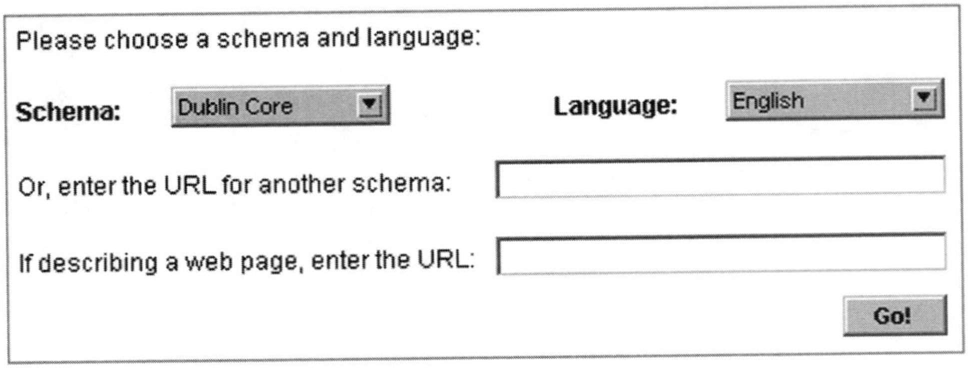

Please choose a schema and language:

Schema: Dublin Core **Language:** English

Or, enter the URL for another schema:

If describing a web page, enter the URL:

Go!

Figure 4.4 The input fields of the dc.dot metadata analyzer.

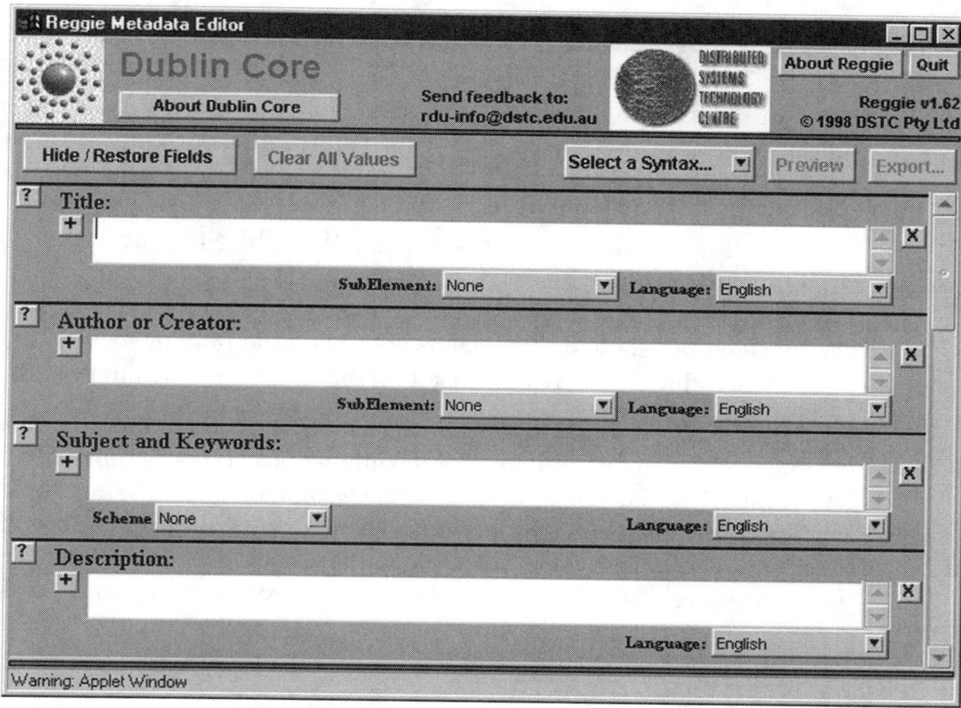

Figure 4.5. The input fields of the Reggie metadata analyzer.

The result looks like this:

```
<?xml version = "1.0"?>
<RDF xmlns = "http://www.w3.org/TR/1999/REC-rdf-syntax-19990222#"
     xmlns:DC = "http://metadata.net/dstc/DC-10-EN/#">
 <Description xml:lang="en">
  <DC:Title>
    Designing Wireless Information Services
  </DC:Title>
  <DC:Creator>
    Johan Hjelm
  </DC:Creator>
  <DC:Subject>
    HTML, HTTP, XHTML, XML, WAP
  </DC:Subject>
  <DC:Description>
    The site for the book
  </DC:Description>
 </Description>
</RDF>
```

Metadata Profiles in Your Documents

Some of the metadata analyzers we have looked at allow for the generation of output other than RDF, such as HTML. The HTML 4.0 specification defines an attribute on the HEAD element, the `profile` attribute. This attribute specifies the location of a metadata profile. The value of the `profile` attribute is a URI. The intention is that user agents can use this URI either as a globally unique name for the profile, without retrieving it; or they can use it as a link. The first way is similar to how a URI would be used by XML namespaces to identify a namespace. The second way means retrieving the document identified by the URI, and conducting activities based on the definitions within the profile.

A simple HTML example of the latter could be a profile that defines some basic information for the document. The profile would hold a number of properties, but because this is HTML, you would have to define them using the `META` declaration. In essence, you would define the elements in the content declarations of the `META` element. This means that there would be no schema, and there would be no repeatability of the properties. Here is what it would look like:

```
<HEAD profile="http://www.historybuff.org/profiles/core">
 <TITLE>Basics: The Napoleonic wars</TITLE>
 <META name="author" content="Johan Hjelm">
 <META name="copyright" content="&copy; 2000, johanhjelm.com, Inc.">
 <META name="keywords" content="history,introduction,Napoleonic wars">
 <META name="date" content="2000-11-06T08:49:37+00:00">
</HEAD>
```

If the document was XHTML instead, it would still use `profile`, because that is defined as part of the XML mapping of HTML. Here is what the W3C home page looks like, if you view the source:

```
<!DOCTYPE html PUBLIC "-//W3C//DTD XHTML 1.0 Transitional//EN"
"http://www.w3.org/TR/xhtml1/DTD/xhtml1-transitional.dtd">
<html xmlns="http://www.w3.org/1999/xhtml" lang="en-US" xml:lang="en-US">
<head profile="http://www.w3.org/2000/08/w3c-synd/#">
<meta http-equiv="PICS-Label" content='(PICS-1.1
"http://www.classify.org/safesurf/" l gen true for http://www.w3.org by
"philipd@w3.org" r (SS~~000 1 SS~~100 1))' />
<meta http-equiv="PICS-Label" content='(PICS-1.1
"http://www.rsac.org/ratingsv01.html" l gen true comment "RSACi North
America Server" by "philipd@w3.org" for "http://www.w3.org" on
"1996.04.16T08:15-0500" r (n 0 s 0 v 0 l 0))' />
<meta name="keywords" content="W3C, World Wide Web, Web, WWW,
Consortium, computer, access, accessibility, semantic, worldwide, W3,
HTML, XML, standard, language, technology, link, CSS, RDF, XSL, Berners-
Lee, Berners, Lee, style sheet, cascading, schema, XHTML, mobile, SVG,
```

```
PNG, PICS, DOM, SMIL, MathML, markup, Amaya, Jigsaw, free, open source,
software" />
<meta name="description" content="W3C is over 400 organizations leading
the World Wide Web to its full potential. Founded by Tim Berners-Lee,
the Web's inventor. The W3C Web site hosts specifications, guidelines,
software and tools. Public participation is welcome. W3C supports
universal access, the semantic Web, trust, interoperability,
evolvability, decentralization, and cooler multimedia." />
<title>The World Wide Web Consortium</title>
<link rel="stylesheet" type="text/css" href="StyleSheets/home" />
<link rel="bookmark" href="#technologies" title="Technologies |" />
<link rel="bookmark" href="#news" title="News |" />
<link rel="contents" href="#contents" title="Contents |" />
<link rel="bookmark" href="#search" title="Search" />
```

As you can see, it also includes a number of other metainformation items, such as PICS labels. But the most interesting thing is the profile. If you look at http://www.w3.org/2000/08/w3c-synd/#, you will find a page describing how the W3C is transforming its page from XHTML to an RSS profile. The profile for the W3C page looks like this (I have abbreviated it, since it would fill several pages in this book otherwise):

```
<?xml version="1.0" encoding="utf-8" ?>
- <rdf:RDF xmlns:dc="http://purl.org/dc/elements/1.1/"
xmlns:h="http://www.w3.org/1999/xhtml"
xmlns:rdf="http://www.w3.org/1999/02/22-rdf-syntax-ns#"
xmlns="http://purl.org/rss/1.0/">
- <channel rdf:about="http://www.w3.org/2000/08/w3c-synd/home.rss">
<title>The World Wide Web Consortium</title>
<description>Leading the Web to its Full Potential...</description>
<link>http://www.w3.org/</link>
<dc:date>2000-12-05T21:31:29Z</dc:date>
- <items>
- <rdf:Seq>
<rdf:li resource="http://www.w3.org/Consortium/Prospectus/Joining" />
<rdf:li resource="http://www.w3.org/TR/2000/WD-voice-intro-20001204/" />
<rdf:li resource="http://www.w3.org/TR/2000/WD-query-algebra-20001204/" />
<rdf:li
resource="http://www.gca.org/attend/2000_conferences/XML_2000/default.
htm" />
<rdf:li resource="http://www.w3.org/2000/11/w3c-drm-cfp" />
<rdf:li resource="http://www.mdbl.sfc.keio.ac.jp/IPSJ-
DBS/Symposium/DBWeb2000.html" />
<rdf:li resource="http://www.chez.com/ailf/LP2000.htm" />
<rdf:li resource="http://www.w3.org/Jigsaw/Doc/User/webdav" />
<rdf:li resource="http://www.w3.org/Amaya/" />
<rdf:li resource="http://www.w3.org/TR/2000/CR-xsl-20001121/" />
<rdf:li resource="http://www.w3.org/TR/2000/WD-nl-spec-20001120/" />
<rdf:li resource="http://www.vqfoundation.org/" />
```

```
</rdf:Seq>
</items>
</channel>
- <item rdf:about="http://www.w3.org/Consortium/Prospectus/Joining">
<title>W3C Welcomes Members at Advisory Committee Meeting</title>
<description>5 December 2000: W3C held its semi-annual Advisory
Committee Meeting on 28-30 November, 2000, in Cambridge, Massachusetts,
USA. W3C Member Organizations participated in two days of presentations
and discussions on the range of W3C Activities. If you would like to
join W3C, visit the W3C Membership page, and please consider attending
the next Advisory Committee Meeting to be held 30 April - 1 May 2001, in
Hong Kong.</description>
<link>http://www.w3.org/Consortium/Prospectus/Joining</link>
<dc:date>2000-12-05</dc:date>
</item>
</rdf:RDF>
```

This profile is used by other sites that syndicate the information, using a robot to retrieve the information and present it in the context the site provider has decided is relevant. This can, of course, be used to construct portal sites that are current, as well as news sites that are accurate, when the information is retrieved automatically. It should be obvious how useful this could be in an intranet, where you could create constant updates of the sites maintained in your company, or the sites linked to yours. Creating site profiles and then using a simple search robot, such as the robot which is included in libwww (the demonstration library for World Wide Web applications), allows you to keep track of what is going on in your company. Assuming your colleagues update their sites, of course.

You do not have to construct this information on your own, however. The W3C uses RDF Site Summary (RSS) to describe its site. It is intended to be generated automatically, and that is exactly what happens. Dan Connolly of the W3C has written an XSLT transformation sheet that takes information from the page and creates a profile (and there are a couple of others linked from the site). You can apply the transformation sheets yourself, if you want to, and generate an automated translation from XHTML to RSS. It takes the `<h1>` elements and puts the content in the `<title>` elements, and then it takes the text and puts it in the `<description>`. The `<link>` element comes from the links on the page, and the `<dc:date>` is derived from the date of the page.

Vocabularies for Site Information

The profile above contains three namespaces: RDF (prefixed with `rdf:`), RSS (which is default), and Dublin Core (prefixed with `dc:`). Typically, those give you all the elements you need to describe your site. In essence, Dublin Core enables you to give information about the author and other related information, while RSS gives you the syndication information.

RDF Site Summary (RSS)

RSS is a format specially intended to give the gist of the site and enable syndication. An RSS summary, at a minimum, is a document describing a *channel*, with items that can be retrieved following the URIs in the document. Each item consists of a title, link, and brief description. Traditionally, RSS has been used for news headlines, but there is no real restriction on what it can be used for.

RSS 0.9 was introduced in 1999 by Netscape as a channel description framework and content-gathering mechanism for its My Netscape Network (MNN) portal. The intent was for Web site owners to provide a simple snapshot of their site, and get an audience through My Netscape. This did not work out as expected, because Web site owners were reluctant to provide metainformation. However, RSS began to see use as a syndication format. The alternatives were (and are still) ad hoc solutions (such as those most often used for HTML-based Web site syndication), which may work for a special case but do not generalize well; and special purpose protocols like XML News and ICE, recently developed into PRISM. RSS, however, is not an entire framework, but only an XML document. This makes it easier to use for Webmasters, and more lightweight to transport. It is also versatile enough to handle a number of different formats and content types, including news headlines, discussion forums, software announcements, and proprietary data.

However, this is also one of its weaknesses. RSS became overloaded, and the need for an enhanced framework started to grow. There are even ad hoc elements in some descriptions. The format, intended to be sparse, is growing to be more like full-fledged frameworks such as ICE. It had also dropped the RDF elements as Netscape discontinued its support and others took over.

A group of "concerned citizens"—prominent in the Web world, to be sure—decided to do something about this and created a specification which divides the functionalities into pluggable RSS modules. Modularization is achieved by using XML Namespaces for partitioning vocabularies, which means that functionalities can be included or removed by selecting the relevant namespaces. The RSS core does not have to change. The modularization is included in RSS 1.0, which uses RSS 0.9 to provide a basic (although limited) RDF base for further structure. It enables repurposing of content. Of course, it does not involve copyright management, but it can let a local newspaper, say, get the weather information automatically from the local meterological office.

An RSS document is a RDF document, and as such, an XML document. It should begin with the XML declaration, and the top-level element in the document is RDF, in which all the following elements nest. The opening RDF tag associates the `rdf:` namespace prefix with the RDF syntax schema and establishes the RSS 1.0 schema as the default namespace for the document. Normally, you should use "`rdf:`" as the document namespace. The default namespace of the document, however, is the RSS namespace, so you write xmlns= "http://purl.org/rss/1.0/".

The elements of the RSS core module are shown in Table 4.1.

The only modules originally supplied with RSS are the Dublin Core and Syndication modules. However, other modules can be added at will. The syndication module has only three elements: `updatePeriod`, `updateFrequency`, and `updateBase`.

`UpdatePeriod` describes the period over which the channel is updated. It can be hourly, daily, weekly, monthly, yearly. If there is no other value, it is assumed that "`daily`" applies.

`UpdateFrequency` is used to describe how often the site is updated during the update period. The value is a number, which of course has to be positive. If the updateFrequency is 1, and the updatePeriod is weekly, the site is updated once a week. However, there is no way to express that the site is updated every now and then, as with most small sites. The default value is 1.

`UpdateBase` is the date used to calculate the period and frequency of updates (i.e., the date when the updates start). It is in the date and time format yyyy-mm-ddThh:mm.

One example of a site that uses RSS to create summary information and make it public is the O'Reilly Meerkat site (www.oreillynet.com/meerkat/). It is a jumble of everything from news of the Middle East peace process to new implementations of Linux drivers. The stories are strictly chronologically ordered, and there is no attempt to editorialize—the summary of the story is always presented as is.

Dublin Core

One of the most important uses of RDF in the near future will most likely be to map existing vocabularies into a structured, machine-understandable format. The reason for this is simple: The established description of the thing (whatever it is) will fit into the object structure of RDF. Another reason is that you as a metadata author do not want to have to write new vocabularies for things that other people have already described.

The biggest user of metadata today is the library world, not because metadata is inherently limited to libraries but because the library world has an inherent

Table 4.1 RSS Core Elements

ELEMENT	SUBELEMENT	DESCRIPTION
<channel>		Contains metadata describing the channel itself, including a title, brief description, and URI for the described resource (the channel provider's home page, for instance). Note that *channel* here does not mean that there is streaming data or anything similar. This is simply a name for the syndicated object. Channel has a number of subelements (all are required, except the `image` and `textinput` elements)
	<title>	A descriptive title for the channel
	<link>	The URI for the HTML rendering of the channel. For instance, the channel providers home page.
	<description>	Brief description of the content, function, source, etc. of the channel, in free text (PCDATA, strictly speaking)
	<image>	Associates an image to the channel. Can be used for logotypes, etc.; optional (the channel can, of course, in itself contain images)
	<items>	A table of contents in RDF which associates the items in the document with this particular channel. The items used to be headlines, but can be basically anything (house prices, melon sizes, water pipe lengths–you name it). There is a minimum of one and a maximum of fifteen items per object. Each item must be identified with a unique URI.
	<textinput>	Associates the (optional) `textinput` element to this particular channel.
<image>		An image associated with the HTML rendering of the channel. If it is present here, it must also be present inside the channel element. The `image` element has a number of subelements:
	<title>	The alternative text (alt) of the image.
	<url>	The URI of the image as given in the src attribute of the channel image tag, when rendered as HTML.
	<link>	The URL that links to an HTML rendering of the channel.
<item>		Can be just about anything: a discussion posting, job listing, software patches–any object with a URI. Which is to say, any object. There must be a minimum of one and a maximum of fifteen per document.

continues

Table 4.1 RSS Core Elements (Continued)

ELEMENT	SUBELEMENT	DESCRIPTION
	<title>	The title of the item. For a page, the title, for an image, the alt text.
	<link>	The URI for the item.
	<description>	A brief description or abstract of the item. Not `description about` in the RDF sense.
<textinput>		With the `textinput` element, you can submit forms data to any URI. The field is typically used as a search box or subscription form. It is not very useful today, however, because forms mechanisms are well established. In the future, used together with some kind of resource discovery mechanism, it might come in handy.
	<title>	The title for the field. For instance, search.
	<description>	Brief (free-form) description of the fields purpose.
	<name>	The name of the field.
	<link>	The URI that receives the submission.

need to define the properties of the information objects. The library community has defined its own metadata vocabulary, the Dublin Core (named after Dublin, Ohio, not Dublin, Ireland), which contains the things you normally would find on a library card, and then some. In the Dublin Core `DC:Coverage` element, the place name is used to designate the location relevance of the information. However using the place name presents a problem when we are talking about position-relevant information, because it is unclear what is meant by the `DC:Coverage` element. Is the coverage the location of the information, or the location in which it was written, or some other location? Such location ambiguities make it impossible to decide the relevance of the information properly.

However, there are several elements that it makes sense to reuse in other descriptions. `Author`, `Publisher`, and elements that directly describe other aspects of document management seem unnecessary to reinvent. But when the document describes something that is not related to information, such as a handheld computer or a mobile phone, it makes more sense to use other elements.

The Dublin Core classification is not constructed out of thin air: It is assigned by the librarian (or other resource classifier) classifying the resource. In some cases, such as the *location* property, this means that the person assigning the information must have a very good knowledge of the resource to be classified (as this more or less requires you to read the document itself).

Dublin Core and its associated description format, as well as many other previous attempts at classification, have been an inspiration for RDF. RDF relies heavily on a lot of the thinking that has gone into Dublin Core. Essentially, Dublin Core defines a schema language much like the RDF Schema language for creating new attribute values for a given set of elements. However, the values are quite limited, compared to RDF, and you have no freedom to define your own. The framework that is spelled out in the RDF Grammar and Syntax document is also implicit in the Dublin Core definition.

The latest version of the Dublin Core metadata element set is version 1.1, which has been published as a recommendation from OCLC.

The elements are defined using a set of ten attributes from the ISO/IEC 11179 standard for the description of data elements, namely:

- *Name* The label assigned to the data element
- *Identifier* The unique identifier assigned to the data element
- *Definition* A statement that clearly represents the concept and the essential nature of the data element
- *Comment* A remark concerning the application of the data element
- *Version* The version of the data element
- *Registration Authority* The entity authorized to register the data element
- *Language* The language in which the data element is specified
- *Obligation* Indicates whether the data element is required to always or sometimes be present (contain a value)
- *Datatype* Indicates the type of data that can be represented in the value of the data element
- *Maximum Occurrence* Indicates any limit to the repeatability of the data element

In XML encoding, the language will, of course, be superseded by the `xml:lang` attribute; the maximum occurrence, as well as the datatype, can be defined in the DTD. In a RDF encoding, these can be defined either in the DTD (which actually complicates things), or—in case of the datatype—in the RDF Schema. However, the datatypes available in RDF are very limited, so this is not a very good way of defining datatypes.

Six of the ten attributes are common to all Dublin Core elements, as are the values of the attributes. If you wanted to create a different Dublin Core vocabulary, they would change, as follows:

- *Version* The value is always "1.1" (if you are using the latest version of Dublin Core, of course).
- *Registration Authority* The value is always "Dublin Core Metadata Initiative" because there is no other registration authority for Dublin Core elements and attribute values.

- *Language* The value is always "en," meaning that Dublin Core always uses English. Note that this is an ambiguous value, because it does not declare which of the different regional English variants it uses (spelling, for instance, varies between British English and U.S. English). It is also quite possible that people speaking other languages might want to create their own description formats, in which case this value would very likely not be "en."
- *Obligation* The value would be "Optional," which is to say that Dublin Core elements do not have to be present, but can be excluded on the whim of the author.
- *Datatype* The value would be "Character String," which is something RDF has borrowed, because RDF elements are also always character strings. If you need a more precise datatype (say, integer), you could use an XML Schema language definition, but XML Schema is still under development.
- *Maximum Occurrence* The value would be "Unlimited." In RDF, this is defined by the schema, which determines how often a property value may occur.

These attributes are part of the formal definition of the elements, but are often excluded as part of shorthand definitions.

The Dublin Core specification describes a number of elements which can be used to create descriptions (the element descriptions are defined in what essentially corresponds to the Dublin Core schema language—the elements we just defined—although the distinction between a formal schema language and element names does not exist in Dublin Core).

- *Title* This element is most often the name given to the resource (by which it is formally known). It corresponds to the title of the book, rather than the title you put on the top of the Web page (which was intended to work in the same way, but often does not).
- *Creator* This element is the creator of the resource, that is, whoever is responsible for the content of the service. It can be a person, an organization, a service, or another entity. If it has a name, that should be used as the identifier.
- *Subject* Subject and Keywords describe the topic of the content. If there is an established vocabulary, for instance keywords, classification codes, or something similar, that should be used.
- *Description* This element is not the RDF `Description` element. Here, you describe the content of the resource. This description could contain a table of contents, the abstract, or a reference to some other kind of description.

- *Publisher* This element is the entity that makes the resource available. It could be a person, an organization, or a service. If it has a name, that should be included. Note that this is not necessarily the publisher in the formal sense (e.g., the magazine publisher).
- *Contributor* This element is someone who has made contributions to the content of the resource. It can be a person, an organization, or a service. The definition of content is not clear: It could also be style.
- *Date* This element is a date in YYYY-MM-DD (ISO 8061) format. It is a date in the life cycle of the resource, which could be the creation date, the date it was changed, or another significant date.
- *Type* This element is the resource type of the content (its nature or genre, according to some predefined thesaurus).
- *Format* This element includes the physical or digital manifestation of the resource, such as the media type, size, duration, typeface, and so forth. Usually, this will be selected from a vocabulary, for intstance, the IANA list of media types.
- *Identifier* The resource identifier is supposed to be an unambiguous reference to the resource, which applies within a given context. It could be the XML ID, the URI, or some other form of identification, such as the ISBN number.
- *Source* This element identifies the resource from which the current resource is derived. For instance, if the current resource is a summary of a document, this element should refer to the document that was summarized. Referencing is done in the same way as for the Identifier.
- *Language* This element is the human language of the content of the resource. It is best to qualify it, so you do not think that this is some XML variant. The language names are defined in RFC 1766, which gives each language a two-letter code (taken from the ISO 639 standard), followed, if desired, by a two-letter country code for local variants; for example, "en-uk" is the way to refer to English as used in the United Kingdom. Note that this element will normally be superseded by the `xml:lang` element, which shows the language used directly in the XML encoding. Another possibility is that there can be a conflict between these two elements, for instance if the Dublin Core encoding gives a language variant, but you have a different language in one section of the document, which would then have to override the `xml:lang` on the root element, as well as the `dc:language` element. The `xml:lang` element should normally have precedence.
- *Relation* This element contains some kind of reference to a related resource (how the relation occurs is not specified). This element should be an ISBN number, a URI, or some other type of structured reference.

- *Coverage* This element implies the temporal and/or geographic extent (scope) of the resource content. This element is intended to include a spatial location (a place name or geographic coordinate), a temporal period (a period label, date, or date range) or a jurisdiction (such as a named administrative entity). You can either give the coverage as a value from a well-established vocabulary (for instance, the Thesaurus of Geographic Names), or you could use coordinates and numeric identifiers for the dates. However, there is no mechanism to convey geographic polygons (i.e., cities), or to show that different locations apply at different times (e.g., the memoirs of Benjamin Franklin, which recount events in Boston, London, Philadelphia, and Paris, depending on the time).
- *Rights* This element is intended to convey the rights management aspects of the resource. For instance, a book is sold on the condition that it cannot be copied indiscriminately. There will either be a rights management statement for the resource or a reference to a service providing such information. The current types of rights that may be included in this element are patents, pattern protections, copyrights, rights to perform, and any other type of intellectual property right. These are well defined, and there is a large body of information around how they occur, when, and so forth.
- *Comment* A remark concerning the application of the data element; this attribute captures the data representation together with the `Datatype` element (which is, as you saw above, always a character string). This is the same mechanism as is used in the RDF Schema language, where the datatype of the element is always a character string, and the comment is used to determine further constraints (such as whether the character string defines a value of a different kind, such as an integer, a floating-point value, or another kind of number).

In practice, only four elements are required to create a Dublin Core definition: `Name`, `Identifier`, `Definition`, and `Comment`. This is especially true for documents that do not have a traditional author, such as documents generated by a computer.

CHAPTER 5

RDF Schemas

RDF provides a general model for describing resources. Resources in RDF are any objects that can be uniquely identified by a Uniform Resource Identifier (URI). The objects can have properties, which then have values (which may be another resource, i.e., they are atomic, which means they are text strings (literals), numbers, etc.). The properties can be of different types, which express the values associated with the resources. The types, as well as the vocabulary (i.e., the names of the properties) are defined in the vocabulary. A collection of properties that refer to a resource is called a description.

RDF in itself is just a framework; it does not contain any vocabularies for authoring the metadata itself. Anyone can design a new vocabulary, as long as it conforms to the XML and RDF syntaxes. The only requirement for using it is that it is pointed to by a URI, which is included in the metadata instances using this vocabulary. This makes vocabularies unique, without creating a central registry, by using the XML namespace mechanism. Note that the URI in itself does not have to point to anything for namespace purposes (although for a vocabulary, there has to be an RDF schema defining it).

Since you can specify your own vocabularies, RDF does not have to make any assumptions about any particular application domain. It does not define the semantics of any domains either (this is, for instance, not true about the Dublin Core metadata mechanism, which assumes that the domain described is a library). This enables it to avoid one of the biggest traps in the development of artificial intelligence technology, namely creating both structures and vocabularies that are domain-specific.

The reason it is useful to have specialized vocabularies that are mapped into RDF is, of course, that when you want to create a meta-description of your information object, you do not have to either invent your own language or use a dedicated description language (which would include creating specialized software for it). Imagine the nightmare of having to use the Corporate Special Description Language for your intranet site, at the same time as you describe it in the Enormously Good HTML Authoring Language, and the Railroad Hobbyist Description Language, plus the Incredibly Refined Domain Knowledge Language. Each of these languages would require a different processor, and there would be no simple way of translating between them. That is how it works in the world of expert systems today. The alternative is to use a single language for the structure of your knowledge representation and vary the vocabularies you are using. That is what you do when you use RDF with a standard RDF parser to analyze the information. The role of RDF Schema is to provide a definition of the elements you can use and their properties.

When you make an assertion, you say something about something. In order to enable a computer to understand your assertion, you need an address for what you are referring to, and what you say must be comprehensible to the computer. This means that a resource address with a named property and the value of that property together comprise a statement. To illustrate how close this is to normal languages, the resource is the subject of the statement, the property is the predicate, and the value is the object of the statement. Of course, this is a description that works only in terms of formal grammar, since the predicate is a property, not a verb, and the subject is a resource, not a noun.

Wherever there can be a description, there can be a container that contains values. (This is also true for IDs, and a generated URI that the ID signifies can be a container.) A container is a container in the object sense: an object that contains other objects. This means that the contents of the container can in itself be graphs, which create a chain of graphs spawned from the graph containing the container. Another question is why should you use a generalized piece of software, when you could have someone create a program that does the same thing? This might be more efficient (there is no risk that programmers will lose their jobs), but on the other hand, it is inflexible. It is possible to create agents that change their output entirely depending on the input—in effect, act differently depending on what rules you provide them in the form of RDF datastructures. The need to describe how this works is one reason for this book (another is that I find RDF so interesting).

The specialized languages and vocabularies often come from the artificial intelligence world, and while they have been highlighted as one of the major successes of AI (because you are able to describe a specialized area at all), they are also one of its biggest weaknesses (because you either have to create a vocabulary that describes everything in the universe as soon as you go outside the current domain, or resign yourself to incompatibilities between domains). They also touch on another discipline that has received a lot of attention in the last few years: knowledge management. This has become the focus of much attention in the context of intranets in the last few years, as companies have started to regard the knowledge and competence of their associates as a resource, and even list it on their balance sheets. If you want to value your associates' competence, you have to be able to describe it. Knowledge management is a way to formalize the knowledge that exists in the company. This has been done for specialized domains in artificial intelligence work, the most famous being the soup cooker at Campbell Soup, where the knowledge of the chief soup cooker was literally sucked out into a computer system. This knowledge was then input into a rule-based system, enabling less skilled operators to understand at which steam pressure to add 400 liters of milk and at what temperature to pour in a ton of potatoes, so they would not be overboiled when the soup was done.

RDF is a language to make assertions. But if you do not declare the meaning of the elements used in the assertion, you can not be sure that the meaning is the same in one assertion as the other. You have to make sure that the meaning of the elements in one context is the same as in other contexts. By having a unique identifier you make each schema unique, and by referencing it in the RDF document using namespaces, you make sure that you are referring to a specific schema. This means that each time you reference a schema, you declare which unique context you are using to make the assertion—thus avoiding one of the problems that have plagued traditional AI.

Datatypes in RDF

The RDF-type system does not define classes in terms of the properties the instances of the class (the objects) can have. Instead it defines the properties in terms of the classes to which they can apply. This means that the property is central to the definition, instead of the object and the class. In traditional terms, the property is the object and the classes, its properties . . . .

The definition is expressed using the attribute domain (which describes the classes it belongs to), and the range (which defines a type as a resource in a specified class). The RDF Schema language lets you define not only the properties of a resource, but also what kind of resource it is. It gives a type system that enables you to define properties as members of classes and subclasses. It is not a type system in the traditional sense of the word, defining datatypes like integers and strings; rather, it is a language on top of the type system of XML, where these datatypes are defined. All RDF attributes are, by definition, strings in XML, and the RDF Schema-type system rides on top of this.

It is important to be able to express the type of the data item, since this is often the basis for decisions about it. Rule-based systems (expert systems) express decisions in trees: If the soup temperature is above 50 degrees, and the steam pressure is below 200 PSI, add 400 liters of milk and one ton of potatoes (The example is fictitious, by the way. Do not try it at home). If the measurement system gave the temperature in degrees Fahrenheit, and the expert system expected a Celsius value, you had better be making gazpacho. When the type is not clearly expressed, the data cannot be matched.

In RDF, we are confronted with a set of unknown parameters (a new set for each namespace), which have to be defined in order to be usable. The definition is not, however, about providing meaning in the human sense. A computer could not care less whether a property is called *potatoes* or *fuse_distance*. What is important is that the computer has instructions about which values are acceptable for the property.

XML gives you the list of ingredients, RDF gives you the instructions for how they relate together. It makes for a poor cake if you add the frosting before you put the batter into the oven. But the ingredients have to be expressed in a way that you (if you are baking a cake) or your computer (if you are shooting down aircraft) can understand. For instance, there can be an arbitrary quantity of flour in a cake, but only in the correct proportions with eggs, milk, sugar and baking soda does it become a cake. You have to define what you mean by eggs and flour. This is what you do in the RDF Schema. (It is then possible to chain further definitions off this, so that you not only define the measurement type for flour, but the grinding, the crop type, and so on).

RDF expresses how different elements relate together; that is the reason RDF data are triples, not attribute-value pairs. The actual datatypes, however, cannot be expressed in RDF, because there are only two types of data: strings and URIs. The typing mechanism has to be added on top. The schema defines the terms that will be used in RDF statements and gives specific meanings to them. The schema is the place where definitions and restrictions of usage for property types are documented. In order to avoid confusion between independent- and possibly conflicting-definitions of the same term, RDF uses XML namespaces to ensure elements are unique. Schemas define how a name can be used, including restrictions on the property. Each property type used in a statement must be identified with exactly one namespace, or schema. However, a `<description>` element may contain property statements from many schemas, as we have seen.

In the RDF documentation, a number of basic RDF elements and properties are defined, but anyone can create their own elements by defining a schema for them (within the constraints of the schema, of course). The RDF syntax provides ways of building data structures (the directed graphs), and the schema language provides a way to populate the structures with entities. A schema defines the terms used in RDF statements, the way you use a dictionary when you write letters in a foreign language. The idea is that the terms should hold the same meaning for all users, which is why the elements defined in a schema are globally unique, by virtue of using XML namespaces. A schema can appear a number of ways, but the RDF schema specification defines how a schema should look for RDF to be able to interpret it automatically.

There is no need to reinvent descriptions of your concepts every time you want to use them. You will most likely use existing vocabularies (and thus, schemas) most of the time. But from time to time, you will find that you need to define a new term. You cannot just throw that up on the Web in any old way and hope that the computer that retrieves it will understand it, however. You have to define in a way that all RDF processors will understand. That way is described in the RDF schema specification, which really provides a format for descriptions of vocabularies so that they can be shared with other communities (and once you have done that, you can throw it up on the Web and others can use it). The intention is that RDF should enable automated processing of descriptions of Web resources (in the W3C parlance, anything that can be given a URI).

Schemas in Other Communities

In knowledge representation theory, a schema is a way of representing what an individual knows. Schemas became popular in the artificial intelligence community when they were used to construct rule bases for the knowledge of an expert (in what were often known as expert systems). It turned out to be much harder (and therefore much more expensive) to capture all the relevant knowledge than was previously thought. While some expert systems became successes, in most cases there was simply no need for them.

In the database world, a schema describes the datatypes and relations for the fields in a column or row in a table (in a relational database). RDF schemas define the meaning, characteristics, and relationships for a set of properties. These characteristics may include constraints on the values of the properties, and whether they can inherit from other schemas. The RDF schema language is a declarative representation language influenced by knowledge representation, database schemas, and graph data models.

In XML, the content of the elements, the attributes, and the ordering and structuring of the elements (e.g., which elements can nest in each other) for a given document type are described in the DTD (Document Type Description) or the schema (the document describing the element structures). But there is nothing that describes the relation between different resources, be they objects in a container, documents, or something else. That is what RDF does.

The Basic RDF Data Model

The basic RDF data model consists of three object types describing the types of triples: resources, property types, and statements. The RDF data model can resemble an entity-relationship diagram. But it provides no mechanisms for declaring the properties about which it makes statements, nor does it provide any mechanisms for defining the relationships between the properties and other resources—that is the role of RDF Schema.

In the RDF "Model and Syntax" specification, there are only two types of property values: a string of characters and a URI. The character string must itself be well-formed XML. This means that the same quoting rules, escape mechanisms, and so on, that apply otherwise in XML also apply here. It is possible to have a literal attribute, which means that the attribute's markup will not be interpreted as RDF, but rather as is: a string (XML markup that will not be further evaluated by the RDF processor). The RDF Schema specification goes further, and specifies how datatypes can be declared. If the value is a URI referencing another resource, the property value is the resource with the URI in the attribute. If the content is a string with XML in it, the rule is that it has to be well-formed.

The data model of RDF, the directed graph from resource to property value, can only handle binary relations (a statement can only specify the relation between two resources). To get around this, the specification recommends that you create a higher-level resource with no function other than having properties that give the relations between the two resources in the statement. If the value could be several different units, there would be one arc for each of the different units containing the measurement, plus one to the resource. When you use `xml:lang` to declare that a property value is in a certain language, this does not add anything to the description, but is considered part of the literal (the text string).

Property types are the names of the properties (attributes or relations, expressed as arcs in graph theory) in a RDF expression. The property type defines the specific meaning of the property, which values for the property are permitted, which types of objects that can be described with the property, and the relationship(s) between properties of one type and properties of other types. A resource may have multiple properties with the same property type. This is not the same as having a single property whose value is a container containing multiple members.

Property types are also resources, for instance when the property type defines a relationship between two resources. The RDF specification recommends that property names always be qualified with a namespace prefix to unambiguously connect the property definition with the corresponding RDF schema.

Statements are the third object type. They consist of a specific resource together with a named property, plus the value of that property for that resource. Property values can be other resources or they can be atomic (simple strings or other primitive datatypes defined by XML).

If I say "the folo is frogler than the ecks," I have described a relation between two objects; but you are probably wondering what the objects and the relation really are. The RDF Schema specification describes how I define folo, frogler, and ecks, while the RDF Syntax and Model specification describes how the new terms can be related in a statement.

RDF is a general format for metadata encoding. It does not define the semantics for the topic in question. What it defines is the rules for defining and expressing the semantics. Each author is free to define his own semantics and vocabulary, as long as he puts the schema declaring that semantic at the URI he uses to declare the element names. Then it is possible for the computer which tries to resolve what the element name means to retrieve its definition and use it in the correct way. Because it is possible to have more than one namespace in a document, it is possible to have more than one vocabulary describing the object that the metadata is attached to. The author can pick and choose from existing vocabularies, or invent his own.

A schema for folos, frogler, and ecks does not have to provide any human-understandable meaning, however. As long as it declares that a folo can have a range of 1 to 5, and an ecks of 2 to 54, and to be frogler is to be 3.5 larger than something, the statement is completely valid and works matematically (for the values 1 and 3.5, for instance). If, however, the values were subjective (for instance, to be frogler meant "to be nicer to"), the computer would not be able to process it.

The ordering and nesting of elements is often significant, which makes it hard to express multidimensional relations in the XML serialization, even though it is no problem to create n-dimensional graphs (i.e., you can create an infinite number of arcs from a node). Visualizing them, of course, may be a different thing. It is also possible to mix and nest elements with different properties using XML namespaces (strictly speaking, there is a separate namespace mechanism in RDF as well; but let us forget that, because in practice, you are going to use the XML namespace mechanism).

The independence of assertions may bring another problem. I can state "It is June" and "It is winter" in the same breath, and the fact that I may be lying cannot be detected. All that can be detected is that I am making these statements, and by creating a mechanism for applying digital signatures to metadata you can make sure that it was I who made those statements. If I happened to live in Australia, it would of course be true. But there is no way for you to know if I am fibbing, or if this is a valid statement. This is a problem with the way the W3C metadata system is designed.

All RDF elements are of the type "string," that is, they are sequences of characters. More type information can be added at the schema level by introducing constraints, but there are no datatypes in RDF Schema. The type information and other information about an element comes from the XML level of the system. The information about the datatypes is found in the DTD or the schema. (The metadocument describing the information types in the document, their ordering, and how to manage them.) It can also contain other types of classifications, including those added by the user. To describe the composition of RDF assertions, you use RDF Schemas. The RDF schema works at a much higher level than the XML schema. XML defines whether a character is a numeral or a letter; RDF determines how they belong together in words.

RDF lets you represent the relationships between objects as a directed labeled graph. The resources are the nodes, the property types the arcs, and the values are the nodes at the other end of the arcs. This also means that there is an unambiguous direction in the representation. The property type points from the resource to the value, not the other way around. The statement "This document was written by Ora Lassila" is a directed labelled graph with the URI for "this document" as the node, the property type author pointing to the value "Ora Lassila" (who is a real person, by the way, although he became famous for being part of a specification. Hi, Ora.).

If you want to describe Ora Lassila further (e.g., give his phone number and e-mail), you have to create a unique resource representing him. This is a URI from which the property arcs `telephone_number`, `name`, and `e-mail` point to the values of the respective properties.

This may seem cumbersome, but it means that the value "Ora Lassila" of this particular property is unique, since it is tied to a URI, which is unique. That, in turn, means there can be no discussion about what the property values refer to.

On the other hand, there may not be any limit to the chain. Say we created a unique resource for the telephone number, the author's name, and his e-mail address. This would mean inserting another set of nodes and arcs. We could then insert even more nodes, for instance splitting up the e-mail address into hostname and username, and so on. This may seem like a disadvantage, but it is not. It allows for the definition of different vocabularies of property types to fit the situation. They may share the same values, but the values are atomic, and it is clear that they only describe an association in this particular case.

RDF as Class Structures

The schema specifies the datatypes in the document and how they should be handled. It is quite possible to create a document without a schema, but it is not possible to process it. Schemas actually exist for most documents and DTDs, but they may not be formally described (although in some sense, a DTD is actually a schema). But in XML and RDF, there is a special format to describe schemas. Unlike an XML DTD, which gives specific constraints on the structure of a document, an RDF Schema provides information about the interpretation of the statements given in an RDF data model.

When you take a document and remove the element names to create a generalized structure, you describe elements in terms of what their types are. The RDF types are properties and resources, providing information about how the statements should be interpreted. The RDF datatypes are not the same as the datatypes you are used to as a programmer. In RDF, there is only one datatype: strings. The intent is that for other types, RDF should use XML datatypes (as given in the DTD or the XML schema), which provides a constraint mechanism on the document. When you validate an XML document against an XML schema, the validator makes sure that the content of the datatypes does not violate the declarations in the DTD (by making sure that they really say what they were supposed to say in the way they were supposed to). RDF schemas declare not only the syntax of a document (they do not just describe how a document should be organized to be valid RDF), but also how it should be interpreted. The intention is, however, that RDF Schema should reuse the datatypes in XML Schema. Before you can say anything about an object, you must declare a resource that represents the object. This means that we are now three steps removed from the object in reality: You are describing a resource representing an information object representing an object.

A way of looking at the structure of RDF is that it has a class system, not unlike many object-oriented programming and modeling systems. A collection of classes is called a schema. (Classes are generalizations of instances of objects, typically authored for a specific purpose or domain.) Classes are organized in a hierarchy, and offer extensibility through subclass refinement. This way, in order to create a schema slightly different from an existing one, you can just provide incremental modifications to the base schema. The XML and RDF schemas provide a typing system for the datatypes that are described in the nodes and relationships. This typing system can be regarded as a basic set of nodes and relations that express properties of the schema classes. It is possible to map the RDF schema to other schema descriptions, for instance in Universal Modeling Language (UML).

The RDF schema makes it possible to indicate that certain classes are subclasses of others, and provides a small number of basic classes. It also contains a facility for specifying a small number of constraints such as the cardinality (number of occurrences) required and permitted of the properties of instances of classes. Property names must always be associated with a schema, such as by qualifying the element names with a namespace prefix to unambiguously connect the property definition with the corresponding RDF schema.

Resources may be instances of a class (or of more than one class). This is indicated using the type property. Classes and subclasses are often organized as hierarchies, and the `SubClassOf` property describes the relationship between classes and subclasses: You declare all Web sites about history to be of the class historySite, for instance, and all sites of the Napoleonic wars to be members of the class `NapoleonicWars`, which is a subclass of that class (and also, of course, of the classes `WarSites` and `SitesAboutNapoleon`).

RDF schemas may also specify consistency constraints that should be followed by these data models, such as the meaning of classes in a schema. The meaning of classes includes properties (attributes) and relationships between classes as described in the schema of the document.

In addition to using the namespace URI as a reference for the RDF specification, it also serves as the reference to the RDF schema for the specification itself.

Reusing Vocabularies

There are some property names that many different communities may want to use. For instance, the property type `Creator` may have very different values in a religious context and in the context of your child's first clay model (even though there are some people who will claim the opposite). To distinguish which property type the value refers to, the XML encoding of RDF uses the XML namespace mechanism. Namespaces are made unique by using a URI as the namespace identifier. Having done so, you can then declare whatever names you want for your property types, since by definition they will be unique.

This means that you have to declare them in the XML encoding of the graph. The namespace declaration follows directly after the XML declaration:

```
<RDF xmlns="http://www.w3.org/RDF/RDF/"
xmlns:dc="http://purl.oclc.org/dc/">
```

This declares that in the context of this document, `dc:` is the prefix for Dublin Core elements. You must always declare the default namespace for the document (here, the RDF namespace) as well as the namespaces for all the other property types you are using. If you are using only one namespace in the document, you don't have to use the prefix; otherwise, you have to.

The assertion "Johan Hjelm is the author of the book *Designing Wireless Information Services*" will look like this (without the XML declaration and the namespace declaration):

```
<?xml version="1.0"?>
<rdf:RDF xmlns:rdf="http://www.w3.org/1999/02/22-rdf-syntax-ns#"
            xmlns:dc="http://purl.org/dc/elements/1.1/">
  <rdf:Description about="http://www.wireless-information.net/">
    <dc:Creator rdf:resource="http://johanhjelm.com/whois/"/>
  </rdf:Description>
</rdf:RDF>
```

The namespace prefixes `rdf:` and `dc:` are used to distinguish which elements belong to which namespace. The `rdf:RDF` element is used to show where the RDF begins and ends, and the `rdf:Description` element declares that this is a description about the resource identified by the URI.

The URI that identifies a namespace points to a schema, which describes the vocabulary being used. Anyone can define their own schema, as the Dublin Core group did for their description format. Having a schema that expresses your vocabulary is useful if you want to extract information automatically and have information in an XML-based format. Then, you can use an XSLT transformation sheet to take content from elements in the document format and put it into another format.

RDF Syntax Elements in RDF Schema

The RDF Schema also contains a number of properties that express RDF syntax in RDF Schema, as shown in Table 5.1. For the most part, we have covered them already.

Things to Remember When Building Schemas

When constructing RDF schemas, there are a few things you need to think about. New vocabularies are introduced through XML namespaces. This means that you have to take into account all the rules that apply for XML namespaces.

To understand how to create a schema, take a normal document tree and describe the elements you are using. Then, remove the element names. Do the same for the properties and the property values. A schema is nothing but a generalization of a document structure, which can be reapplied to other documents. Schemas are meta-descriptions, whereas DTDs just describe the ordering and internal structure of the elements, for instance which datatypes they can contain, which values those datatypes can have, and in which order

Table 5.1 The RDF Syntax Elements in RDF Schema

ELEMENT	FUNCTION
rdfs:Literal	Corresponds to `Literals` in the Model and Syntax specification. Examples include atomic values such as text strings.
rdf:Statement	Corresponds to `Statement` in the Model and Syntax specification. In essence the same as `DescriptionAbout` or `DescriptionID`.
rdf:subject	Corresponds to `subject` in the Model and Syntax specification. This is used to specify the resource described by a reified statement. In essence, the same as `DescriptionID` with an anonymous ID. Its `rdfs:domain` is `rdf:Statement` and `rdfs:range` is `rdfs:Resource`.
rdf:predicate	Corresponds to predicate in the Model and Syntax specification. This is used to identify the property used in the modeled statement. Its `rdfs:domain` is `rdf:Statement` and `rdfs:range` is `rdf:Property`.
rdf:object	Corresponds to `object` in the Model and Syntax specification. This is used to identify the property value in the statement. Its `rdfs:domain` is `rdf:Statement`.
rdfs:Container	Represents the `Container` classes (`bag`, `alternative`, and `sequence`) of the Model and Syntax specification. It is an instance of `rdfs:Class` and `rdfs:subClassOf` `rdfs:Resource`.
rdf:Bag	Corresponds to `Bag` in the Model and Syntax specification. It is an instance of `rdfs:Class` and `rdfs:subClassOf` `rdfs:Container`.
rdf:Seq	Corresponds to `Sequence` in the Model and Syntax specification. It is an instance of `rdfs:Class` and `rdfs:subClassOf` `rdfs:Container`.
rdf:Alt	Corresponds to `Alternative` in the Model and Syntax specification. It is an instance of `rdfs:Class` and `rdfs:subClassOf` `rdfs:Container`.

Table 5.1 The RDF Syntax Elements in RDF Schema (Continued)

ELEMENT	FUNCTION
rdfs:ContainerMembershipProperty	A class which has as members the properties _1, _2, _3 . . . which are used to indicate container membership as described the Model and Syntax specification. This is an `rdfs:subClassOf rdf:Property`.
rdf:value	Corresponds to the `value` property of the Model and Syntax specification.

and how often they can occur. (The chain never stops: Schemas describe what the elements mean, using the RDF schema language.)

When you name your elements, they will have to be unique within the schema, but they do not have to be globally unique—that is the job of namespaces. The RDF Model and Syntax specification recommends the use of *interCap* name styles for RDF property names (starting with a lower case letter, and having the second and subsequent words within a name started with a capital letter and no internal punctuation). So that is good practice. Names for elements and attributes follow the XML namespace rules, so you also need to make sure that the names do not contain any of the reserved XML characters, such as `&` and `;` , which have to be escaped if you insist on using them. The definitions of your attributes and elements should indicate the type and interpretation of the associated value. Ultimately, it is a matter for agreement between generating and receiving applications as to how any particular attribute value is to be interpreted. Where element or attribute content expresses a quantity, the units of that quantity should be clearly associated with the definition. There is, however, no separate mechanism for indicating the units in which an attribute value is expressed.

The meaning of every element or attribute must be defined in isolation. It is not possible to create an element or attribute with a value that is dependent on the value of some other attribute. For example, an attribute called `page-width` must always be expressed using the same units: it is not acceptable for this attribute to be expressed in characters for one class of device, millimeters for another, and inches for another. There is no way of expressing this disparity in RDF Schema. But you can define attributes in *layers* so that simple capabilities (e.g., the ability to handle color photographic images) can be described by a simple attribute, with additional attributes used to provide more detailed or arcane capabilities (e.g., exact color matching capabilities).

Now, say we want to create a schema for the French emperor Napoleon. It might look like this, if you want to create a schema that can be used in documents with an element called `Napoleon`.

```
<? xml version='1.0'?>
  <rdf:RDF
     xmlns:rdf="http://www.w3.org/TR/REC-rdf-syntax#"
     xmlns:rdfs="http://www.w3.org/TR/WD-rdf-schema#"
     xmlns:n="">
  <rdf:Description ID="napoleon">
    <rdf:type rdf:resource="http://www.w3.org/TR/REC-rdf-
syntax#Property"/>
    <rdfs:label>Napoleon</rdfs:label>
    <rdfs:comment>The French emperor of the same name.</rdfs:comment>
    <rdfs:isDefinedBy = ""/>
  </rdf:Description>
</rdf:RDF>
```

Let us see what we did: first, the XML declaration and the namespace declarations. (As you will note, the `n:` prefix applies to the current document.)

```
<? xml version='1.0'?>
  <rdf:RDF
     xmlns:rdf="http://www.w3.org/TR/REC-rdf-syntax#"
     xmlns:rdfs="http://www.w3.org/TR/WD-rdf-schema#"
     xmlns:n="">
```

Then, we have an ID for the description about the element. It is defined as a property by the URI in `resource`, and is of the type `Property`. The label for the element is `Napoleon`.

```
<rdf:Description ID="napoleon">
  <rdf:type rdf:resource="http://www.w3.org/TR/REC-rdf-syntax#Property"/>
  <rdfs:label>Napoleon</rdfs:label>
```

I think you understand `comment`. And finally, there needs to be an `isDefinedBy` declaration, to make sure a parser can understand that this was the element it was reading. This is an *empty* element, where the content of the element is an attribute value. In this case, it refers to the current document and so can itself be empty. And the document ends by closing all the elements.

```
    <rdfs:comment>The French emperor of the same name.</rdfs:comment>
    <rdfs:isDefinedBy = ""/>
  </rdf:Description>
</rdf:RDF>
```

It is, as we saw in Chapter 3, very easy to read an RDF schema (and to write one). To show you an example, here is a piece of the RDF schema for Dublin Core:

```
<? xml version='1.0'?>
  <rdf:RDF
     xmlns:rdf="http://www.w3.org/TR/REC-rdf-syntax#"
     xmlns:rdfs="http://www.w3.org/TR/WD-rdf-schema#"
     xmlns:dc="">
```

```
<rdf:Description rdf:about = "">
  <dc:title> The Dublin Core Element Set </dc:title>
  <dc:creator> The Dublin Core Metadata Inititative </dc:creator>
  <dc:description> The Dublin Core is a simple metadata element
      set intended to facilitate discovery of electronic
      resources. </dc:description>
  <dc:date> 1995-03-01 </dc:date>
</rdf:Description>
<rdf:Description ID="title">
  <rdf:type rdf:resource="http://www.w3.org/TR/REC-rdf-
syntax#Property"/>
  <rdfs:label>Title</rdfs:label>
  <rdfs:comment>The name given to the resource, usually by the Creator
  or Publisher.</rdfs:comment>
  <rdfs:isDefinedBy = ""/>
</rdf:Description>
```

(It of course goes on to list all the elements, but these are sufficient for demonstration purposes).

As you can see, the schema starts with the XML declaration and the namespace declaration. It may look funny to have a namespace declaration that is empty, but it refers to the current document. This schema is recursive, using elements from itself, as you can see a bit further on (of course this is perfectly legal: a schema, like any other XML document, needs to be read in its entirety before it can be used).

If we look at the schema for the title element, you will see how it is defined in RDF Schema. First, there is an `rdf:Description` that defines the ID for the item. Then, the type and the URI for the resource. After that comes the label of the element, and a comment that explains what it is. And, finally, `isDefinedBy`, which is the current document.

This is one vocabulary. As you can understand, even if there is a very large number of RDF descriptions, it is simply not possible to describe everything to everybody's satisfaction. There will always be occasions when you feel you have a vocabulary that describes a topic better than someone else does. It may even be that you are part of a standards group that has designed a specific vocabulary for your area. The good thing is that there is nothing to stop you from writing your own schemas and publishing them. When the RDF processor comes to your new element, it will have to resolve the namespace and use the element it found in your profile.

There are a few things required to publish the information. The first is a URI at which to publish it. That needs to be persistent, since you need to be able to guarantee that other people can download your schema even after several days or weeks-or years, in the worst case. There will not be any copies of your schema, since HTTP caching rules mandate that the cached items be refreshed after a time. If your schema becomes popular, it will also be the target of quite a lot of traffic from servers and clients who are trying to use it. You may want to make sure the machine at which you are locating it can take the strain. Apart from that, it only requires a bit of sweat, a Web server, and a reasonably good XML editor.

RDF Schema is an object system that you add to the RDF model, and it lets you express constraints in the relationships between resources and properties using the object structure of classes and subclasses.

The object system includes classes, types, and subclasses. In essence, you are defining the properties and resources you are going to use in your descriptions. It is not a full-blown object system, however. The RDF Schema mechanism is specified as RDF resources (including classes and properties), and constraints on their relationships. The RDF Schema core vocabulary can be used to make statements defining and describing application-specific vocabularies such as the Dublin Core Element Set, which we will look at in the next chapter.

RDF Schema has three different types of resources: the properties, the constraint properties (which are a subset of the properties), and the classes. It is a collection of RDF resources that can be used to describe properties of other RDF resources (including properties) which can then be used to define application-specific RDF vocabularies.

The RDF Schema has three core classes that are used to define the elements under discussion: `Resource`, `Property`, and `Class` (see Table 5.2). Essentially, they represent the node, the arc, and the type of arc.

The `Property` class has a number of instances (which, of course, means that they are properties) that are considered core properties of RDF Schema, and

Table 5.2 The Elements of RDF Schema

ELEMENT	MEANING
rdfs:Resource	Everything that is being described by RDF (the roots of the graphs) are resources, and as such, are instances of the class `rdfs:Resource`.
rdf:Property	The properties are a subset of the resources, i.e., they are resources in their own right, but they are not the subjects of the description.
rdfs:Class	`Class` here is a class in the object-oriented sense. When the schema defines a new class, an `rdf:type` property with the value `rdfs:class` must be created. Classes can essentially represent anything (just as classes in an object-oriented system can represent anything).

Table 5.3 The Properties of RDF Schema

PROPERTY	MEANING
rdf:type	The type indicates that a resource is a member of a class. The value of the type property is the class.
rdfs:subClassOf	A class can be a part of another class, which is what this property expresses (the class dogs is a subclass of animals, for instance). A class can never be a subclass of itself nor any of the subclasses it contains. This property is transitive, i.e., subclasses of subclasses are considered subclasses of the class (Dalmatian is a subclass of dog is a subclass of animal, so Dalmatian is a subclass of animal).
rdfs:subPropertyOf	`subPropertyOf` is an instance of `rdf:property`, and is used to create a specialization of that. It is a subclass of property, in the same way as `subClassOf`.
rdfs:seeAlso	`rdfs:seeAlso` is intended to give additional information about the resource in the subject. It can be defined as a `rdfs:subPropertyOf`, if you want to define the subject resource better. Both object and subject must be instances of `rdfs:resource`.
rdfs:isDefinedBy	`rdfs:isDefinedBy` is a subproperty of `rdfs:seeAlso`. It indicates the resource defining the subject resource. The idea is that when you use a property or class defined in another RDF schema, this property can be used to point to it, in case additional assistance is needed beyond the XML namespace mechanism.

they express the relationships between classes, instances of classes, and superclasses (see Table 5.3).

Validating Against Schemas

When the document has been read into the XML processor, it is validated against the document schema (an optional step, because documents need only be well-formed, not valid). The DTD describes which tags the document should contain, but the schema describes how they should be handled. The schema is a description of the data model of the tags: Data models are descriptions of the datatypes the tags can contain, how long they can be, how often they can occur, and so on. Schemas are intended to replace DTDs. Applying stylesheets to the document (if stylesheets are referenced or included) then formats the resulting data. Other semantics, such as actions for forms, applets, and other objects, are also applied. This process produces a hierarchy of formatting objects, which are rendered on the screen (or the selected output medium, voice or paper) of the user. XML documents do not have to be displayed; they can be used for communication between computer systems, because it is possible to create machine-understandable information in XML. In that case, the document is handed over to the RDF processor for further processing, since it will have been identified as RDF in the process.

This processing model means that you really cannot display an XML document as it is received from the network, as HTML browsers usually do; you have to parse the entire document first, resolve any URIs that require resolving, look up unknown elements in the schema, and so on.

RDF is a graph-based system, and as such, the matching of different graphs—one of the most powerful features of RDF—can be done using topological algorithms. If it was possible to transport and handle information as graphs, you could do that and not worry about the XML encoding.

XML is, as we stated in Chapter 3, a markup language for documents containing structured information. Structured information contains both content (words, pictures, etc.) and markup, which are indicators to show the role of the content piece (a fragment, in the correct terminology). Content can have different roles in different places in a document: The same word in a heading has a different meaning from when it occurs in a footnote. Almost all documents have some structure.

The XML DTD

XML inherited DTDs from SGML, where they are the schema mechanism. XML Schemas are the first widespread attempt to replace DTDs with something better. XML is, in some sense, an SGML application. (Each markup language defined in SGML is called an SGML application.) An SGML application has an SGML declaration specifying which characters and delimiters may appear in the application. The DTD defines the syntax of markup constructs, including additional definitions such as character entity references (Character references are numeric or symbolic names for characters that may be included in a document. They are useful for referring to rarely used characters, or those which are difficult or impossible to enter using authoring tools). It is also a specification that describes the semantics to be ascribed to the markup. A document instance containing data (content) and markup also contains a reference to the DTD to be used to interpret it.

An SGML document type definition declares element types that represent structures or desired behavior. Elements may have associated properties, called attributes, which may have values (by default, or set by authors or scripts). Attribute-value pairs appear before the final > of an element's start tag. Any number of (legal) attribute-value pairs, separated by spaces, may appear in an element's start tag, in any order.

DTDs can be used to define content models (the valid order and nesting of elements) and, to a limited extent, the datatypes of attributes. They provide a grammar for a class of documents. The DTD can point to an external subset (a special kind of external entity) containing markup declarations, it can contain the markup declarations directly in an internal subset, or it can do both. The DTD for a document consists of both subsets taken together.

There are some problems with DTDs, however. They are written in the SGML syntax, which is not XML. They have no support for namespaces. There are only limited datatypes. DTDs can only express the datatype of attributes in terms of explicit enumerations and a few coarse string formats: There's no facility for describing numbers, dates, currency values, and so forth. Furthermore, DTDs have no ability to express the datatype of character data in elements.

The markup declarations may be made up, in whole or in part, of the replacement text of parameter entities, which are replaced by the XML processor when the DTD is read. However, this extension mechanism is based on little more than string substitution. The DTD extension mechanism (parameter entities) doesn't really make relationships explicit, such that two elements defined to have the same content models aren't the same thing in any explicit way. The content models define constraints on the logical structure and to support the use of predefined storage units. The function of the markup in an XML document is to describe its storage and logical structure, and to associate the attribute-value pairs in the document with its logical structure.

XML Schema was developed to overcome these limitations and to be much more expressive than DTDs. However, it also managed to be more complex and vastly larger (the specification runs to more than a hundred pages if you print it, whereas the XML specification is only some 10 pages). However, you can do much more when the encoding is in the XML Schema language, such as exchanging XML data much more robustly without relying on ad hoc validation tools. Although XML schemas will replace DTDs, in the short term DTDs still have a number of advantages. A large number of tools—all SGML tools and many XML tools—can process DTDs. They are also widely deployed, which means that there is widespread expertise among developers with many years of practical application.

XML documents should begin with an XML declaration specifying the version of XML being used, the DTD used, and the namespaces used in the document. The XML document is valid if it has a document-type declaration appearing before the first element in the document, and the document complies with the constraints expressed in it. Markup declarations can affect the content of the document, as passed from an XML processor to an application; examples are attribute defaults and entity declarations. Attributes are used to associate name-value pairs with elements, but attribute specifications may appear only within start-tags and empty-element tags. Attribute-list declarations may be used to define the set of attributes (names) pertaining to a given element type, to establish type constraints (datatypes) for these attributes, and to provide a default value (if any) for each attribute associated with a given element type.

An XML document may consist of one or many storage units called entities; they all have content and are all identified by name (except for the document entity and the external DTD subset). Each XML document has one entity called the document entity, which serves as the starting point for the XML processor and may contain the whole document.

Entities may be either parsed or unparsed. A parsed entity's contents are referred to as its replacement text; this text is considered an integral part of the document. The text is a sequence of characters, which may represent markup or character data. Markup takes the form of start-tags, end-tags, empty-element tags, entity references, character references, comments, CDATA section delimiters, document type declarations, and processing instructions.

An unparsed entity is a resource whose contents may or may not be text, and if text, may not be XML. Each unparsed entity has an associated notation, identified by name. Beyond a requirement that an XML processor make the identifiers for the entity and notation available to the application, XML places no constraints on the contents of unparsed entities.

Parsed entities are invoked by name using entity references; unparsed entities are invoked by the name given in the value of `ENTITY` or `ENTITIES` attributes.

General entities are entities for use within the document content. In this specification, general entities are sometimes referred to with the unqualified term `entity` when this leads to no ambiguity. Parameter entities are parsed entities for use within the DTD. These two types of entities use different forms of reference and are recognized in different contexts. Furthermore, they occupy different namespaces; a parameter entity and a general entity with the same name are two distinct entities.

A character reference refers to a specific character in the ISO/IEC 10646 character set, for example one not directly accessible from available input devices. An entity reference refers to the content of a named entity. References to parsed general entities use ampersand (`&`) and semicolon (`;`) as delimiters. Parameter-entity references use percent-sign (`%`) and semicolon (`;`) as delimiters.

As an example, the following is a complete XML document (taken from the XML specification), well-formed but not valid:

```
<?xml version="1.0"?> <greeting>Hello, world!</greeting>
```

and so is this:

```
<greeting>Hello, world!</greeting>
```

This is an example of an XML document with a document type declaration:

```
<?xml version="1.0"?> <!DOCTYPE greeting SYSTEM "hello.dtd">
<greeting>Hello, world!</greeting>
```

The system identifier "hello.dtd" gives the URI of a DTD for the document.

The declarations can also be given locally, as in this example:

```
<?xml version="1.0" encoding="UTF-8" ?> <!DOCTYPE greeting [   <!ELEMENT
greeting (#PCDATA)> ]> <greeting>Hello, world!</greeting>
```

XML Schemas

In the context of XML, a schema describes a model for describing the structure of the information in a whole class of documents. The model describes the possible arrangement of elements and content. A document that follows it is a valid document. A schema might also be viewed as an agreement on a common vocabulary for a particular application that involves exchanging documents. The word *schema* comes from the database world, where it is used to describe the structure of a table in a relational database (i.e., the column headers). Since it has nothing to do with schemes, it is often used in its Greek root form, so we refer to a schema or several schemata.

The relationship between XML Schema and RDF Schema has been the root of a lot of confusion, both inside the W3C and for the rest of us. Basically, the XML Schema replaces the DTD, describing the document in terms of basic datatypes. RDF Schema defines the properties at the application level, and not only the properties of the resource (Title, Author, Subject, Size, Color, etc.) but also the kinds of resources being described (books, Web pages, people, companies, etc.). The role of RDF Schema is to provide a mechanism for declaring the properties of elements as well as relationships between properties and resources, and the semantics for these. The data model of RDF defines only a simple model for relationships between resources, as named properties and values. RDF properties may be thought of as attributes of resources and in this sense correspond to traditional attribute-value pairs. RDF properties also represent relationships between resources. As such, the RDF data model can therefore resemble an entity-relationship diagram.

In database schemas, models are described in terms of constraints, which define what can appear in any given context. In XML Schema, you can basically use two kinds of constraints to create the model of the document infrastructure. These are the content model constraints, which describe the order and sequence of elements (in effect, the semantics of the data model), and a datatype constraint that describes what constitutes valid units of data.

XML Schema and Datatypes

RDF Schema does not have a datatype mechanism, and the intent is that it should use the datatype mechanism in XML Schema at some stage. But because you declare your schema as constraints, you can declare the datatypes as constraints on the data model of the RDF application you are defining.

The XML Schema defines the datatypes for the XML document, and so does not get read by the RDF application. XML Schema documents are XML documents. This means that they use elements and attributes to express the semantics of the schema and that they can be edited and processed with the same tools that you use to process other XML documents. This is contrary to the DTD, which is an SGML document (there is also a DTD for XML Schema). It is also possible to vary the syntax in the data model of RDF a great deal within the specification, but since the RDF data model describes graphs, you may have to constrain the representation to fit into the graph model. The RDF/XML syntax itself provides considerable flexibility in the syntactic expression of the data model but a syntactic schema alone is not sufficient for RDF purposes. RDF Schemas may also specify consistency constraints that should be followed by these data models.

XML Schema allows you to specify your own XML elements, just as RDF Schema allows you to specify your own RDF elements. The XML Schema element specification has some limited concept of the relations between the elements, but not as much as the RDF Schema. Most likely, however, you will use a schema which someone else has defined for you, as part of a document class. The most frequently used schema definition is likely to be the one for XHTML, which will be implicitly used by everyone who wants to write better HTML documents. But there are also schemas for e-commerce, catalogs, news, and lots of other things. The hard part is really finding out for which document types there are schemas defined.

Just as documents were validated against the DTD, they can be validated against the XML Schema. An XML Schema document itself is only valid if it conforms to the schema for XML Schema. Validity is going to be more important in a world of machine-to-machine communication, and when you receive and send information to and from lots of sources, you want to make sure the information you receive is valid before you try to import it into your system. If you can catch problems before they enter your database or even before they enter your computer system, you'll be better off.

As I mentioned before, XML Schema allows you to define datatypes for the elements in the document, which is a major difference from RDF Schema. The basic difference is between complex types, which allow elements in their content and may carry attributes, and simple types, which cannot have element content or attributes. Another important distinction is between type definitions that call in already-existing datatypes (for instance, from other schemata), and definitions which create entirely new types. This can be done using the include element, for instance `<include schemaLocation="http://www.example.com/schemas/address.xsd"/>`. This means that you are, in effect, replacing the include element with all the definitions and declarations from address.xsd.

Just so you do not get confused, since XML Schema is an XML document, it is possible to have inline references and use namespaces, just like in any other XML document. We will not go through how to actually create an XML schema, since that would not be particularly useful when you are working with RDF (which, of course, is an XML application and ought to have its own schema, although since it came about before schemas were specified, it has only a DTD).

Datatypes are defined by having a distinct set of values, called the value space, that are characteristic in some way. They also have a valid lexical representation for each value in the value space. A value space is an abstract collection of permitted values for the datatype. Value spaces have certain properties: for example, they always have the concept of cardinality and equality and may have the concept of order, by which individual values within the value space can be compared to one another. Value spaces may also support operations on values, such as addition. The lexical space for a datatype consists of a set of valid literals (text strings). Each value in the datatypes value space maps to one or more valid literals in its lexical space.

The vocabulary in the XML Schema specification consists of only thirty elements and attributes, as shown in Table 5.4. It is actually a schema definition language, although not as advanced as the RDF Schema language. It has a number of simple types built in, and it is also possible to derive new datatypes from existing types (for instance, by constraining them and, of course, giving them a different name). This can mean having a string that can only contain A:s, for instance.

As you see, these datatypes can be combined to create quite complex applications. (For instance, you could build a calendar application using them.) The legal values for each simple type can be constrained through the application of one or more facets. A facet is a single defining aspect of a concept or an object. Each facet is a characterization of the concept independent from others.

Table 5.4 Simple Types Built in the XML Schema

SIMPLE TYPE	EXAMPLE
String	"Confirm this is electric"
Boolean	true, false, 1, 0
Float	-INF, -1E4, -0, 0, 12.78E-2, 12, INF, NaN ("not a number"), equivalent to single-precision 32-bit floating point
Double	-INF, -1E4, -0, 0, 12.78E-2, 12, INF, NaN, equivalent to double-precision 64-bit floating point
Decimal	-1.23, 0, 123.4, 1000.00
TimeInstant	1999-05-31T13:20:00.000-05:00 (May 31st 1999 at 1:20 P.M. Eastern Standard Time, which is 5 hours behind Coordinated Universal Time (UTC))
TimeDuration	P1Y2M3DT10H30M12.3S (1 year, 2 months, 3 days, 10 hours, 30 minutes, 12.3 seconds)
RecurringInstant	-05-31T13:20:00 (May 31st every year at 1:20 P.M. UTC, format similar to `timeInstant`)
Binary	100010
uri-reference	http://www.example.com/, http://www.example.com/doc.html#ID5
ID	an XML 1.0 ID attribute type
IDREF	an XML 1.0 IDREF attribute type
ENTITY	an XML 1.0 ENTITY attribute type
NOTATION	an XML 1.0 NOTATION attribute type
Language	en-GB, en-US, fr, and other valid values for `xml:lang` as defined in XML 1.0
IDREFS	is an XML 1.0 IDREFS attribute type
ENTITIES	is an XML 1.0 ENTITIES attribute type
NMTOKEN	US; an XML 1.0 NMTOKEN attribute type
NMTOKENS	"US UK;" an XML 1.0 NMTOKENS attribute type
Name	shipTo (an XML 1.0 Name type)
Qname	Address (an XML Namespace QName)
NCName	Address (an XML Namespace NCName, i.e., a Qname without the prefix and colon)
Integer	-126789, -1, 0, 1, 126789
non-positive-integer	-126789, -1, 0
Negative-integer	-126789, -1
Long	-1, 12678967543233

Table 5.4 Simple Types Built in the XML Schema (Continued)

SIMPLE TYPE	EXAMPLE
Int	-1, 126789675
Short	-1, 12678
Byte	-1, 126
non-negative-integer	0, 1, 126789
Unsigned-long	0, 12678967543233
Unsigned-int	0, 1267896754
Unsigned-short	0, 12678
Unsigned-byte	0, 126
Positive-integer	1, 126789
Date	1999-05-31, --05 (5th day of every month)
Time	13:20:00.000, 13:20:00.000-05:00

Schemas define not only the datatypes of the content of an element, but also the datatypes of attributes, and so they define empty elements as well. When you do that, however, you cannot, by definition, use the simple datatypes. You have to create more complex datatypes, which further constrain the simple datatypes. It is also possible to have unique data values and combinations of data values. All of this can be declared in the schema.

XML Schema actually gets by with very few element types. The reason is, of course, that when combined with the datatypes and each other, they can be used to create very sophisticated elements in themselves. You have to remember that you constrain the original elements further and further in order to create the new elements. The first four in Table 5.5 are used for setting boundaries in schemas; the others to determine the numeric and literal type of an element.

RDF Constraints

RDF is a constraint on XML, and the types of properties and resources are also constraints on RDF. There is, moreover, a further constraint mechanism in RDF, defining two properties: range (which implies that the value of a property should be a resource of a certain class-in essence, a URI) and domain (which implies that the property can only be used on resources of a certain class). The constraints can be used to define constraints across different namespaces

Table 5.5 The Datatypes in XML Schema

`MaxExclusive`
`MinExclusive`
`MaxInclusive`
`MinInclusive`
`Precision`
`Scale`
`Length`
`MaxLength`
`Enumeration`
`Literal`
`LexicalRepresentation`
`Lexical`

(essentially, in different schemas). It is not defined how they should be implemented, however.

There are three core constraints in RDF Schema (as shown in Table 5.6), defining different aspects of the constraints. Constraint mechanisms, like type mechanisms, are something intended to be enhanced at some later date. However, there is no way to include new constraints automatically, since there is no automated mechanism for discovering new constraints.

Finally, there are two different schema properties that are used to make the schemas human-readable. These are shown in Table 5.7.

Table 5.6 RDF Schema Constraints

CONSTRAINT	EXPLANATION
rdfs:ConstraintProperty	Defines a class that consists only of constraint properties (`rdfs:domain` and `rdfs:range`). It is a subclass of `rdfs:property`.
rdfs:range	Indicates the classes that property values must be members of. Its value is always a class, and it is in itself an instance of `ConstraintProperty`. It can apply only to properties.
rdfs:domain	Indicates the classes on whose members a property can be used. These can rangefrom zero to infinitely many. If there is no domain property, the property can be used with any resource.

Table 5.7 RDF Schema Comments

PROPERTY NAME	PROPERTY PROPERTY
rdfs:comment	Used to provide a human-readable description of the resource
rdfs:label	Used to provide a human-readable version of the resource name

RDF and Databases

Since RDF applications are mostly database applications anyway, you might ask yourself why it is necessary to complicate things by using additional constructs (like triples and graphs). Why not use SQL, the Structured Query Language that all relational database management systems support, to make statements and queries for information?

SQL is a standard, to be sure, but it suffers from its popularity. All vendors have added their own small pieces to it, and they are incompatible. A piece of software working in an Oracle database will not work in a Sybase database. The most important reason, however, is that not all RDF data is stored as SQL. It is perfectly feasible to store a piece of RDF as a text file, another piece as an entry in a database, and the third as a fragment in some object system. XML is already well-established as an excellent method for hiding the underlying application, but RDF enables database engines to exchange structured statements without knowing the structure of their internal representations.

RDF Schema also forces you to do things that most database management systems do not. The `rdfs:subClassOf` and `rdfs:subPropertyOf` predicates are transitive—they are *implied* properties, a notion that the RDF data model includes. It is, however, not something that can easily be expressed with standard relational or document-storage database technology. Storing the base RDF triples is not a problem, though.

RDF schemas can also be used for consistency checks. If the RDF Schema which the data uses contains *constraint resources* (range, domain), the actual RDF triple can be verified to follow these. This would not be a problem if they could not be arbitrarily complex, but database management systems can have a problem processing them.

Another problem is that properties can be used to draw conclusions about resources. If a resource has a property with a range constraint, it can be used to infer that other resources with the same property have the same range (e.g., if Napoleon I has a property Emperor, and this has a range constraint France, we can conclude that if Napoleon III has the property Emperor, he was also emperor of France). To use schemas in this way is especially useful in the Web environment, where information is often incomplete. However, a database management system cannot handle complex inferences like this (unless specially programmed to do so).

Rules can express basically any operation, like searches. RDF does not contain a construct for sets, so the language has to extend RDF Schema with a set construct to enable searches, for example (because search operations in an index are a matter of identifying all instances of an object that conform to a certain set of properties out of the set of total instances, the object in the case of traditional search engines being Web pages). Of course, the subject of the operation can be any object. Since rules can be arbitrarily complex, a specialized parser is usually insufficient, if they are going beyond a limited set of primitives. You have to use a special application to process them. This can be either a database application geared toward processing information using the database management system (such that operations take place in the database management engine, using SQL) or a specialized application (often known as an intelligent agent).

Relational databases are structured in columns containing the properties of the objects, and rows containing the property values. Each field contains an instance of a property. Using this model, RDF graphs can be mapped into relational databases. However, this is not the only approach to implementing RDF in relational databases. Optimizing databases is an entire science in itself, and the layout of the database tables is directly reflected in the performance of the application.

The simplest (most naive) way of storing RDF in a database is likely to break down when the database gets large. It is probably fine for several thousand triples (depending on the database engine, of course), but when the data set becomes larger, there need to be other solutions. One is to create a series of tables containing the statements, data model, literals, resources, and the keys to the statements. These make it easier to do searches based on the key values. Another way is to create a different set of tables, containing the resources, statements, and prefixes. There are probably even further optimizations that are possible, depending on what you want to do with the data.

CHAPTER 6

More Metadata Vocabularies

Your site probably has some very nice metadata by now. But you also probably perceive it to be somewhat limited. The information elements available are rather few, as you have probably noticed. While the author of a Web site may be unambiguous, the content is not at all as clear. Is your site about Paris, Texas, or Paris, France?

That is not all. To enable the metainformation to be comparable, you need information that is defined in a schema. And to describe different aspects, you need several schemas. There is more to site information than RSS. After all, it just gives a description of some aspects of the site. There are a large number of different description formats for information—as many as there are possible descriptions. Here I will highlight some more, but you can choose which you want to include in the profile of your site.

Open Directory

Yahoo came about as an attempt to classify the chaotic proliferation of Web sites that was then emerging. There are a variety of other classification schemes available today, albeit far fewer for information objects. Yahoo was already mentioned, but its classification terms are somewhat abstruse and often the reason why a document or site has been placed in a certain category is impenetrable. That goes for all other sites that use the same classification method; that is, a human reading and verifying the pages.

The Open Directory Project takes the same idea, but attempts to apply Open Source methods and classifies the information using RDF. This probably brings to mind one of the oldest and still best working systems on the Internet: Usenet. There are a large number of experts in the Usenet discussion groups, but to be able to tell what is good or bad, right or wrong, you have to be an expert yourself. The Open Directory is intended to be a self-regulating republic where experts can collect their recommendations, without including noise and misinformation.

Each person (or editor) can organize a small portion of the Web and present it back to the rest of the population, culling out the bad and useless and keeping only the best content.

The goal is to produce a comprehensive directory of the Web, by relying on volunteer editors. The premise is that it is better to work together than to work alone: As the Web grows, automated search engines and directories with small editorial staffs will be unable to cope with the volume of sites.

Like Open Source software (and perhaps even more democratically, because no programming competence is required), everyone is invited to contribute. Signing up is easy: choose a topic you know something about and join. There is a comprehensive set of tools for adding, deleting, and updating links, which generate the RDF behind the directory structure. Essentially, it creates a database with statements about the sites, including your statements.

However, there is no distributed markup, because all the information is stored in a central database. The fact that it is an RDF database is interesting enough in itself, of course. But there is no simple way for you to select a piece of Open Directory markup and put it on your pages. Part of that is due to the fact that editors manage the Open Directory. What gets put on the different pages reflects the opinions of the editors.

vCard in RDF

Some years ago, a number of companies got together to define a standard for electronic business cards. It became known as vCard, and was later developed by the International Mail Consortium and standardized (as a MIME type) by the IETF in RFC 2425. However, you can only compare a vCard to another vCard, unless you have a piece of software that "understands" both vCard and the other datatype you are comparing it to. Unless you use the RDF mapping, of course.

vCard is used in WAP, as well as in many other places. But today you can handle the vCard items only as fields in a database. If you take a vCard from one database and another from your personal database, you have no way of comparing the different elements and determining whether their address is close to your office, for instance. Presenting your vCard as part of the metadata information for your site makes sense if it is related to yourself, for instance your personal site. There are some RDF vocabularies for personal information, among them vocabularies for resumes that would enable you to search for competent people automatically.

Renato Ianella of DSTC in Australia has written an RDF encoding of the vCard format—without asking the IMC first. It is quite possible to create RDF encodings of structured data without any permission whatsoever from the author.

The namespace for vCard is http://imc.org/vCard/3.0#, which is the current version of vCard. Using a prefix, which contains the version number, means there is no need to provide a special version number among the property types. There is also no need for the *Begin* and *end* types, because the XML encoding of RDF automatically tells when the description starts and ends.

vCard consists of a set of property types describing the different properties a person may want to put on a business card. These include the first name, last name, address, e-mail, fax number, home phone number, work phone number, mobile phone number, title, organization, department, address, city, zip code, country, and URI. This is an example of Johan Hjelm's vCard (abbreviated):

```
<?xml version='1.0'?>
<rdf:RDF xmlns:rdf="http://www.w3.org/1999/02/22-rdf-syntax-ns#"
         xmlns:vcard = "http://www.imc.org/vcard/3.0/">
 <rdf:Description rdf:about = "http://411.com/JoeSmith">
   <vcard:fn>Johan Hjelm</vcard:fn>
   <vcard:email>johan.hjelm@nrj.ericsson.se</vcard:email>
   <vcard:org>Nippon Ericsson KK</vcard:org>
 </rdf:Description>
</rdf:RDF>
```

Event Markup

If your site describes an event, such as your company's Christmas party, using Dublin Core is not good enough. There are no functions referring to opening times, no way of describing that it takes place in the ballroom of the Munich Hilton, and no way of describing which day it happens. However, there are other solutions. The Svenska Kalenderinitiativet (SKi) format is based on VEVENT, which is defined in IETF standard RFC-2445, Internet Calendaring and Scheduling Core Object Specification (iCalendar). A SKi-object can have all the fields that exist in a VEVENT, but also others, defined as a media type starting with "X-SKI-". VEVENT was originally intended to be used for the exchange of information between desktop calendars, but using SKi, it can be extended to contain all those information sets needed to describe an event—which are many more than what you need to describe a meeting. Besides VEVENT, there are a number of other events in the iCalendar format, such as VTODO, VALARM, and so on. They do not relate to descriptions of events, however.

Besides the fields (component properties) that are described in the iCalendar-specification, the iCalendar-files can contain information fields that are extensions to it—which is what SKi is. This also means it uses the same content type (text/calendar) as iCalendar. The file extension of *ics* is used to designate a file containing calendaring and scheduling information consistent with this MIME content type, although you might want to use *ski* as your file type if you are publishing it as metadata.

Typically, the information in an iCalendar file will consist of a single iCalendar object. The calendar properties are attributes that apply to the calendar as a whole, and calendar components are collections of properties that express a particular calendar semantic, in a parameter-specific format. For example, the calendar component can specify an event, a to-do, a journal entry, time zone information, free/busy time information, or an alarm. The first and last line of the iCalendar object must contain a pair of iCalendar object delimiter strings.

The iCal format is a series of objects. The Calendaring and Scheduling Core Object is a collection of calendaring and scheduling information. An iCalendar object is organized into individual lines of text, called content lines; long lines have to be split into multiple lines. The object can have a set of properties, which can have parameters and attributes. Where properties and parameters allow a list of values, a comma character must separate them, but there is no significance to the order of values in a list. (A semicolon must separate some property values, which are defined as multiple parts.) A property can have attributes associated with it. These "property parameters" contain metainformation about the property or the property value, for example, the location of an alternate text representation for a property value, the language of a text property value, the datatype of the property value, and other attributes. The general rule for encoding multi-valued items is to simply create a new content line for each value, including the property name. Binary content information in an iCalendar object should be referenced using a URI within a property value (and indeed, when it is inline, it must be).

The SKi specification is a continuous work in progress, and has been defined by an ad hoc group that creates additions to the iCal standard. It is, in essence, a vocabulary, and it could be changed to an RDF schema.

In the following example, I have created a namespace for both iCal and SKi. Strictly speaking, SKi is a subset of iCal, so I did not really have to do that. But it will illustrate the use of multiple namespaces better. One problem, though, is the collapsed form of RDF. To be able to compare it to other RDF files, you would have to express it as full XML, so this description is in the full XML format. This means, among other things, that the parameter names must be in lowercase. In some cases, such as with the facilities for the disabled, we also have to switch things around: The attribute `TRUE` applies to any handicap facilities available, and we have to give them as the parameter value, while the fact that they exist (`TRUE`) becomes an attribute value.

```
<?xml version='1.0'?>
  <rdf:RDF>
   <xmlns:rdf="http://www.w3.org/1999/02/22-rdf-syntax-ns#"
   xmlns:ski="http://skical.org/metadata/skical#"
   xmlns:ical="ftp://ftp.ietf.org/rfc/rfc-2445.txt">
     <rdf:Description about="http://www.sydneyopera.co.au/concert.html">
       <ski:x-ski-placename>Sydney Opera House</ski:x-ski-placename>
       <ical:geo>37.386013;-122.082932</ical:geo>
       <ski:x-ski-performer>
         <rdf:Bag ID="Performer">
           <rdf:li Victor Borge/>
           <rdf:li James Galway/>
         </rdf:Bag>
        </ski:x-ski-performer>
       <ski:x-ski-openingtimes>
       <rdf:Bag ID="Openingtimes">
         <rdf:li vcal:open>18:00</rdf:li>
         <rdf:li vcal:close>21:00</rdf:li>
       </rdf:Bag>
       </ski:x-ski-openingtimes>
     </rdf:Description>
   </rdf:RDF>
```

Apart from the iCal fields SUMMARY and DESCRIPTION, a SKi-object can contain the fields shown in Table 6.1.

Classifying Site Information

RSS lets you classify site information in ways that enable syndication engines to retrieve it and present it as the author intended. It does not provide information for classifying the information on a site in terms of the intent of the information provided, nor its origin. You have probably done searches and received a hundred hits from e-mail archives, which eventually, in long roundabout ways, led you to the main page of the information you were looking for. This is

Table 6.1 The Elements and Attributes of SKi

FIELD NAME	PURPOSE	CONTENT TYPE	COMMENT
X-SKI-TITLE	The title for the event	Text	
X-SKI-PERFORMER	Provides information about prominent actors in the event: for instance, artists, teams, guides, or speakers	Text	By referring to a register of performers the information can be machine-understandable.
X-SKI-CREATOR	The creator of the work that is being presented during the event: can be the composer, the director, or someone else (not necessarily present during the event)	Text	
X-SKI-PARTOF	Defines that this event is part of a larger event, for instance, a festival	Text	The value should be a unique ID for another SKi-object.
X-SKI-EVENT-LANGUAGE	Language the event is presented in (using two-letter codes)	Text	If the event is translated, the Resource field should be used.
X-SKI-CHECKSUM	A calculated checksum for the object	Integer	
X-SKI-OPENINGTIMES	Defines opening times; may become standardized by the iCal group	Text	
X-SKI-SCHEDULINGTIMES	See the previous item		
X-SKI-VENUE	Gives a list of parameters where the event takes place	Text	Must be one of the following: Internet, Radio, TV, Outdoors, Indoors, Travel-transit. Two can be used for events in parallel venues (e.g., for a football match that is being broadcast).
X-SKI-ORIENTATION	The type of audience primarily concerned	Text	Keywords from a list: The intent is that these should be produced later; can be any type of category: sexual (like Gay), gender (like Female), religious (like Methodist), etc.

Table 6.1 The Elements and Attributes of SKi (Continued)

FIELD NAME	PURPOSE	CONTENT TYPE	COMMENT
X-SKI-DIRECTIONS	Description of a route (in human-readable format)	Text	There are two fields, GEO and LOCATION, that can be used for machine-readable descriptions; can have several parameters, including travelby (which way the transport is accessed), and geo-path (a sequence of coordinates).
X-SKI-PLACENAME	A well-known name for the location of the event	Text	Can be fetched from a canonical list.
X-SKI-QUALIFICATION	Describes qualifications (recommended or necessary) to participate	Text	Keywords can be fetched from a list, followed by RECOMMENDED, REQUIRED, NOT-RECOMMENDED, and FORBIDDEN.
X-SKI-PRICE	Price for participation in the event	Text	Currency codes in ISO 4217 should be used. Parameters from a keyword list can be used, e.g., Admission, Breakfast, Room, Happy Hour, Monthly Fee.
X-SKI-TICKETS-AT	Describes where and how to get tickets	Text	Can be described by start and end times (when the tickets are sold).
X-SKI-RESERVATIONS	Where interest for participation can be registered	Text	Validity can be constrained by DTSTART and DTEND.
X-SKI-AVAILABLE	Provides information about availability for the event (e.g., number of seats)	Text	Can be timestamped with DTSTAMP.
X-SKI-HANDICAP-FACILITIES	Availability for people with special needs	Boolean	Keywords can be fetched from a list; whether they apply is declared by TRUE.
X-SKI-PAYMENT-METHOD	Describes the means of payment for tickets	Text	Under development.

continues

Table 6.1 The Elements and Attributes of SKi (Continued)

FIELD NAME	PURPOSE	CONTENT TYPE	COMMENT
X-SKI-MOTIVATION	Arguments from the arranger for participating	Text	For instance: "This will be a great party!"
X-SKI-ADVERT	Refers to advertisements about the event, possibly in image format	Text	A URI referencing the information.
X-SKI-REVIEW	Gives an address for a third-party review of the event or the artists	Text	A URI referencing the information.
X-SKI-RESPONSIBLE	A person or organization who is responsible for the event	Text	E-mail, name, physical mail address, or other qualified name.
X-SKI-OTHERAGENTS	If there is more than one organizer (e.g., coarranger), this could be used	Text	See the previous field.
X-SKI-ASSOCIATION	Organizations which the arranger is a member of, e.g., Rotary, Lions, Kiwanis	Text	If there is a register of keywords, that can be used; the URI of the organization can also be used.

one of those instances where searches in the wireless environment require you to be more precise than search engines on the Web today can be.

Search engines work by creating an index of the information and listing it on your screen based on a heuristic. Most of them actually use metadata as part of the weight, but not RDF (because they still work with HTML). Some use the frequency of the word in the document as the prime weighting parameter. Others try to compute the pages which are linked most often to each other. But they do not attempt to classify the information in terms of its importance to other information items.

What would solve this would be a simple classification scheme enabling you to declare which information is relevant and which is not. You could also automate metadata creation in e-mail archives, for instance, by including a document type in the metadata declaration and creating properties for it, which could include types like e-mail, specification, information, and so on. To a search engine intelligent enough to use it, this would be a tremendous help.

Using Multiple Vocabularies

It may seem confusing that you can use multiple vocabularies to describe your site. But descriptions are not absolute, and several things can be true at the same time. No two people perceive the world exactly alike, something that becomes noticeable when asking them to describe it. When navigating a new Web site, we will look for information about how to find our way around it, especially if we are looking for something in particular. We will form a mental model of the site. The designer of the site also created a mental model of the site when he built it, and it is possible for the designer to communicate his conception of the mental model. That mental model may be very different from the mental model the user creates of the site, especially if he is looking for something that may have been peripheral to the designer.

How a mental model is communicated represents a cultural convention, as long as you are communicating the description to other people. But if you are communicating the site description to a computer, the important thing is that it be understandable to the other computer. Using multiple vocabularies in RDF descriptions is, as we have seen, a cinch.

RDF is a system to describe properties of objects. As you have seen in the previous chapters, this means using one or more vocabularies to describe what an object is. To understand which vocabularies you should use, you first have to understand what the objects are, and which properties they have.

When you describe a site, you choose which aspects about it are central. You may think it is very important that it has information about your board members' hobbies, but to anyone looking for information about your company's products, your company's board members are really secondary. Determining what will constitute objects and elements in your information is not an exact science. All categorizations by humans are necessarily arbitrary. There are no such things as absolutes in classification, not even in physics. (Is a quark a standing wave or a material object? You tell me.)

The user is likely to have a different view of the objects. Each user has his own operational world and his own conceptual model of the underlying objects, with its own set of use cases. Each user would like to see a model based upon his role in the problem domain, the role of the domain objects in his world, and his view of the system. However, the models cannot be constructed in isolation of each other. Labels make us exclude whatever doesn't fit and apply the information labeled in one way to all situations that are labeled in the same way. We are built to scan the environment leisurely and make sense of it by translating the patterns into concepts. Today, we are in too much of a hurry to allow ourselves to scan the environment and make sense of it.

When describing an object, the description becomes very difficult to understand if one person talks about fulks and the other about holks, when they in reality mean the same thing. You will comprehend neither, because you were thinking about golms.

A language is a social contract about which words map to which concepts (and, of course, a host of other things). The dictionary of concept descriptions is called an ontology. Creating ontologies to describe concepts is one of the biggest remaining challenges of artificial intelligence research.

But, as in a language, you cannot just cut words out of a dictionary and use them in random combinations. The ontology has to fit into a framework that makes the content understandable and processable by the machine.

Language describes reality, but it does not map directly onto reality. Computers are stupid: they need a description that is precise to be able to act on a concept. Our languages are fuzzy. We can understand them, because we are intelligent. But our computers are stupid.

An ontology (called a vocabulary in RDF) consists of the words you use. But a language does not consist of dictionaries. The order of the words and the grammar of the sentences also convey meaning. These are the semantics of the statement, the rules to which it conforms in order to be meaningful. In RDF, the Syntax and Grammar document describes the semantics, and RDF Schema describes how to create a vocabulary. RDF in itself is not a finished application, however, but rather a framework for creating mini-languages in which you can make statements about objects.

The important thing, as you probably understand from the reasoning above, is that your language, the expression of your mental model, overlaps that of your readers. One way of doing this is to identify the user group you intend the site for, and then determine which tasks you intend them to perform on the site. Once this is done, you have to structure the canonical representation of your information accordingly. This representation can be a database table or it can be an XML file, generated by whatever means necessary. You can also start creating representations for your users.

Handling elements from several vocabularies at the same time is not the real problem. You define them using name spaces. The problem is when the content is diverging. If your `dc:coverage` element says Stockholm, and your `ski:geo` element says Munich, which applies? Of course, they may apply to different things (for instance, it would be perfectly feasible to have it that way for a talk held in Munich about a trip to Stockholm). But you have to keep track of the content of the elements yourself, to make sure that you are not presenting inconsistent information. Today, there is no simple automated way to check the information you are going to present. It is probably easier to use one single element that represents a specific topic, for instance `ski:geo` for the position of the site. It is really up to you to select the relevant vocabularies, and up to the providers of the vocabularies to provide a proper definition of the concept the element represents (in the comments).

It is important to be able to express the type of a data item, because this is often the basis for decisions about it. Rule-based systems, often called expert systems, express the decisions in trees: If the soup temperature is above 50 degrees, and the steam pressure is below 200 PSI, add 400 liters of milk and one ton of potatoes. (The example is fictitious, by the way. Do not try it at home.) If the measurement system gave the temperature in degrees Fahrenheit, and the expert system expected a Celsius value, you had better be making gazpacho. When the type is not clearly expressed, trying to achieve a match will result in a mismatch.

This of course assumes that the decisions can be formulated as trees, but it also assumes that the description of the properties can be formulated in a rigid and formal way. If you say, “When it sort of starts to simmer, pour in some milk and throw in a few potatoes,” you will find that different chefs get very different results, not to speak of one very expensive boiler explosion. It must be possible to describe the properties of the soup in measurable quantities of well-defined entities (e.g., temperature in degrees, volume in liters), and these descriptions can then be used as input at different stages of the cooking process. The tasks that each decision entails must also be expressible in a formal description format, so that the computer can interpret it (and you can apply mathematical formalisms to it).

Remember, the first computers were used for the calculation of anti-aircraft artillery shell trajectories, and strange as it sounds, shooting down airplanes with anti-aircraft cannon is very similar to cooking soup—from the viewpoint of the computer. You have to take into account the amount of gunpowder, the temperature of the ammunition, wind direction and speed, the angular and absolute distance of the aircraft, and the aircraft speed. All these factors determine the elevation and direction of the gun (the gunpowder temperature determines how fast it will burn, and thus the velocity of the shell—which is important, because the idea is to create a ballistic trajectory that meets the aircraft at the distance equivalent to the time for which the fuse is set), and whether the shell will hit the aircraft or not (actually, the ideal is to have it explode close to the aircraft, to achieve maximum shrapnel). It is possible to measure all these parameters, describe their relation mathematically, and have it output into the direction system for the anti-aircraft cannon. Or the soup boiler.

To the computer, the names of the elements do not matter, after all, as long as they are different. A computer does not understand that a banana is yellow, any more than you understand that a flurb is brogg. It understands that the element banana has an attribute whose value is yellow, and if it is in the same name space as the attribute value yellow for an orange, they must be the same.

This illustrates the importance of using shared vocabularies, because if your computer has to look up the value of yellow when it is going to process it, it will take time and it is very unlikely that it will find your yellow to be the same as mine. Using a shared vocabulary means sharing concepts, and the important thing is not just that it speeds up computing drastically when elements and attribute values can be cached, it is more important than anything else for the author in making statements about his site.

Analyzing the information by breaking it down into its smallest parts allows you to capture commonalities between objects, by grouping them into classes (a class is a supergroup of objects). If we look at a class as a set of instances of an object, then it becomes relatively easy to identify subclasses and to partition the set into groups based on the differences in their properties. States are configurations of such instances. When you are describing your site in metadata, you are actually creating a model of it. As a modeler, you must sometimes choose between modeling some differences between objects as distinct patterns of attribute and association values, or as instances of distinct subclasses. It all depends on your point of view.

In reality, it is usually relatively easy to identify what are objects and what are properties—or, in the case of RDF, resources and attributes. Remember that this may be different the next time around. If the object is Napoleon, being emperor of France is a property; if the object is the French emperor, Napoleon is the property. This will change depending on the view you are taking of the system, and it can mean that one view may result in a set of attributes completely different from another view. If your statements are very large, it will mean that it will be hard to repeat them from a different view (even if they are generated automatically). This implies that it makes sense to keep the statements relatively short (and instead combine several statements using, for instance, a Bag).

Once you have identified the resources and attributes, you will probably also find a logical set of attribute values. It makes sense to conduct a preliminary analysis, because it is not at all unusual to have some attributes become resources and the reverse in the final analysis. It will also turn out to be relatively easy to tell which attributes are tied to which resources.

The unit of interchange between object management systems is the transaction; this means that when you build the statements, you have to think in terms of statements that can be interchanged in transactions. They should be self-contained, they have to be relatively short (in the tens of lines), and the vocabulary you create should not contain any ambiguities. It is somewhat different if the statements are supposed to be used in a different context, for instance, as an information plane attached to a map.

Some theories point to the important role of language for the development of the human mind, and if those are true, questions and answers are our natural way of receiving complex information that requires an interpretation of our environment. If you look at our most frequent queries, they relate to simple, everyday information. If you do not wear a watch, how many times in a day do you have to ask a passerby the time? Simple information such as weather forecasts and the time of day have been available in databases for a long time; the Web presented us with a comprehensive gateway to the databases. The Web-based queries we pose are transactions against an information set.

Interacting with information, however, is different in another way. To enable you to interact, the services rely on the user affecting the information and changing it according to their preferences. This customization requires the service to remember what they did and when they did it—maintaining a user state. State maintenance is easiest to do in a database system, where the interaction can be shaped using templates and variable substitution. Creating the interactivity in a way that makes sense is another matter, and something that will be a challenge to many Web designers.

Applications in the mobile environment must be different, by virtue of the different environment, if nothing else. The terminal and the use cases for the mobile environment cannot afford the flashy, graphical environment of Web advertising, which like all advertising is intended to be disruptive—interrupting the user's experience to entice him to the site that bought the advertisement (if it is not intended to sell a product, like most advertising). To effect the disruption, advertising is presented in a horizontal cascade instead of a vertical one, which is more natural to read. In many ways, mobile applications resemble the early uses of the Web rather what the Web has become.

When modeling communications in terms of transactions, it makes sense to separate the content of the transaction and its intended effect on the receiver. This is the same type of modeling as in the theory of language called speech act theory, and it is also reminiscent of the separation of content and presentation.

One way to enable modeling is to associate each message with one of a set of predefined communication types. This implies that you have been able to break down the communications protocol into a few types of interactions, or that one of the emerging protocols such as the Simple Object Access Protocol (SOAP) is able to do so. Unfortunately, this area is still developing very fast, and it is not very easy to come up with a definitive list. There are standardization efforts underway, but they may be too early to have any effect. Still, for e-commerce systems, it is meaningful to look at a division in purpose (determining what the message is for) and commitment (determining how bound the receiver and sender are). Together, these can be said to comprise the intent of the message.

The intents of different information types are different, but it is quite possible to have a protocol with a generalized message type, communicating the intent of the transaction using primitives contained in the message itself (or as metainformation in a header of the message, instead of in the message body).

There is probably a limited set of possible intents of messages, but a total generalization into a comprehensive set of primitives has not been done. However, it is relatively easy to do for e-commerce. There is a limited set of communication models, actually; according to the CommonKADS model, only three different models for communication: task delegation, task adoption, and pure information exchange. The models of commercial transactions are actually quite well researched, and can be divided into twelve types of messages (see Table 6.2), which have different purposes and degrees of commitment.

This table describes how communication types map onto commitment and involvement by the parties of a transaction. The parties are more committed the further right you go. The further down you go, the lower involvement there is. According to this typology, the least committed message type in the pure information exchange category is a message with the purpose only to inform.

Table 6.2 Communication Models and Predefined Communication Types

COMMUNICATION TYPE	NEGATIVE COMMITMENT	LOW COMMITMENT	MEDIUM COMMITMENT	HIGH COMMITMENT
Task delegation	Reject-td	Request	Require	Order
Task adoption	Reject-ta	Propose	Offer	Agree
Pure information exchange	Inform	Ask	Reply	Report

The messages with the least degree of involvement are in the bottom row and the ones with the highest degree of involvement in the top row. One way of looking at it is that in the lower row, you do not have to do anything as a result of the message (other than reply), whereas in the top row, you request an action to be taken (or not taken, in the case of rejection). On the other hand, the purpose of the message is more general in the leftmost column, and more specific in the rightmost. This means that the three basic primitives can be mapped onto a contiguous field, which indicates the intent.

Now we see why this discipline is called knowledge representation. These messages map well onto electronic commerce transactions (actually, onto all commercial transactions). Commercial transactions are probably the most analyzed transactions of all, and while they may possibly differ from that, the interaction between the legal framework and the practice results in transactions being tightly mapped onto the table above (anyone interested is directed to the Swedish law of acquisitions—the translation is actually precise—which contains a very thorough analysis of commercial transactions).

The table above can be used to decide how two agents want to interact, but it is interesting to see that while the actual acquisition takes place in the upper row, there is room for a number of information transactions in the bottom row. HTTP, the protocol of the Web, is actually a transactional protocol, using requests and responses to transmit information. A query by a client can be seen as a transaction of the type *ask*, and the reply from the server as a transaction of the type *respond*. Thus, mapping these transactions to RDF primitives is relatively easy, and it allows us to denote the purpose of the transaction—which then becomes disembodied, separated from the transport. In traditional protocols, the transport was tightly mapped onto a purpose (a WAP Push message can be only of the type *inform*, for instance). This is still an area of research, to be sure; it is known as conversation policies.

However, up to now conversation policies have been expressed as a part of the transport protocol. Having a type framework for a protocol that is separated from the transport is new, but not entirely. It allows us to parameterize the transactions further: If a transaction can be of several types, then those types can be further parameterized.

For instance, CC/PP allows us to parameterize request–response messages with terminal capability and user preference information. It should be quite simple to parameterize messages with other information as well. If we have a message of the type *offer*, we can parameterize it according to the policy that our company has (e.g., we reserve the right to refuse to serve anyone; only customers with credit ratings above AA receive discounts; etc.).

These statements are assertions, and as such, they can be expressed in RDF. Having expressed them in RDF, we can match them with the assertions of the client (or server, as the case may be), arriving at a best compromise and creating a transaction that is optimized for both parties. This means that we can build agent systems that can truly negotiate by first exchanging assertions, then comparing them to a hidden set of policies, then returning a compromise, and so on until both parties are exchanging identical assertions. It also means that we do not need to expose our policies to all and sundry, as we do not need to express them to the receiving party. Only the assertion of the current transaction needs to be expressed. (This is a considerable bone of contention, if you think about it. For instance, most banks do not want private persons with a balance below $100,000 as clients, because they really are unprofitable over their lifetime. However, they cannot say so outright, becauses that would mean legal action and possible boycott by the profitable customers as well.)

Communication model construction is usually done in a six-step model. Here, I have modified it somewhat (and removed two steps), because the only task is to exchange assertions; this means that a specific transfer function is not needed for each of the different communication types (as is the case in traditional agent construction). Instead, specific functions are invoked by a general agent, which has as its only purpose to be an interface to other objects.

The Four Steps of Communication Model Construction

1. Identify the core information objects (i.e., the assertions) that are to be exchanged between agents. Do this by listing the leaf tasks from the task model and the knowledge model.
2. Create assertions for the policies and objects that are to be interchanged.
3. Identify the transactions and express the type of each transaction by asserting the type.
4. Compose the parameterized message. (In the traditional communications modeling, you would create a communications diagram here, but because that would be tantamount to reinventing the protocol, that is not necessary.)

Note that sometimes, especially in the case of information messages, it can be hard to separate an assertion, the content, and the formatting of the content (and the desired action). For instance, Web pages (unless they contain interaction elements such as scripts or forms) either propose, offer, reply, report, or inform. The intent of the information can be expressed in different ways, and formatting is often used to do so. This can cause awkward problems in cases where you need to transform the content into another medium, such as from text to speech. It is far better to express the intent in the content (maybe in addition to the formatting). Otherwise, you risk locking your presentation into a single modality (way of presentation); that means not only that you may lose customers, but also that your message, when translated into another modality, is ambiguous. Remember, on the Web, the user rules, and can always change the presentation format. You have no way of knowing that the user is blind and uses a screen reader, for instance. But if you get sued for millions of dollars not only for not conforming to the Americans with Disabilities Act, but also for leaving out important information from your offer (because it was only available as a GIF image), you will learn fast. On the other hand, it would seem that being forewarned is being forearmed, and paying a design agency to redo your Web site correctly does not cost much. It also means that you can reach mobile customers, and there are potentially more of those than customers with fixed access, anyway. I will not go deeper into this topic, as I already wrote a book about it, but you do see how it can be important.

Creating a Vocabulary

To describe something, you need to have a vocabulary. Syntax (the word order and structure of sentences, or assertions, as the case may be) is not enough. You need words to talk about things. However, do not think that those words necessarily need to have anything to do with the words you use every day. The mapping between words and concepts is the result of a social contract among the users of the language that certain sequences of signs (spoken sounds, signs with the hands, characters on paper or on a computer screen) should represent a concept. How concepts themselves occur is a matter of discussion among philosophers (I myself lean toward the theory of Peter Gärdenfors, stating essentially that concepts are derived from our environment, and that they are created by a kind of statistical mapping of similar objects—but we do not need to discuss this here). Suffice to say that concepts exist and are essentially arbitrarily mapped to signs (in the very broad sense). This means that you can call a spade a rose, if everyone in your language family accepts that.

How to describe concepts is one of the thorniest matters in artificial intelligence. And not just to create descriptions of the concepts, but descriptions of the descriptions—or assertions about the description, if you will.

Today, there is no easy way of finding out which vocabularies are available. There are a number of them floating around, and the W3C does a valiant effort to gather them up. But there are still more which they do not know of, and cannot know of, because there is no registry for RDF. Anyone can construct his or her own vocabularies.

CHAPTER 7

Device Descriptions and User Profiles

The description of the content on the server is only one third of the equation. If you want to be able to adapt the presentation of the content to the device the user is retrieving it with, you have to have a declaration of the properties of the device. (I will, by the way, use the words *terminal* and *device* interchangeably in this chapter.) If you want to adapt content by filtering, you have to have a description of the user (and the situation of the user). You will also need a set of rules for the adaptation, but we cover that aspect in Chapter 8.

For the adaptation of content and presentation to be effective, there has to be a way to describe both the content of a document and how to match it with the characteristics of the device. As we saw in Chapter 5, there are simple and efficient ways of creating a profile of a site. On the other side, CC/PP is a way of describing profiles of devices, which is as close as you get to a standard. It is also defined in RDF, which makes the matching easier. There are a variety of capability formats that are used to describe the capabilities of a receiving device, though. It is also likely that other formats will emerge in the future. Just to make you aware of them, we will look at some of them in this chapter.

Traditional World Wide Web content and applications have assumed a homogeneous client environment consisting of a PC connected to a network with relatively high capacity running a full-function HTML browser, attached to a graphical display, and supporting a range of user input devices. Of course, this is true only for a majority of users. If you are disabled (e.g., have problems seeing), your view of the information will be very different. If you are using a modem with a maximum speed of 300 bits per second (remember, 10 years ago this was very high-end), you are disabled in the way you can access the network.

As the Web continues to develop, the assumption that there will be a majority using homogeneous devices is no longer universally valid. Already, the number of users of mobile phones surpasses the number of Internet users, and mobile phone vendors will assure you that in a few years, the number of users accessing information on mobile phones will surpass the number of PC users. Other devices will be used for access to the Web: for instance, TVs, printers, and non-PC computers such as "Web appliances." Mobile devices such as cellular phones, palmtop computers, and automotive computing systems also have different sets of characteristics, for instance a widely divergent range of input and output modalities, network connectivity, content, and scripting languages. Content adapted for presentation on the desktop PC with a fully functional HTML browser cannot be delivered to all mobile devices without some sort of modification.

It is also probable that the user will have larger control over how information is accessed and what information is accessed (e.g., which information is paid for). This is specifically true for the mobile market, but likely to extend to all Web access devices.

Content customization may depend on any or all of the following parameters:

- Device screen resolution, color depth, and other display parameters
- Supported scripting languages and installed libraries and versions
- Supported tag sets and versions
- Installed plug-ins and versions, supported datatypes
- Output modalities (text vs. images vs. audio only)
- Network capabilities such as bandwidth and latency
- Input modalities (keyboard vs. mouse vs. voice)
- Security
- Device hardware (memory, processor, etc.)
- Cost of content
- Device type (phone, PDA, PC, etc.)
- Acceptable language, character encoding
- User agent identity and manufacturer
- Proxies or gateways deployed in the network
- User preferences (e.g., payment mechanisms)

The description of the physical device is one thing, but it may not necessarily determine the configuration of the device. Users may have content presentation preferences that should be transferred to the server for consideration: For instance, price of content and sound (on or off) are aspects of the user's preferences. If you have problems understanding how this works, think of the Ericsson R380. This smartphone has a one-inch-square screen, but when the keypad is flipped down, it has a one-eight VGA screen (100 by 75 pixels), and becomes a PDA. The user is in control and, by flipping down the lid, can change preferences.

One way of regarding the capabilities and preferences of the user is as a set of components, which can be overridden by the user changing the defaults. This is exactly the way CC/PP, the Composite Capabilities/Preferences Profile specification, works.

Composite Capabilities/Preferences Profile (CC/PP)

As a result of the heterogeneity of the devices used to access the information on the Web, and the limited ability of users to convey their content presentation preferences to the server with the present systems, clients may receive content that they cannot store, that they cannot display, that violates the desires of the user, or that takes too long to convey over the network to the client device. What is needed is a way to describe the terminal in such a way that the server can adapt the content to it and make sure the user gets the best possible presentation.

User agent capabilities and references can be thought of as metadata, or as properties and descriptions of the user agent hardware and software. The basic data model for a CC/PP is a collection of tables. These are described as assertions in RDF. In the simplest form each table in the CC/PP is a collection of RDF statements with simple, atomic properties. These tables may be constructed from default settings, persistent local changes, or temporary changes made by a user.

Current mechanisms, such as the HTTP User Agent header field and HTTP content negotiation, are somewhat limited. While they are sufficient to select from a set of variants, they do not enable a richer description of the capabilities of the device, such as its screen size, the user agent or agents it has which can receive the information, and so on. These factors (especially the properties of the device, such as its position) are crucial in creating an optimal presentation, especially when this presentation involves filtering the content because the presentation format selected may require a change of navigational paradigm (e.g., if the user is retrieving an XHTML presentation on a WAP device).

Given an RDF representation of the document profile data, this will, generally speaking, be a converse of the RDF tree for the user device and preferences. If the profile information and the CC/PP information are provided with each request, the matching can be integrated with the Web server. This does not require an extensive amount of roundtrip traffic; the CC/PP profile can be cached in the server and re-used as long as it is valid.

When you describe the capabilities of a terminal, you do not start by talking about the size of its hard disk, then mention that it has an IMAP client, and follow by stating that it has a USB connector and is watertight. You tend to describe the terminal in terms of its logical components (granted, the logic of the order depends on custom). The ways that we are accustomed to thinking about our computers are in terms of hardware and software (although the distinction is largely irrelevant). CC/PP is intended for you to be able to create a description that follows the established way of describing terminals. The CC/PP profile is a collection of the capabilities and preferences associated with the user and the user agents for accessing the World Wide Web. These user agents include the user's hardware platform, system software, and applications.

CC/PP Data Model

CC/PP profiles are structured into named *components*, each containing a collection of attribute-value pairs, or properties. The components of the profile have been specified by a W3C working group and may include the hardware characteristics (screen size, color capabilities, image capabilities, manufacturer, etc.), software characteristics (operating system vendor and version, support for the Mobile Execution Environment (MExE), a list of audio and video encoders, etc.), the application and user preferences (browser manufacturer and version, markup languages and versions supported, scripting languages supported, etc.), WAP characteristics (WML script libraries, WAP version, WML deck size, etc.), and network characteristics (device location, bearer characteristics such as latency and reliability, etc.). However, these are logical components, and they are by no means the only way of describing a terminal (in the future, we may well use things we do not consider either hardware or software, for instance).

Each component can provide a default description block containing either a set of default values for attributes of that component, or a URI that refers to a document containing those default values. Some collections of properties and property values may be common to a particular component. For example: a specific model of a smartphone may come with a specific CPU, screen size and amount of memory by default. Gathering these "default" properties together as a distinct RDF resource makes it possible to independently retrieve and cache those properties. A collection of default properties is not mandatory, but it may improve network performance, especially the performance of relatively slow wireless networks.

The data model for the capabilities and preferences profile is similar to a table of tables. Each individual table roughly corresponds to a significant hardware or software component. There are a few important assumptions that the CC/PP working group made in the course of the work: For instance, the information contained within the profile is provided on behalf of the user who will be receiving the content. The profile information consists of information gathered from the device hardware, active user agent software, and user preferences. In many cases, much of this information must be pre-installed directly on the device, possibly in the firmware. For instance, the device may publish a single URI that points to default device capability information made available by the device manufacturer. Similarly, the user agent may publish a single URI that points to default software information made available by the software developer. This makes it possible to send a very compact profile, but it has to be resolved in the server. This has turned out to be a very cost-efficient and fast method of communicating large data sets, especially the more similar the devices are, because the profile can be cached by the server and does not have to be downloaded every time.

The user preferences involved are related to the device capabilities, such as preferred language, sound on or off, images on or off, privacy preferences (like P3P), scripting on or off, cookies on or off, and so forth. You would also want to assert hardware platform attributes, like the vendor, model, class of device (phone, PDA, printer, and so on), screen size, colors, available bandwidth, CPU, memory, and a number of other parameters.

Apart from this, users will also want to include software-defined variables. These can include application brand and version, level of HTML support, supported XML vocabularies, level of CSS support, level of WAP support, and so forth. One important item is very likely to be the XHTML modules supported in the device. In principle, in XML, using namespaces you can add any tagset to your content (as you saw in the RDF example). However, the device does not necessarily have to support tagsets. If XHTML modules are used, it is quite possible that some XHTML modules are not supported, and then they will not work.

The introduction of "defaults" makes the graph of each major component more of a simple tree than a table. In UAProf over WSP, to take a WAP example, the major components are associated with the current network session. In this case, the network session is serving as the root of a tree that includes the trees of each major component. The closest thing to a "document" associated with a CC/PP is the current network session. In HTTP, the root of the tree will be the current transaction (because HTTP is stateless, but WSP is not).

Any attributes explicitly provided in the component description will override the default values. This means that changes in the user preferences for how the components should be used (such as the example with the open and shut lid of the R380) will be taken into account. It means, for instance, that users with bad eyesight can mandate that the terminal should present the information as sound instead of text.

The CC/PP specification does not mandate a particular set of components or attributes. It is a framework, and the definition of the exact vocabulary falls on other bodies—or whomever wants to do it, because the mechanism for this is XML namespaces.

Another aspect of the CC/PP profile is that it can describe the capabilities of proxies. A proxy is an entity that inserts itself between the client and the server and can conduct functions on behalf of either. Usually it stores copies of documents to enable the client to retrieve the documents from the proxy, instead of from the origin server. It can, however, perform operations like transcoding content (from an XML format to another using XSLT, for instance). If the proxy is placed between the client and the server, and content will pass it on the way back, it is a part of the client from the server's point of view (because it extends the client with its capabilities). For that reason, the proxy capabilities can be included in the capabilities of the terminal as part of its profile.

Content negotiation, as it exists and is implemented today, is limited to the preferences you have set in the browser (plus a limited set which is derived automatically, such as by the brand of the browser). But it is quite possible for your computer to provide a much larger set of profile information, which the origin server—the computer providing the data—could use to enhance your experience, for instance by personalizing the information, transforming it so that it fits the presentation capabilities of your device, or adapting the information to your current context. The CC/PP framework will do what the User Agent header field in HTTP does today, but it will enable a vastly richer and more precise description of the device. The capabilities of a terminal are integral with network entities such as proxies and firewalls, which may add capabilities such as transcoding and provide for the removal of certain offending file types (e.g., many firewalls will not let MP3 files through). The entire chain of proxies from the client to the origin server constitutes the client capabilities.

Conversely, the reverse chain constitutes the capabilities of the server. The server will be able to utilize these capabilities in formatting the content, even though the functions may not be embodied in the same physical machine as the Web server. By reversing the profile it received from the client, the server can assure that the capabilities described are the capabilities it gets.

However, the framework is not intended only for the transport of capabilities information from a client (and its associated proxies) to a server (and its associated proxies). It is intended for contextualization (often called situation dependency) that makes the information adapt not only to the current terminal and user preferences, but also to information about the user's surroundings—for instance, the weather. This means that it should comprise more than the device description. There are two reasons for this. One is that it is not at all clear what a device profile, as opposed to a personal profile, is. This is probably something that can be clarified only with time, as a best practice starts to establish itself. In the original paper on contextualized information, Bill Schilicht (then at Columbia University) described two types of adaptation: environmental and personal. The problem is to distinguish between the components that go into these two, especially in the borderland between them.

It is reasonably clear that some things, where we share the details with others, are environmental. The screen size, for instance, is most likely something I share with millions of other users. Some things are no doubt personal, such as my credit card number. But there are some things that are not as certain, such as the position. It may be regarded as something personal, but it may also be regarded as a part of the environment of my situation, because—until resolution reaches 30 centimeters—I will share my position with others.

If an application can act on information about the user and his environment, such as location, time, temperature, or user identity, it can become a context-aware application. The information that the terminal provides (probably using CC/PP) can be used not only to tag information that is being collected, but also to enable selection and content generation responses, such as triggering alarms or retrieving information relevant to the task at hand. Context awareness builds on situated information spaces, where information objects are embedded in an environment, either virtually or in reality. Central to the idea of situated information spaces is the idea of enhancing everyday tasks by embedding computer infrastructure without sacrificing the benefits of the existing technology. As such, it shares a great deal in common with ubiquitous computing.

If the content is to be adapted as the result of a request (meaning that each transaction, just as on the Web today, will be a one-to-one transaction between the client and the server; i.e., there will be one copy of the document sent out from the server for each client), the consequence of the ability to receive a profile which describes the capabilities of the client and the preferences of the user is that it is possible to adapt content to the client to a much higher degree than was previously possible, as well as adapt it to the preferences of the user. The same framework can be applied to a much wider scope of contextualizations of information, for instance, adapting information to the current position of the user, the current weather, and so on.

The framework can carry all the properties of the terminal and those preferences of the user that affect these properties, plus any other information that is necessary for contextualization. This framework, needless to say, must be compatible with other information required by the user. This is one of the main reasons that RDF was selected to design the framework. Other reasons are the flexibility of RDF and the fact that information is constructed as a set as graphs. Comparing graphs, merging graphs, and attaching graphs to each other are relatively simple operations (at least in theory), as we saw in Chapter 1. This means that attaching a graph describing the proxy capabilities gives a collective description of the aggregate, for instance.

The mobile environment is different from the traditional Web environment. The network is slower, and mobile devices are expected to have an ever-divergent range of input and output capabilities, network connectivity, and levels of scripting language support. Moreover, users may have content presentation preferences that cannot be transferred to the server for consideration. As a result of this device heterogeneity and the limited ability of users to convey their content presentation preferences to the server, clients may receive content that they cannot store, that they cannot display, that violates the desires of the user, or that takes too long to convey over the network to the client device.

The History of CC/PP

The history of CC/PP started in July 1998, when a group of interested people met at the face-to-face meeting of the W3C mobile access interest group and decided to create a profile framework for the description of devices in RDF. This led to a report and the subsequent development of the CC/PP Exchange Framework.

The CC/PP working group was formed in 1999 in the W3C. At the same time, the WAP Forum had decided to set up a committee to create a vocabulary for the CC/PP format, which became known as UAProf. WAP was developed by a consortium of companies from the mobile communications industries with the primary intent of bringing information to mobile telephones. They adopted CC/PP for the structure of UAProf, developing and maintaining the most comprehensive schema available for it.

The W3C working group is expected to finish its work in 2001, and the protocol has been brought to the Internet Engineering Task Force (IETF), now responsible for the development of HTTP, for standardization.

CC/PP Structure

CC/PP is a framework, and within that framework different groups should develop vocabularies for describing their devices. A vocabulary consists of a set of classes (essentially names for entities) in RDF, expressed in RDF Schema. The CC/PP core vocabulary at present has only seven entries, but is intended to be infinitely extensible (the WAP Forum vocabulary has more than 40 entries, and several groups in the WAP Forum has created vocabularies of their own, by creating their own namespaces). The CC/PP vocabulary is more or less a demonstration vocabulary.

To say that vocabularies are infinitely extensible may seem like a high claim. However, infinite extensibility is achievable using RDF and XML, because when the RDF processor comes upon an unknown property or resource, it will look up that element in the schema associated with the namespace declared in the document. This means that whoever wants to declare an element can do so, declare a schema, set up a Web server, and wait for the world to find out what it means—automatically (although, as we discussed in Chapter 6, things are not that easy in reality).

The CC/PP framework makes it possible to provide information about the capabilities and characteristics of a device and a network. These capabilities and characteristics are referred to as attributes, and together they form a vocabulary. The semantics associated with these attributes are identified in a schema for that vocabulary. A profile is an instance of the schema and contains one or more attributes from the vocabulary. The attributes in the schema are classified into one of several components, each of which represents a distinguished set of characteristics.

One extension of the simple table of properties data model is the notion of a separate, subordinate collection of default properties. Each major component, such as the hardware platform, the software platform, and the applications, may have its own collection of attributes or preferences. Default settings could be properties defined by the vendor. In the case of hardware the vendor often has a very good idea of the physical properties of any given model of their product. However, the current owner of the product may be able to add options, such as memory, persistent store, or additional I/O devices, that add new properties or change the values of some original properties. These would be persistent local changes. An example of a temporary change would be turning sound on or off.

The kind of data that will be encoded in these profiles includes the amount of memory, what the CPU is, the screen size, whether the device has a keyboard, whether it is Bluetooth-enabled, and so on. Some collections of properties and property values may be default properties for a component. Gathering these default properties together as a distinct RDF resource makes it possible to independently retrieve and cache those properties.

An RDF description consists of a structured collection of RDF properties, each of which is associated with a property type and value and expressed as a directed labeled graph with nodes, leaves, and arcs or an object-oriented data model with tuples (object/attribute/value).

The basic data model for CC/PP is a collection of tables. In the simplest form, each table in the CC/PP is a collection of RDF statements with simple, atomic properties. These tables may be constructed from default settings, persistent local changes, or temporary changes made by a user. The introduction of `Defaults` makes the graph of each major component more of a simple tree than a table. When the parameters are associated with the current network session, the network session is serving as the root of a tree that includes the trees of each major component.

Each attribute is limited in its scope to the component it is describing. For example, each software application can define a value for a `Version` attribute. This attribute indicates the version of the particular application being described. In general, side effects that extend beyond the bounds of a particular component are not defined in this document. The relationship between components is system- and application-dependent.

A sample CC/PP description is as follows:

```
<RDF xmlns="http://www.w3.org/1999/02/22-rdf-syntax-ns#"
     xmlns:rdf="http://www.w3.org/1999/02/22-rdf-syntax-ns#"
     xmlns:ccpp="http://www.w3.org/2000/07/04-ccpp#"
     xmlns:uaprof="http://www.wapforum.org/UAPROF/ccppschema-19991014#">
  <Description about="http://www.devicecapabilities.org/MyProfile">
    <ccpp:component>
      <Description about="http://www.devicecapabilities.org/
TerminalHardware">
        <type resource="http://www.devicecapabilities.org/
Schema#HardwarePlatform" />
        <ccpp:Defaults>
          <Description>
            <type resource="http://www.devicecapabilities.org/
Schema#HardwarePlatform" />
            <uaprof:CPU>PPC</uaprof:CPU>
            <uaprof:ScreenSize>320x200</uaprof:ScreenSize>
          </Description>
        </ccpp:Defaults>
        <uaprof:ScreenSize>640x400</uaprof:ScreenSize>
      </Description>
    </ccpp:component>
    <ccpp:component>
      <Description
about="http://www.devicecapabilities.org/TerminalSoftware">
        <type resource="http://www.devicecapabilities.org/
Schema#SoftwarePlatform" />
        <ccpp:Defaults>
          <Description>
            <type resource="http://www.devicecapabilities.org/
Schema#SoftwarePlatform" />
            <uaprof:OSName>EPOC</uaprof:OSName>
            <uaprof:OSVersion>2.0</uaprof:OSVersion>
            <uaprof:OSVendor>Symbian</uaprof:OSVendor>
          </Description>
```

```
        </ccpp:Defaults>
      </Description>
    </ccpp:component>
    <ccpp:component>
      <Description about="http://www.devicecapabilities.org/Browser">
        <type resource="http://www.devicecapabilities.org/
Schema#BrowserUA" />
        <ccpp:Defaults>
          <Description>
            <type resource="http://www.devicecapabilities.org/
Schema#BrowserUA" />
            <uaprof:BrowserName>Mozilla</uaprof:BrowserName>
            <uaprof:BrowserVersion>5.0</uaprof:BrowserVersion>
            <uaprof:CcppAccept>
              <Bag>
                <li>text/plain</li>
                <li>text/vnd.wap.wml</li>
              </Bag>
            </uaprof:CcppAccept>
          </Description>
        </ccpp:Defaults>
        <uaprof:CcppAccept>
          <Bag>
            <li>text/plain</li>
            <li>text/vnd.wap.wml</li>
            <li>text/html</li>
          </Bag>
        </uaprof:CcppAccept>
      </Description>
    </ccpp:component>
  </Description>
</RDF>
```

As you can see, this profile mixes four namespaces: The two RDF namespaces, the CC/PP namespace, and the UAProf namespace. In the profiles developed by the WAP Forum, the `prf:` tag is mostly used for the CC/PP namespace, but again, the namespace declaration is local to the document, so there is nothing that binds the `prf:` prefix firmly to the profile.

The CC/PP Schema

If you want to define your own schema for your own terminals, you should know that the definition of a CC/PP schema is governed by the following rules:

- The schema must be associated with a well-defined vocabulary. A unique URI (identified as `prf` above) in the XML namespace must serve as an unambiguous identifier for the particular vocabulary.
- The schema for a profile must consist of one or more components, each describing a set of attributes within one or more description blocks.

- All components in a CC/PP profile must have the same schema structure (layout).
- Each component must be an object of type `Class` and may contain a subordinate description block for default attributes.
- Attributes considered to be default capabilities or characteristics must be described within the `Default` description block. Typically, these include attributes that are common to a group or class of devices or user agents across multiple profiles. For example, profiles for users of a Palm III device would all have the same `Default` hardware characteristics specified by the vendor.
- Descriptions to override the default values must also be included in the component description but outside the `Default` description block. The final value of an attribute described in the profile is resolved based on the semantics associated with the attribute.

The CC/PP working group defined only two basic components:

HardwarePlatform. A collection of properties that adequately describe the hardware characteristics of the terminal device. This includes the type of device, model number, display size, input and output methods, and so on.

SoftwarePlatform. A collection of properties associated with the operating environment of the device. These provide information on the operating system software, video and audio encoders supported by the device, and user preferences on language to be used, for instance.

The WAP Forum UAProf drafting committee has gone on to define a number of additional blocks:

BrowserUA. A set of attributes to describe the HTML (or XHTML) browser application.

NetworkCharacteristics. Information about the network-related infrastructure and environment such as bearer information and roaming/location information. These properties can influence the resulting content, for instance when the bandwidth is low and information is being transcoded to a less rich representation (e.g., a video program is transformed into a slide show).

WapCharacteristics. A set of attributes pertaining to WAP capabilities supported on the device. This includes details on the capabilities and characteristics related to the WML Browser, Wireless Telephony Agent (WTA), and so on.

Additional components can be added by other groups, simply by adding namespaces to the schema to describe capabilities pertaining to other user agents such as an e-mail application or hardware extensions. It is also possible to add entire component sections, for instance for location, mood, or other information that can be derived from the terminal that is relevant to the current situation of the user.

Modification of Properties

It is important to be able to add to and modify attributes associated with the current CC/PP information. This includes those properties that can be influenced by the user, such as turning sound on and off, and persistent changes to reflect things like a memory upgrade. The default profile provided by the vendor will need to be overridden. However, we need to concern ourselves only with changes to the current profile (that is associated with the current request).

The problem boils down to transmitting the information without resending the whole profile. If `Sound` were to be changed from Off to On, the only data that would need to be sent would be as shown in the following example.

```
<?xml version="1.0"?>
<RDF
xmlns:RDF="http://www.w3C.org/TR/WD-rdf-syntax#"
xmlns:PRF="http://www.w3C.org/TR/WD-profile-vocabulary#">
<Description ID="SoftwarePlatform"
PRF:Sound="On" />
</RDF>
```

Of course it is not enough to have a framework. You must also transport the contextualization information between the client and the server. While the CC/PP datastructure architecture is protocol-independent, one way of doing this is to use the CC/PP Exchange Protocol, an application of the HTTP Extension Framework. In the WAP environment, the WAP Session Protocol (WSP) has been enabled to carry CC/PP.

Transporting Client Profiles

From the point of view of any particular network transaction, the only property or capability information that is important is whatever is current. The network transaction does not care about the differences between defaults or persistent local changes, it only cares about the capabilities and preferences that apply to the current network transaction (because HTTP is a stateless protocol, in principle the client does not exist between transactions, from the point of view of the server). Because the profile information may originate from multiple sources and because different parts of the capabilities profile may be differentially cached, the various components must be explicitly described in the network transaction.

In its WAP incarnation, the system uses WSP to request content from an origin server. WSP is different from HTTP in that it has a session concept, something that does not exist in HTTP (although it can be added using cookies, database markers that the receiving server can use as a pointer into a database of profile information; there is, however, nothing that specifies how this information should look, and what should be done with it). The profile is then transmitted and maintained using designated WSP headers. This profile information is initially conveyed when a WSP session is established with a compliant WAP protocol gateway. The client then assumes that the WAP gateway caches the profile information and will apply it on all requests initiated during the lifetime of the WSP session. This caching saves on transmissions over the air.

The CC/PP Exchange Protocol enables CC/PP profiles to be transported over HTTP 1.1 using the HTTP Extension Framework. It enables effective profile caching at Web servers and proxies, in addition to overrides of URIs as sketched above. The profile is associated with the current network session or transaction, but can be independent of these. Because the profile information may originate from multiple sources and because different parts of the capabilities profile may be differentially cached, the various components must be explicitly described in the network transaction.

Remote Referencing

Instead of enumerating each set of attributes, a remote reference (a URI) can be used to name a collection of attributes, such as the hardware platform defaults. This remote referencing has the advantage of enabling the separate fetching and caching of functional subsets. If an application in the server/gateway/proxy uses RDF to process the CC/PP, it may encounter attributes with default values and user-specified values. It is up to the application to enforce the rule that user-specified attributes override default values. RDF does not provide a convenient mechanism for implementing the override rule.

Delivering all of the CC/PP at one time and inline makes some simplifications possible. If the user has overridden some default property, then there is no reason to send the default—all that is needed is to send the current value for that attribute. In the example above, there is no reason to send the hardware platform's default setting of "Memory=16mb" because the user has upgraded the memory to 32MB. The CC/PP Exchange Protocol provides for such updates.

Bandwidth and Caching

One reason for WSP was the limited bandwidth available in wireless networks. Wireless networks are more expensive, provide less bandwidth, with higher latency and less reliability. SMS data service on GSM networks provides 22 bytes per second to a typical mobile host. Tomorrow's wireless networks will also be slow, compared to tomorrow's wireline networks.

In the WAP environment, WSP is used to carry the information between the client and the WAP gateway. But the gateway translates the information to HTTP, and sends it out on the Internet, if the origin server is not a WAP server. The HTTP requests generated by the WAP gateway are conveyed over a network using TCP/IP, which can be the Internet or a corporate intranet. As it passes through the network, the request may pass through one or more proxies, each responsible for forwarding the request toward the particular origin server designated in the request. Currently, proxies can conform either to the HTTP 1.0 or 1.1 standards. (There are also a number of proxy implementations which do not implement all of HTTP 1.1, but only parts of it; and even some which are HTTP 0.9.) This lack of conformance to the specifications may be a cause for problems, as HTTP 1.0 proxies will discard all profile information in the HTTP request. The specification states that they should strip out information that they do not recognize. HTTP 1.1 proxies can forward the profile information, depending on whether it is conveyed in `Mandatory` or `Optional` headers. It is also possible for proxies to add information to the profile, and to manipulate the content, for instance formatting it for presentation according to what the device specifies.

Proxies can also cache both the information and the profile, as can origin servers. This can cause problems for transcoding proxies, which change the formatting of the information—the presentation—depending on the parameters presented by the terminal. The same URI will be returned using one set of presentation and filtering parameters to users with one parameterization, but as a different presentation and filtered in a different way to users with another set. Users with PDAs will see different things from users with PCs. Applying different filtering rules means that users in marketing may also see different things from users in engineering, even though they are retrieving information from the same address. This lack of consistency presents a general problem in parametrizing URIs, and is actually something on which Tim Berners-Lee, the inventor of the Web, has strong opinions. It is quite possible that the use of CC/PP and other profile formats will force the Web to change.

WAP sessions are intended to be very long-lived, and can be suspended and resumed. This feature can be used when the user changes the presentation functions of the device. For example, if the user enters his car and puts the telephone in the hands-free cradle, the action can trigger a suspend of the session using graphic presentation parameters, and resume the session in voice only. Each active WSP session of a client can be associated with different profile information, which means that the resume and suspend of WSP sessions can be used to change information about the user.

The WAP gateway is a crucial part in the architecture. WAP gateways represent an intermediary between the Internet and the mobile network, and while many of their functions could be conducted using standard protocols and IP over the wireless link, the WAP specification is intended to optimize the transactions so that they take up minimal bandwidth over the network. It is a gateway on several levels, not only translating the transport layer from Wireless Datagram Protocol (WDP) to User Datagram Protocol (UDP), but also translating the request from a client device over WSP into an HTTP request with an extended header containing the profile information. When it forwards these requests, the gateway must also forward the current profile information associated with the session or request. The gateway can add information to the profile with additional data obtained from local databases. This can be network-related information, such as position information. The WAP gateway is also responsible for translating HTTP responses into appropriate WSP responses for delivery over the wireless network to the requesting client device.

Proxy Interaction

The assumption throughout this work is that the server or proxy (endpoint) does content negotiation and/or personalization work, while the device does presentation. This makes it possible to have very dumb terminals, should that be desired. If we want to have the profile in the client, there is nothing to stop us from having a server in the client (actually, it is possible to imagine an architecture where there are only servers and very stupid clients, and the local server in the client device handles all caching, etc.).

An HTTP proxy or origin server will deliver content from its cache only if the content has not expired from the cache (in accordance with standard HTTP caching semantics, for instance, if the `NOCACHE` parameter is not set, as is recommended if the caches between the origin server and the client are not HTTP 1.1-compliant), and the profile information associated with the cached request exactly matches the profile information associated with the new request (which ensures that the idempotency—the capability of a method to always return the same result if the same parameters are used—is maintained). One problem, however, is that many caches used today do not actually use HTTP 1.1, so if you want to use CC/PP, you had better make sure all your proxies and caches implement it.

The request from the client is intended for the origin server, by way of the WAP gateway and possibly other proxies in between. It is the responsibility of the origin server to receive the request and generate appropriate content, which is then delivered as an HTTP response to the WAP gateway (and from there, forwarded to the client).

As a request travels over the network from the client device to the origin server, each network element may, optionally, add additional profile information to the transmitted profile. These additions may provide information available solely to that particular network element. Alternatively, this information may override the capabilities exposed by the client, particularly in cases where that network element is capable of performing in-band content transformations to meet the capability requirements of the requesting client device.

The origin server extracts the profile information sent along with the HTTP request; resolves all indirect references to information stored at other repositories in the network and fetches the profile elements from them, if necessary; and uses that information to select or otherwise customize the content being delivered to the client. Using the CC/PP Exchange Protocol over HTTP, the origin server can indicate how much it used the profile information to produce the content in the response.

The customization method is not specified anywhere, and depends on the implementation in the origin server. It may be anything from traditional content negotiation, in which a variant that fits the user preferences is selected, to a full contextualization, in which information from a database is filtered depending on the user location.

Because there is a one-to-one relation between the request and the response (as per the definition in the HTTP protocol), this list-matching method is the most efficient way of creating an optimized presentation. If the information had been broadcast, then the adaptation might have worked differently. As it is, you cannot be sure that the user preferences, or even the hardware capabilities, are constantly the same. The hardware vendor might have profile information available for its products, the software vendor might supply a default profile, and the user's preferences might apply across multiple applications (preferred language) or change during a session (sound on or off).

There are significant privacy and security problems associated with these profiles, of course. We will discuss the privacy problems in another section of this chapter, but let us just mention a few of the security problems:

- The CC/PP repository storing the profile is assumed to be secure, meaning that it does not permit unauthorized modification to stored profile information.
- WSP/HTTP headers are generally not encrypted. Therefore, information is transported in clear text. While the selection of the CC/PP elements is intended to not be sensitive, the very fact that all the information is collected may create a problem if the information is aggregated by a malicious third party.
- An implicit chain of trust exists between the client and origin server. The integrity of the profile is maintained (in other words, not compromised) as it is transmitted through or cached within the network. It is assumed that

the network elements that contribute property descriptions to the profile are trusted. Network elements will not assemble a "history" about users by tracking the deltas in their profile over time. These assumptions are, of course, weak. To ensure the integrity of the profile, lower-level mechanisms such as Transport Level Security (TLS, formerly known as SSL), must be used.

Although there may be a long-term threat to user integrity, this should not be a short-term problem. The origin server is intended to use the profile information to enhance the user experience. Should the profile be discarded, corrupted, or otherwise inaccessible, then the origin server will still provide and deliver content to the client in a best-efforts fashion (i.e., as good as it gets today).

Contextualization and Environmental Adaptation

Although the adaptation of content to a certain set of device capabilities is a fairly well-described process (e.g., using style sheets with different resolutions and formatting parameters to match different device capabilities), the adaptation of content to other parameters has so far been investigated mostly in isolated systems that do not attempt to aggregate content from different sites. Positioning has been the starting point for several trials with context-aware mobile devices. Several methods exist for sensing the user location, such as GPS, network-based positioning, active badges, and others. If, however, a topical search engine can discover content with certain properties in its metadata—for example, content relevant at a particular location—this content can be matched with the location preference of the user (a real or "pretended" location).

Contextualization means that the HTML model of encapsulating metadata in the document itself no longer holds, primarily due to the fact that if the representation is device- and user-independent, it becomes possible to link in a multitude of style sheets, as well as other relevance metadescriptors.

Users may have preferences for content that cannot be communicated to the server for consideration today. This lack of communication may cause problems in future information retrieval, when increased parameterization becomes available. Clients may receive content that they cannot store, that they cannot display, that violates the desires of the user, or that takes too long to convey over the network to the client device.

Many users of desktop and mobile computer systems are familiar with diary and personal organizer software that provides reminders of meetings and other events through a limited temporal awareness (that is, synchronizing with the clock of the system). With a computer that is also able to determine location, such systems could be extended to provide only those reminders that are appropriate to a location: for example, a reminder to go to a particular shop next time the user visits London.

There are a vast number of possible context variables that can be used to adapt the information. Context-aware applications can derive the information from environmental sensors attached to the mobile device. These could be location sensors, for example, GPS, active badges, mobile phones, or ultrasonic devices. The sensors could present data about companions or objects near the user, as detected by active badges or tags; orientation, as detected by an electronic compass; and time and date, derived from the system clock. Environmental information can also be data captured by specialized sensors for particular applications: temperature, radiation level, or even mental environmental variables, such as share prices (where the sensor is an information feed from a stock exchange). Data can also be aggregated by super-sensors which correlate information from lower-level sensors in order to deduce some higher-level state; for instance one may detect whether the occupant of an office is busy by looking at sensors that record what equipment is being used, who else is in the office, and so on.

GPS, user input, and beacons all deliver the position directly into the terminal. Network-based positioning delivers the position information to a proxy, from which it can be retrieved to the terminal. If the position is handled as the `TerminalLocation` attribute of the CC/PP profile, it can be derived from the device and transmitted as a CC/PP Exchange override; in case it is derived from the network, it can be referenced as a URI and resolved by the XML processor when the profile document arrives at the server.

The values of these sensors together constitute the present context of the user. One inherent feature of mobile systems is the ability to derive the position of a device. The network itself can be used to find out the position of the user. There are several ways of doing this: some are based on communication with the user's device, retrieving either network information or position from a GPS device; others measure the user's terminal position in the network (essentially, using the radio transmitters to triangulate it). In the United States, this is used in the enhanced 911 feature; in Europe, it is used to locate stolen vehicles and missing persons.

If involving data from sensors, the data will be fed to the context-aware application in a steady (continuous) stream. This stream may mean that the user interface is continually changing as the user changes context. Continuous applications require a significant programming effort and provide a totally different authorship challenge. They will also produce a quite different load on the network. One of the most important examples of context dependency is the user's location.

If the profile contains the position information, it can be updated for each request, because HTTP is stateless—it does not retain any information about the user between requests. The updates can be done using the mechanisms described above, by sending only the change in the information.

The CC/PP profile is not a user preference profile. If it were, it could contain information that the user was interested in receiving sports scores and, if so, the particular teams; or which payment systems the user wants. Instead, the CC/PP profile is intended to enable not just adaptation of presentation, but contextualization of the information.

Contextualization is far more than content negotiation, where a variant of a document is selected based on request parameters, such as the type of user agent (e.g., Mozilla or Internet Explorer). While content adaptation to a certain set of device capabilities is a fairly well described process (e.g., using style sheets with different resolutions and formatting parameters to match different device capabilities), the adaptation of content to other parameters has so far been investigated mostly in isolated systems, which do not attempt to aggregate content from different sites. If, however, a topical search engine can discover content with certain properties in its metadata, e.g. that is relevant at a particular location, this content can be matched with the location preference of the user (real location or "pretended"). The work of Jason Pascoe and others, as well as the GUIDE Project at Lancaster University, demonstrates clearly the importance of position information in determining the information set to be transmitted to the user. Items such as temperature, whether the sun is shining or it is raining, the weather forecast, and other environmental parameters (such as traffic) will also affect the decisions of the user, and therefore the context. Different information sets can be generated for different circumstances, which is a part of the personalization of the information set for the user.

In the Internet architecture, information retrieval is a request-response architecture. In other words, the user initiates the request for information. The computer monitors various aspects of the user environment and includes them as parameterizations on the request. The environmental factors can be both physical and logical. Apart from parameters that are properties of the device, such as location, they can include physical criteria such as date and time, temperature, ambient light level, and other physical characteristics of the environment, measured by attached sensors.

Logical criteria include the user's current preferences, to be used in the adaptation of content presentation to the current user situation and the capabilities of the device. This can be exemplified by your communicating PDA switching over from graphic presentation to voice presentation when you enter your car. The capabilities of the device are the same, but your preferences have changed, from watching the device to watching the road.

As long as there is a one-to-one relationship between the request and response, it is more efficient from a computational and networks view to adapt information at the origin server or in the network than at the client. It is also possible to exclude information that should not be transmitted to the receiver, enabling the conversion proxy to act as a "semantic firewall."

Position relevance is expected to be one of the primary drivers for context-dependent information. The exact position of a user (or, more accurately, the terminal) is in itself, however, rarely relevant to the user; what is relevant is the information that relates to that position. How it relates to the position is irrelevant to the current discussion, but the relevance may occur in a variety of ways: describing the physical object at the position, describing an event occurring at the position, and so forth.

The determination of which information objects are relevant in the current context of the user can take place in the same way as traditional content negotiation: The device reports its position to a server, which identifies documents relevant to that position, and forwards them to the user. The real problem is to determine the information objects that are relevant to the user in the position. Users may also make requests for information that is not currently relevant, but will be at the time of the validity of the request.

An information set is location-relevant if it can provide the user (or an agent acting on his behalf) with information that can affect his situation. The user perceives physical objects as having different degrees of relevance depending on the current context and the distance of the object from the user.

Relevance may also depend on the role of the user. For instance, at lunchtime, we may be interested in finding the restaurant that is within the nearest few blocks to our work; but if we are tourists in a foreign city, we may be interested in the location of all the museums in the city. This can also be time-dependent (we are more interested in which museums exist in the morning, when planning our day; and interest in lunch increases around noon) and dependent of the mode of locomotion. (When traveling by car, we will not have the same ability to stop suddenly as would a user on foot, nor will we be able to use restaurants without parking space.)

The problem of providing the information that is relevant in the user context cannot be solved with traditional full-text indexing. Full-text indices, while flexible, do not contain structured information about the location relevance of the information. If a file contains a location (in coordinates, as a placename, or in any other description format), how can we determined what it refers to without retrieving the file? The same goes for the update frequency. If the location relevance of the information, the time of update of the information, and the time the information is relevant were accessible in a structured format, as metadata or in a metafile, it would be possible for an indexing robot to create a meta-index which could be used in the same manner as robots today to retrieve information relevant to the current context of the user. Enabling access to information from the World Wide Web, while maintaining the relevance in the current context, is the goal of the system.

In the Dublin Core `DC:Coverage` variable, the place name is used to designate the location relevance of the information. Place names are ambiguous: the place "Stockholm" has at least six possible interpretations (polygons), for example (the capital of Sweden as the community of Stockholm; the "greater Stockholm area"; the current city of Stockholm; the historic city (inside the city wall); and the cities of Stockholm, Minnesota and Stockholm, Papua New Guinea). This will lead to ambiguities and make it impossible to decide the relevance of the information properly, because there will most likely be several registers of place names, which means that the variable must designate which register it uses along with the place name. If the metainformation is presented as RDF, this is less of a problem, because the namespace has to be declared anyway; if a text format is used, it will be more difficult to express.

If any precision is to be available in the processing of the positional relevance, the place name must also be defined by its coordinates as a polygon. Again, it does not matter greatly which coordinate system is used as long as this definition format is declared. If it is not declared, the granularity of the place-name will be doubtful. Specifically, the SKi format expressed in RDF can easily be matched with the position and temporal preferences of the user. The content of the `ical:geo` tag can be matched with the UAProf property `TerminalLocation`, because the two can have the same datatype.

Position-relevant applications can also be context-dependent applications, where a script is triggered to perform an action as an event occurs, for instance, as the user reaches a location. Simple applications can be tourist guides, where information is given about sights that the user is passing, and in maintenance, where the user is automatically given information about nearby equipment.

The triggering can be more related to the user's needs if it is dependent on several contextual elements. An example could be information presented to a tourist that depends not only on the location, but also on the time of day, the season of the year, and the current temperature (e.g., giving recommendations for museums if it is raining or winter, and for beaches if the weather is nice and it is summer).

The best user interface for a location-aware application still has not been determined. How to represent the context visually is something for which there is no convention. For location, the established convention for representing position on a map is a polygon (dot, circle, rectangle). The marker should be dynamic, because it depends on the context of the user. Placing one such marker at each position where information can be triggered makes the user aware that information is available. On the other hand, if there are too many dots on the map, this will in itself constitute an information overload. Using context dependency to represent the information objects in the user's vicinity will help by minimizing the cognitive load on the user.

Other Formats: CONNEG, RESCAP, and SDP

While CC/PP is designed specifically to fit into the semantic web, by virtue both of being RDF and being extensible with new components, there are a few other formats for parameterization information that can be useful to know about.

The CONNEG Format

CONNEG is a format using feature-tags from a registry maintained by the Internet Assigned Numbers Authority (IANA). The feature set syntax is built upon the principle of using feature set predicates as "mathematical relations" which define constraints on feature-handling capabilities. This allows the same form of feature set expression to be used to describe sender, receiver, and file format capabilities. It has been loosely modeled on the way that relational databases use Boolean expressions to describe a set of result values, and a syntax based on LDAP search filters (which in turn are based on Prolog-based predicate logic).

A part of this framework is a way to describe the range of media features, which can be handled by the sender, recipient, or document transmission format of a message. Descriptions of media feature capabilities need to be based on some underlying vocabulary of individual media features.

Resource Capability Protocol (RESCAP)

The Resource Capability Protocol (RESCAP) consists of two protocol parts:

- A general resolution protocol that will translate resource identifiers to a list of attributes
- An administrative model and update protocol that can be used to set up and maintain the information the resolution protocol accesses

Web sites and other data resources may have associated metadata. A combination of Domain Name Service (DNS) and RESCAP protocols might be used to access this resource metadata. HTTP might be used instead of RESCAP, but the RESCAP goals suggest two possible advantages over HTTP: lightweight access for small items of information that are accessed frequently, and easier administration of metadata about families of related resources. In fact, RESCAP is foreseen to be extremely lightweight (only a few bytes per transaction).

Session Description Protocol (SDP)

The Session Description Protocol (SDP) is intended for describing multimedia sessions for the purposes of session announcement, session invitation, and other forms of multimedia session initiation. It is intended for use with the Session Initiation Protocol (SIP), which is used to set up multimedia sessions (e.g., streaming sessions). Session directories assist in the advertisement of conference sessions and communicate the relevant conference setup information to prospective participants. SDP is designed to convey such information to recipients.

Session descriptions can be conveyed using methods that include electronic mail and HTTP. For both e-mail and HTTP distribution, the MIME content type `application/sdp` should be used. This enables the automatic launching of applications for participation in the session from the WWW client or mail reader in a standard manner.

It is interesting to note that RFC 2327 does not define how the data should be conveyed over HTTP. It is, however, conceptually no different from any other capability exchange information (because the session setup actually takes place using another protocol). That implies that SDP could be transported as part of the CNHTTP `accept-profile` header as well.

This is an example SDP description of an ITU H.332 session:

```
c=IN IP4 224.5.6.7
a=type:H332
m=audio 49230 RTP/AVP 0
m=video 49232 RTP/AVP 31
m=application 12349 udp wb
m=control 49234 H323 mc
c=IN IP4 134.134.157.81
```

Privacy and Profiles: An Unsolved Problem

When you request information from a site using the techniques described above, you are giving it a lot of information about yourself. It is, of course, even worse when you connect to an e-commerce site and gladly give out your credit card number, home address, and everything else the site owner wants to know about you.

How should the information you give out be protected against misuse by the owner of the server or proxy that receives and personalizes the information? Already, there is concern about misuse of the information you give out.

Platform for Privacy Preferences (P3P)

Security has two dimensions: the safeguard of the user's privacy and the safeguard of the integrity of the information. Using encryption solves both these problems, but introduces a lot of other problems—for instance, it becomes impossible for intermediaries to insert information into the profile. Solutions are possible, however, that let information be transmitted in clear text, yet safeguard the user's privacy and the information integrity. The best effort so far for the safeguard of the user's privacy is the W3C Platform for Privacy Preferences (P3P) framework.

P3P is a format for a server to declare what information it will require from a user (and his device), and how that information will be used. Strictly speaking, it is not an automated system: The goal was scaled down from plans for an automated integrity watch system to a way to alert the user about ways the information will be used. There are no guarantees against the service provider lying, of course. The relation between the user and the origin server is a contractual relationship, and such relationships can be established in other ways, such as by simply signing a contract when the subscription to the service is set up. However, the real problem remains: how to know that the service provider is not lying when he declares what he intends to do with the information. The P3P is forced to rely on societal pressures and bodies such as the Better Business Bureau to police the policies.

P3P contains a set of data elements that declare the information the server wants and what it will do with it. As this dataset is in XML (although not in RDF as of this writing, a mapping is planned to be released before this book is published but after it is sent to the printer), it is extensible using namespaces, but also by using a built-in extension mechanism. It defines a header to transport the information, and messages to pass back and forth between client and server. It does not define what the application should do internally, either at the server or client side.

The P3P policies identify the legal entity behind the service, describe the types of data or data elements collected, and explain how the data will be used. In addition, they identify the data recipients and describe how disputes should be resolved, and the address of a site's human-readable privacy policy. P3P declarations are positive: Sites state what they do. The vocabulary is designed to describe a site practice rather than indicate compliance with a particular law or code of conduct. Intermediaries, such as proxies, gateway operators, ISPs, and others are not covered by the policies, even if they can have access to the exchange between the user and the site.

It is relatively easy to create a P3P policy: Take the existing, human-readable privacy policy (or formulate a new one), and express it in the P3P vocabulary. Publish the result files along with a policy reference file that indicates the parts of the site to which the policy applies. As a site owner, you can decide whether you want one policy to cover the entire site, or you can designate different policies for different parts of the site (essentially, different directories). There are restrictions to how this can be done.

Servers may publish policy reference files at a well-known location, or they may reference their P3P policy reference files in HTML content using a link tag. The specification simply declares that the well-known location is the sites /w3c directory, under the name p3p.xml. A user agent could request this policy reference file by using a GET request for the resource /w3c/p3p.xml. Because advertisements are, in principle, not part of the pages in the server (mostly, they are inline references to some other site), there is a way for the site owner to include them in the policy. There are also elements to declare that cookies apply, and what those cookies are. The advantage of this is, of course, that the user is not confronted with unknown cookies.

Alternatively, sites can insert a P3P extension header into all HTTP responses that indicate the location of a site's P3P policy reference file. A P3P policy must cover all data generated or exchanged as part of a site's HTTP interactions with visitors. Currently, P3P is bound to HTTP, and can be implemented on existing HTTP/1.1-compliant Web servers without additional or upgraded software. It is possible to declare separate policies for different HTTP methods.

The policy reference file describes which policies apply to which directories (or, really, URIs). They have an expiry date, which works the same as the HTTP cache expiry; that is, after that date, they must be retrieved again to be valid. The policy in the file describes all the effects of performing any of the HTTP methods listed in the policy reference file against the given URI. The referenced policy must cover all actions that the user's client software is expected to perform as a result of requesting that URI. This not only means data collection performed by the site (e.g., getting the CC/PP profile, or requesting the credit card number of the user). It also includes setting client-side cookies or other state-management mechanisms invoked by the response, as well as any executable code that may be downloaded as a result of the URI being accessed. The user does not have to activate the actions for them to be covered by the profile. This includes applets, scripts, and forms that may be linked to an entire database management system at the server side.

Just like CC/PP, P3P consists of structural elements (describing, for instance, the policy reference file) and vocabulary elements (describing the data elements that will be collected). The difference is that they are bound together in one specification (see Table 7.1), and there is no plan for groups other than the P3P working group to publish element names.

As a user, you must be able to know what information about the site's policy you can get, and how you can get it. This is the function of the access elements in P3P, as shown in Table 7.2.

Having access to a policy is well and good, but you have to know what to do if you want to use it or disagree with something it says. That is the function of the elements in the `Disputes` element, shown in Table 7.3. Several dispute instances can be gathered in a `Disputesgroup` element.

The `Statement` element declares what the receiving organization will do with the information it gets, as shown in Table 7.4.

Because data elements often come in groups that have something in common (e.g., the street address, street number, city and zip code constitute an address), they can be grouped into data structures. A structure is a collection of specified data elements. There are also a number of predefined data structures in P3P: the P3P Base Data Schema, which defines a wide variety of commonly used data elements. Other schemas can reuse the elements, as well. Data schemas describe specific data elements, which may be grouped into hierarchical data sets. Data schemas can be embedded in a policy. They can also be in a standalone XML file, in which case the namespace declaration must make clear that this is a P3P data schema file. P3P uses the `<DATA-DEF>` and `<DATA-STRUCT>` elements to declare a schema or a data structure. Data elements and structures can be classified according to whether or not they are in some fixed category (using the category element). All data, which an individual has to provide, can be described as data structures, and can be connected to forms, for instance. If mapped into RDF, this could be used to infer other things about the user and the visit, such as whether people living in Pittsburgh visit certain pages more often.

I do not intend to teach you the P3P schema language, because RDF will most likely supersede it anyway. The mere fact that the specifiers of P3P have found it necessary to create a schema language of their own actually illustrates how useful it is to have a standardized language. Imagine if you had to learn first the P3P language, then the CC/PP language, and finally the RSS and Dublin Core languages to provide site information: as good a case as any for RDF.

Still, there are some useful things in the P3P schema language. Most of the elements in the P3P base data schema belong to one or at most two category

Table 7.1 P3P Structural Policy Elements

ELEMENT NAME	FUNCTION	SUBELEMENTS	ATTRIBUTES	FUNCTION
<POLICIES>	Gathers several policies in one single file; functions as a wrapper element			
<POLICY>	Contains the complete policy	<discuri>		URI of the human-readable privacy statement
		<opturi>		URI for instructions that describe how the user can decline to have data used for a particular purpose
		<name>		Policy name
<TEST>	If present in the policy, it must be ignored, because the policy is to be regarded as for testing only			
<EXTENSION>	Describes an extension to the syntax		optional	Whether the extension is optional or mandatory (if mandatory="yes" and the application does not understand the extension, it will not understand the entire schema)

Table 7.2 P3P Elements Determining Access to the Policy

ELEMENT NAME	FUNCTION	SUBELEMENTS	ATTRIBUTES	FUNCTION
<ENTITY>	The legal entity that makes the statement (i.e., the company or organization behind the Web site); must contain elements from the `business` data set (see Table 7.6) that makes it traceable			
<ACCESS>	How the user is enabled to see information and where to address questions; one way must be specified, but can also have the value `all`, in which case the user can call, fax, e-mail, or use any other way of retrieving information	<noident/>		Identifiable data is not used
		<all/>		Access is given to all identifiable information
		<contact-and-other/>		Access is given to identifiable online and physical contact information as well as to other information linked to an identifiable person
		<ident-contact/>		Access is given to identifiable online and physical contact information (e.g., users can access things such as a postal address)
		<other-ident/>		Access is given to certain other information linked to an identifiable person (e.g., users can access things such as their online account charges)
		<none/>		No access to identifiable information is given

Table 7.3 The Disputesgroup Element

ELEMENT NAME	FUNCTION	SUBELEMENTS	ATTRIBUTES	FUNCTION
<DISPUTES-GROUP>	Container for the DISPUTES elements			
<DISPUTES>	Dispute resolution procedures that may be followed for disputes about a service's privacy practice, e.g., sue them, go to the Better Business Bureau, or whatever		Resolution-type	Can have one of four values: **Customer service** `[service]`; **Independent organization** `[independent]`; **Court** `[court]`; **Applicable law** `[law]`
			service	URI where the customer services, independent organization, or court of law can be reached
			verification	URI or certificate that can be used for verification purposes, e.g., of seal from an independent organization
			short-description	Short human-readable description of the name of the appropriate legal forum, applicable law, or third-party organization (max 255 characters)
		<LONG-DESCRIPTION>		Long description of the organization that resolves disputes

Table 7.3 The Disputesgroup Element (Continued)

ELEMENT NAME	FUNCTION	SUBELEMENTS	ATTRIBUTES	FUNCTION
		<IMG>		e.g., a logo
			src	URI of the image
			width	Image width in pixels
			Height	Image height in pixels
			Alt	Very short text description of the image
<REMEDIES>	Each DISPUTES element must contain a REMEDIES element that describes what to do in case of a policy breach	<correct/>		
		The service will correct the problem		
		<money/>		The service provider will pay a sum of money
		<law/>		In the human-readable policy, the applicable law is declared

Table 7.4 The Statement Element

ELEMENT NAME	FUNCTION	SUBELEMENTS	ATTRIBUTES	FUNCTION
<STATEMENT>	Groups together a PURPOSE element, a RECIPIENT element, a RETENTION element, a DATA-GROUP element, and optionally a CONSEQUENCE element and one or more extensions. This means that all the data that is collected in the DATA-GROUP element follows the same policies; if not, a separate element has to be used for each data element.			
		<CONSEQUENCE>		Tries to explain to a user why he should give up information he normally would not, because it would have the consequences described
		<NON-IDENTIFIABLE/>		If there is no reasonable way for the entity or a third party to attach the collected data to the identity of a natural person, the information is considered nonidentifiable, e.g., if information is anonymized using a randomizing algorithm; if this element is present, there must be a human-readable explanation of how it is achieved

Table 7.4 The Statement Element (Continued)

ELEMENT NAME	FUNCTION	SUBELEMENTS	ATTRIBUTES	FUNCTION
		<PURPOSE>		Declares the purpose of the collection of the information; must contain one or more of the following subelements
		<current/>		The service provider will use the information to complete the current activity (e.g., a search or a device-dependent presentation) but not for anything else
		<admin/>		Information will be used for technical support and administration of the Web site
		<develop/>		Information will be used for research purposes , e.g., developing the service
		<customization/>		Information (after user approval) may be used to customize the site for the user over several visits (e.g., "Welcome back, Johan!")
		<tailoring/>		Information may be used during the present visit only to tailor the user experience (e.g., recommend goods based on content in shopping basket)
		<pseudo-analysis/>		Analysis is done pseudonymously, i.e., the user is not identifiable as the person giving the information; only for analysis of the site and traffic, etc.

(continues)

Table 7.4 The Statement Element (Continued)

ELEMENT NAME	FUNCTION	SUBELEMENTS	ATTRIBUTES	FUNCTION
		<pseudo-decision/>		Information is used to customize the site to the visitor, but the visitor is anonymous to the site; the record is persistent
		<individual-analysis/>		Personal information is used, but only to analyze buying patterns, etc.
		<individual-decision/>		Personal information is used, e.g., to recommend goods based on previous purchases, street address, etc.
		<contact/>		Information may be used to contact the individual. The contact will be personal (e.g., when you give your information at the luxurycar.com Web site a salesperson will drop by with a Jaguar and offer you a test-drive)
		<historical/>		Information must be archived for legal reasons
		<telemarketing/>		Someone will call you
		<other-purpose>_*string* </other-purpose>		The string declares for what other purposes the information will be used, e.g., hanging yellow ribbons around a tree in your front yard
			required	Can be an attribute on all the subelements in this group; can have the following values: always (users have no choice); opt-in_ (users can say yes to the data being used that way); opt-out_ (users can say they do not want data to be used that way)

Table 7.4 The Statement Element (Continued)

ELEMENT NAME	FUNCTION	SUBELEMENTS	ATTRIBUTES	FUNCTION
		<RECIPIENT>		The legal entity behind the Web site; must contain one of the following subelements; each of them can contain one or more recipient-description elements.
		<ours>		Information will be used by the organization, or by another organization acting on its behalf (e.g., a credit bureau)
		<delivery>		Delivery services may receive the information
		<same>		Others receiving the information will follow the same practices as the site
		<other-recipient>		Information may be given out to someone doing something totally different with it
		<unrelated>		Information may be given out to someone who the service provider does not know anything about
		<public>		Information may become public
		<RETENTION>		The Retention element describes how long the information will be kept. It can have the following subelements
		<no-retention/>		Information is only retained during one single transaction
		<stated-purpose/>		Information is retained for a reason, and will be destroyed after that reason is fulfilled (e.g., individual analysis)

(continues)

Table 7.4 The Statement Element (Continued)

ELEMENT NAME	FUNCTION	SUBELEMENTS	ATTRIBUTES	FUNCTION
		<legal-requirement/>		Information is kept for the period required by law
		<business-practices/>		The amount of time information is kept depends on the business practices of the site
		<indefinitely/>		Ought to be self-explanatory
		<DATA-GROUP>		Describes the data to be transferred or inferred. Container for one or more DATA elements
			base	Base URI for referenced data
		<DATA>		Describes the data to be transferred or inferred
			ref	The fragment identifier part denotes the name of a data element/set, and the URI part denotes the corresponding data schema
			optional	Indicates whether submission is required by the user

classes (they are *fixed*). This means that a user or a program can avoid certain element categories, for instance those related to health. When creating data schemas for fixed data elements, schema creators have to explicitly declare the categories that these elements belong to. For example,

```
<DATA-STRUCT name="postal.street" structref="#text"
short-description="Street Address">
<CATEGORIES><physical/></CATEGORIES>
</DATA-STRUCT>
```

If an element or structure belongs to multiple categories, multiple elements referencing the appropriate categories can be used. For example, the following piece of XML can be used to declare that the data elements in user.name have both categories `physical` and `demographic`:

```
<DATA-STRUCT name="user.name" structref="#personname"
short-description="User's Name">
<CATEGORIES><physical/><demographic/></CATEGORIES>
</DATA-STRUCT>
```

Not all data elements/structures in the base data schema belong to a predetermined category class. Some can contain information from a range of categories, depending on a particular situation. Such elements/structures are called variable-category data elements/structures in P3P (or "variable data elements/structures" for short). User preferences can list such variable data elements without any additional category information (effectively expressing preferences over any usage of this element); services must always explicitly specify the categories that apply to the usage of a variable data element in their particular policy. This information has to appear as a category element in the corresponding DATA element listed in the policy, as for example in

```
<POLICY ... >
...
<DATA ref="#dynamic.cookies"><CATEGORIES><uniqueid/></CATEGORIES></DATA>
...
</POLICY>
```

Where a service declares that cookies are used for identifying the user at this site (i.e., category Unique Identifiers). If a service wants to declare a data element that is in multiple categories, it simply declares the corresponding categories.

```
<POLICY ... >
...
```

```
<DATA
ref="#dynamic.cookies"><CATEGORIES><uniqueid/><preference/></CATEGORIES>
</DATA>
...
</POLICY>
```

With the above declaration a service announces that it uses cookies both for identifying the user at this site and for storing user preference data. Note that for the purpose of P3P there is no difference whether this information is stored in two separate cookies or in a single one. Categories can also be inherited downward when a field is structured, but only into fields, which have no predefined category.

Categories are declared using the `Category` element in P3P, which can have a number of subelements, all declaring the type of data in the structure being described. They are necessarily arbitrary, however.

- **<physical/>** Information that allows an individual to be contacted or located; for example, telephone number or address
- **<online/>** Information that allows an individual to be contacted or located on the Internet (the W3C does not consider other networks); for instance, an e-mail address
- **<uniqueid/>** Specific identifiers that are not related to financial matters (e.g., credit card) or government-issued identifiers (e.g., social security number); used to consistently identify the individual; these include identifiers issued by a Web site or service
- **<purchase/>** Information resulting from the individual making a purchase, including information about the method of payment
- **<financial/>** Information about an individual's finances, including account status and activity information such as account balance, payment or overdraft history, and information about an individual's purchase or use of financial instruments, including credit or debit card information; information about a discrete purchase by an individual, as described in "Purchase Information," does not alone come under the definition of "Financial Information"
- **<computer/>** Identifiers that describe the computer system being used to access the network, such as the IP number, domain name, browser type, or operating system
- **<navigation/>** Data that can be gathered from a log file without active data gathering, such as which pages have been visited for how long
- **<interactive/>** Data generated by the service from user actions, or by interactions with a service that requires the user to provide some information, such as queries to a search engine

- **<demographic/>** Information about the individual, such as gender, age, and income
- **<content/>** Information that has been provided as part of a communication, such as the text of e-mail, bulletin board postings, or chat room communications
- **<state/>** Information used to maintain the identity of the user between visits, such as HTTP cookies
- **<political/>** Membership in or affiliation with groups such as religious organizations, trade unions, professional associations, political parties, and so forth
- **<health/>** Information about an individual's physical or mental health, sexual orientation, use or inquiry into health care services or products, and purchase of health care services or products
- **<preference/>** Data about an individual's likes and dislikes, such as favorite color or musical tastes
- **<location/>** Information that can be used to identify an individual's current physical location and track them as their location changes, such as GPS position data
- **<government/>** Identifiers issued by a government for purposes of consistently identifying the individual
- **<other-category> *string* </other-category>** Other types of data not captured by the above definitions. (A human-readable explanation should be provided in these instances, between the two `<other-category>` tags.)

In P3P there is also a base schema for information. All P3P-compliant user agents must be aware of the elements in the base schema. It defines the basic data structures and four data element sets: `user`, `thirdparty`, `business`, and `dynamic`. The `user`, `thirdparty` and `business` sets include elements that users and/or businesses might provide values for, while the `dynamic` set includes elements that are dynamically generated in the course of a user's browsing session. It is possible for a user agent to provide this information automatically, and the user may choose not to provide this information at all.

The user data set includes general information about the user, as shown in Table 7.5. The data in the data structures are actually data structures themselves.

There is also a `thirdparty` data set, intended for use when the information provided does not relate to the user or the service. This applies, for instance, when sending gifts to someone from a service. It is identical with the `user` data set.

Table 7.5 Information about the User

USER	CATEGORY	STRUCTURE	SHORT DISPLAY NAME
Name	Physical Contact Information, Demographic and Socioeconomic Data	Personname	User's Name
Bdate	Demographic and Socioeconomic Data	Date	User's Birth Date
Cert	Unique Identifiers	Certificate	User's Identity Certificate
Gender	Demographic and Socioeconomic Data	*unstructured*	User's Gender (male or female)
Employer	Demographic and Socioeconomic Data	*unstructured*	User's Employer
Department	Demographic and Socioeconomic Data	*unstructured*	Department or division of organization where user is employed
Jobtitle	Demographic and Socioeconomic Data	*unstructured*	User's Job Title
home-info	Physical Contact Information, Online Contact Information, Demographic and Socioeconomic Data	Contact	User's Home Contact Information
Business-info	Physical Contact Information, Online Contact Information, Demographic and Socioeconomic Data	Contact	User's Business Contact Information

There is also a special subset of the `user` information, shown in Table 7.6, which applies to business. This is primarily used for declaring the entity in the policy. In theory, it could be used for business-to-business information, but it is not nearly comprehensive enough for that in practice.

In some cases, there is a need to specify data elements without fixed values that a user might type in or store in a repository. In the P3P Base Data Schema, all such elements are grouped under the `dynamic` data set, as shown in Table 7.7. Sites may refer to the types of data they collect using the `dynamic` data set, instead of all of the specific data elements.

These elements are often implicit in navigation or Web interactions. They should be used with categories to describe the type of information collected through these methods.

Table 7.6 Information about a Business

BUSINESS	CATEGORY	STRUCTURE	SHORT DISPLAY NAME
Name	Demographic and Socioeconomic Data	*unstructured*	Organization Name
Department	Demographic and Socioeconomic Data	*unstructured*	Department or division of organization
Cert	Unique Identifiers	Certificate	Organization Identity Certificate
Contact-info	Physical Contact Information, Online Contact Information, Demographic and Socioeconomic Data	Contact	Contact Information for the organization

- **clickstream** Represents the combination of information typically found in Web server access logs: the IP address or hostname of the user's computer, the URI of the resource requested, the time the request was made, the HTTP method used in the request, the size of the response, and the HTTP status code in the response; Web sites that collect standard server access logs (as well as sites which do URI path analysis) can use this data element to describe how that data will be used.

Table 7.7 Browsing Related Information Gathered in P3P Data Sets

DYNAMIC	CATEGORY	STRUCTURE	SHORT DISPLAY NAME
Clickstream	Navigation and Clickstream Data, Computer Information	Loginfo	Clickstream information
http	Navigation and Click-stream Data, Computer Information	Httpinfo	HTTP information
Clientevents	Navigation and Click-stream Data	*unstructured*	User's interaction with a resource
Cookies	*(variable-category)*	*unstructured*	Use of HTTP cookies
Miscdata	*(variable-category)*	*unstructured*	Miscellaneous non-database schema information
Searchtext	Interactive Data	*unstructured*	Search terms
Interactionrecord	Interactive Data	*unstructured*	Server stores the transaction history

- **http** Contains additional information (other than the clickstream) contained in HTTP.
- **clientevents** Represents data about how the user interacts with their Web browser while interacting with a resource. For example, an application may wish to collect information about whether the user moved their mouse over a certain image on a page, or whether the user ever brought up the Help window in a Java applet. This kind of information is represented by the `dynamic.clientevents` data element. Much of this interaction record is represented by the events and data defined by the Document Object Model (DOM) Level 2 Events, and would have to be reported to the server by Javascript or another application that listens for these events (i.e., a normal Web page cannot gather them). The `clientevents` data element also covers any other data regarding the user's interaction with their browser while the browser is displaying a resource (exempting events that are covered by other elements in the base data schema).
- **cookies** Should be used whenever HTTP cookies are set or retrieved by a site. According to the P3P specification, however, `cookies` is a variable data element and requires the explicit declaration of usage categories in a policy.
- **miscdata** References information collected by the service that is not otherwise referenced.
- **searchtext** References a specific type of solicitation used for searching and indexing sites. For example, if the only fields on a search engine page are search fields, the site needs to disclose only that data element.
- **interactionrecord** Should be used if the server is keeping track of the interaction it has with the user (i.e., information other than clickstream data, such as account transactions, etc.).

The date structure specifies a date. Dates can be used in different ways, which makes it hard to give them a fixed category. They can be used equally well to request your birthday (in which case they are in the `demographic` category) as to create a browsing history (in which case they are in the `clickstream` category). Date formats (shown in Table 7.8) and time formats (shown in Table 7.9) are problematic. They are defined in ISO Standard 8601, but there are various ways they are being used that are not standardized.

The `personname` structure specifies information about the naming of a person. People living in cultures using other name conventions may be interested in inventing their own data structures.

The certificate structure (see Table 7.10) is used to specify identity certificates (for example, X.509). In Sweden, for instance, all new ID cards that are being

Table 7.8 The date Structure

DATE	CATEGORY	STRUCTURE	SHORT DISPLAY NAME
ymd.year	*(variable-category)*	*unstructured*	Year
ymd.month	*(variable-category)*	*unstructured*	Month
ymd.day	*(variable-category)*	*unstructured*	Day
hms.hour	*(variable-category)*	*unstructured*	Hour
hms.minute	*(variable-category)*	*unstructured*	Minute
hms.second	*(variable-category)*	*unstructured*	Second
Fractionsecond	*(variable-category)*	*unstructured*	Fraction of Second
Timezone	*(variable-category)*	*unstructured*	Time Zone

Table 7.9 The personname Structure

PERSONNAME	CATEGORY	STRUCTURE	SHORT DISPLAY NAME
Prefix	Demographic and Socioeconomic Data	*unstructured*	Name Prefix
Given	Physical Contact Information	*unstructured*	Given Name (First Name)
Family	Physical Contact Information	*unstructured*	Family Name (Last Name)
Middle	Physical Contact Information	*unstructured*	Middle Name
Suffix	Demographic and Socioeconomic Data	*unstructured*	Name Suffix
Nickname	Demographic and Socioeconomic Data	*unstructured*	Nickname

Table 7.10 The certificate Structure

CERTIFICATE	CATEGORY	STRUCTURE	SHORT DISPLAY NAME
Key	Unique Identifiers	*unstructured*	Certificate Key
Format	Unique Identifiers	*unstructured*	Certificate Format

issued by the Swedish Post have two X.509 certificates on them, and because the card identifies the person, it is possible to assume that the certificate identifies the individual. It is more likely that companies will use certificates to

Table 7.11 The telephonenum Structure

TELEPHONENUM	CATEGORY	STRUCTURE	SHORT DISPLAY NAME
Intcode	Physical Contact Information	*unstructured*	International Telephone code
Loccode	Physical Contact Information	*unstructured*	Local Telephone Area code
Number	Physical Contact Information	*unstructured*	Telephone Number
Ext	Physical Contact Information	*unstructured*	Telephone Extension
Comment	Physical Contact Information	*unstructured*	Telephone Optional Comments

identify themselves in trading. The `format` field is intended to represent the information of the IANA-registered public-key authentication certificate format, while the `key` field represents the corresponding certificate key.

The `telephonenum` structure (see Table 7.11) specifies the characteristics of a telephone number.

The `contact` structure (see Table 7.12) is used to specify contact information. Services can specify precisely which set of data they need. This includes the postal address, telecommunication, or online address information. Note that this data structure is actually an aggregate of other data structures.

The `postal` structure specifies a postal mailing address, as shown in Table 7.13. Of course, it assumes that you have a street address, so people living in

Table 7.12 The contact Structure

CONTACT	CATEGORY	STRUCTURE	SHORT DISPLAY NAME
postal	Physical Contact Information, Demographic and Socioeconomic Data	postal	Postal Address Information
Telecom	Physical Contact Information	telecom	Telecommunications Information
Online	Online Contact Information	online	Online Address Information

Table 7.13 The postal Structure

POSTAL	CATEGORY	STRUCTURE	SHORT DISPLAY NAME
Name	Physical Contact Information, Demographic and Socioeconomic Data	personname	Name
Street	Physical Contact Information	*unstructured*	Street Address
City	Physical Contact Information	*unstructured*	City
Stateprov	Physical Contact Information	*unstructured*	State or Province
Postalcode	Demographic and Socioeconomic Data	*unstructured*	Postal code
Country	Demographic and Socioeconomic Data	*unstructured*	Country Name
Organization	Physical Contact Information, Demographic and Socioeconomic Data	*unstructured*	Organization Name

Japan will have to substitute a ward address field. Strangely enough, it does not have a provision for post office box addresses either. The list of countries is intended to follow that in ISO Standard 3166.

The `telecom` structure (see Table 7.14) specifies telecommunication information about a person (whereas the `telephonenum` structure only provided information about the structure of the telephone number).

The `online` structure specifies online information about a person, as shown in Table 7.15.

Table 7.14 The telecom Structure

TELECOM	CATEGORY	STRUCTURE	SHORT DISPLAY NAME
Telephone	Physical Contact Information	telephonenum	Telephone number
Fax	Physical Contact Information	telephonenum	Fax number
Mobile	Physical Contact Information	telephonenum	Mobile Telephone number
Pager	Physical Contact Information	telephonenum	Pager number

Table 7.15 The online Structure

ONLINE	CATEGORY	STRUCTURE	SHORT DISPLAY NAME
email	Online Contact Information	*unstructured*	Email Address
uri	Online Contact Information	*unstructured*	Home Page Address

Table 7.16 The uri Structure

URI	CATEGORY	STRUCTURE	SHORT DISPLAY NAME
Authority	*(variable-category)*	*unstructured*	URI authority
Stem	*(variable-category)*	*unstructured*	URI stem
Querystring	*(variable-category)*	*unstructured*	Query-string portion of URI

Table 7.17 The ipaddr Structure

IPADDR	CATEGORY	STRUCTURE	SHORT DISPLAY NAME
Hostname	Unique Identifiers	*unstructured*	Complete host and domain name
Partialhostname	Demographic	*unstructured*	Partial hostname
Fullip	Unique Identifiers	*unstructured*	Full IP address
Partialip	Demographic	*unstructured*	Partial IP address

P3P provides two different structures for addresses on the Internet. One is intended to cover Web addresses, in the form of URIs (see Table 7.16). The data structure actually defines query URIs, because it defines a *stem* component, which is everything up to the `?`. The query string is everything after that. The other structure represents IP addresses and DNS hostnames.

The `ipaddr` structure (see Table 7.17) represents the hostname and IP address of a system. Note that the full IP address can be an IP version 4 or 6 address, whereas the partial IP address can be only an IP version 4 address.

The `loginfo` structure (see Table 7.18) is used to represent information typically stored in Web-server access logs. It is also an aggregate, chiefly of the previously shown data structures.

The `httpinfo` structure (see Table 7.19) represents information carried by the HTTP protocol which is not covered by the `loginfo` structure (i.e., is not collected by all logfile systems). The `useragent` field is derived from the HTTP user agent header and the `referrer` field is the same as the HTTP `referrer`

Table 7.18 The loginfo Structure

LOGINFO	CATEGORY	STRUCTURE	SHORT DISPLAY NAME
Uri	Navigation and clickstream data	uri	URI of requested resource
Timestamp	Navigation and clickstream data	date	Request timestamp
Clientip	Computer Information	ipaddr	Client's IP address or hostname
other.httpmethod	Navigation and clickstream data	*unstructured*	HTTP request method
other.bytes	Navigation and clickstream data	*unstructured*	Data bytes in response
other.statuscode	Navigation and clickstream data	*unstructured*	Response status code

Table 7.19 The httpinfo Structure

HTTPINFO	CATEGORY	STRUCTURE	SHORT DISPLAY NAME
Referrer	Navigation and click-stream data	uri	Last URI requested by the user
Useragent	Computer Information	*unstructured*	User agent information

field, which gives information about the Web page the user previously visited (and is spelled like this in the specification).

The `useragent` field is primarily intended for the HTTP User Agent field, but because it is unstructured, it could also be used for a CC/PP profile. Of course, all this information can be used as a tool for better marketing by the site owner, which does not have to exclude other purposes. But, more importantly, with it we can create a profile of the user, with which we can create a better user experience.

CHAPTER 8

Reasoning about Metadata: Rules and Ontologies

Intelligent agents have been a hot topic in computer science research for at least 50 years. As time has passed, more and more of the functions that intelligent agents were claimed to be able to perform have been integrated into the set of applications we use regularly on the Internet. Search engines and content negotiation are things that were examples of artificial intelligence a few years ago, but today, nobody would claim that they represented the pinnacles of research. This is due to the fact that the presentation is significantly free from the hocus-pocus that has surrounded intelligent agent technologies.

Intelligent agents are software that is capable of executing autonomously (i.e., without active prompting from another piece of software or the user), to realize preset goals. The agent reasons during its selection of actions. It can act on the authority granted by another entity (in the final count, the user). Agents can interact with other agents (through some kind of agent-communication language—although it might as well be through updating profiles when an event occurs). The agents engage in dialogs (with each other and the user) and negotiate and coordinate the transfer of information. Agents are adaptable: they can work on different platforms. They are mobile: they can find information anywhere (on the Internet) that they require to fulfill their goals. The agent is transparent to the user, and they are accountable to him. They are also user-centered. Agents are rugged (i.e., able to deal with errors), and capable of starting themselves.

The usual 80/20 rule applies to agents as well. If we forego 20 percent of the list above, we still get 80 percent functionality. The hard part is telling which 80 percent. But it is relatively easy to construct an agent that uses the Internet to roam for information, executes in one platform only, can fulfill a goal, and follows policies but doesn't act on its own.

Agents on the Internet today are far from the autonomous, goal-oriented, reactive entities envisioned by agent researchers, anthropomorphic front-ends aside. It is a far cry from *The Sims* and artificial life constructs like Norns to Jango and Bargain Finder. It is really more fair to think of them as processors executing policies and inferencing from profiles what the output should be. Which is perfectly fine, because that means they are a good fit with RDF as the language they draw inferences on. RDF gets 80 percent of the functionality of an agent communication language for 20 percent of the complexity.

How Do Agents Make Conclusions?

Agents cannot, of course, make conclusions. They can receive input, make inferences, and generate output.

An inference engine works by using a formal algebra on the text. The simplest such algebra consists of regular expressions (used in, among other things, file search masks in DOS). The computer can compare two strings of text, and based on the rule set provided to it, take an action. If the strings are the same, for instance, it can trigger a rule to add a line. That the strings were a device description and a document description is irrelevant to the process, as is the fact that the line added to the document was a link to a style sheet adapted to the device.

Since RDF is a format for stating predicates of subjects (properties of objects), and the objects are uniquely identified, it is possible to use RDF to draw conclusions. Since each object is uniquely identified, you can know that the properties it has in one statement are the same as its properties in another statement. In other words, if http://historybuff.org/Napoleon has the property French in one statement, and the property Emperor in another, you know that the properties French and Emperor both apply to Napoleon.

That the property of an object can be another object means it can be a class of objects, which means you can state that Napoleon is a member of the class Emperors, for instance. From there, you can continue to use predicate logic, and with that follows all the possibilities that logic implies. Prolog, for instance, is a logic language (predicate logic for computers, actually).

Comparisons of input with stored policies and other input instances can be made using a number of algorithms, string matching being one of the simplest. There are a large number of different algorithms to select information from a set. Applications like this work by comparing the tuples (or triples, in the case of RDF), and not the XML representation.

Predicate logic can handle almost any statements. It was designed to enable expressions of statements in natural language, sentences expressed formally. It includes operands like *and*, *or*, *not*, and *implies*, plus the quantifiers *all* and *some*. This is very similar to RDF, except that there are no logic operands. These would belong in a rules language, which I will talk about later in the chapter, as would the combination of objects into sets. This is a very well-researched area in mathematics, and has been extensively applied to the management of text, in artificial intelligence.

However, a logic language that can express every possible statement—as predicate logic can—will be very complicated. Chomsky's observation is that the grammar of a language (which a rule set is) is a set of generalizations, which comprise a theory that accounts for an individual's observations of the language (which is how children learn grammar by making observations and forming generalizations, otherwise they would not make mistakes). This applies to formal grammars for programming languages, as well as grammars for human languages.

Grammars can be ordered into a hierarchy, from regular grammar to the complex phase-structure grammars that express human languages. Chomsky proved that the less complex a device, the less complex grammars it can handle. A very simple device, which can only receive input and create output, but does not have a memory, can only handle a very simple, regular grammar. For instance, a combination lock can only handle one set of inputs, the combinations; and it can only create one set of outputs, the lock opening or not.

A slightly more complex device, with a one-stack memory, can handle a context-free grammar. Add more memory, and it can handle a context-sensitive grammar. Theoretically speaking, once you add enough memory to have a human, you have the grammar for a human language. And this is precisely where the problem with artificial intelligence is. It assumes that human language can be handled by computers, which in principle would have to be as complicated as humans.

However, computers are not like that. They are simple and stupid. The value of RDF is that it simplifies grammar and language to the extent that it can be handled by a very simple device, such as a mobile telephone.

Languages and Ontologies

Language consists of two main components: words, which express facts, and grammar, which is a set of rules for handling the words. A language is a social contract about which words map to which concepts (and, of course, a host of other things). The rule for the dictionary of concept descriptions is called an ontology. Creating ontologies to describe concepts is one of the biggest remaining challenges of artificial intelligence research.

But, as in a language, you cannot just cut words out of a dictionary and use them in random combinations. The ontology has to fit into a framework that makes the content understandable and processable by the machine. This means it has to follow a grammar. But with computers being stupid, it has to be a simple grammar.

You cannot just start by throwing the dictionary you created out there, however. You need to describe it. A vocabulary is the words you use. But a language does not consist of dictionaries. The order of the words and the grammar of the sentences also convey meaning. You also have to declare what the words are for them to work in the grammar, for instance, whether they are verbs, substantives, or adjectives.

These are the semantics of the statement, the rules to which it conforms in order to be meaningful. In RDF, the Syntax and Grammar document describes the semantics, and RDF Schema describes how you create a vocabulary. RDF in itself is not a finished application, however, but a framework for creating mini-languages in which you can make statements about objects. You create vocabularies that contain your concepts, but they all fit into the same framework. To enable the metainformation to be comparable, you need information that is defined in a schema. And to describe different aspects, you need several schemas.

The important thing, as you probably understand from the reasoning above, is that your language, the expression of your mental model, overlaps that of your readers. One way of doing this is to identify the user group you intend the site for, and then determine which tasks you intend them to perform on the site. Once this is done, you have to structure the canonical representation of your information accordingly. This representation can be a database table, or it can be an XML file, generated by whatever means necessary. You can also start creating representations for your users.

Building Ontologies

The AI crowd will tell you that ontologies will bring world peace, save the whales, and generally be the solution to everything. Just like they told you expert systems would do the same last year. An ontology is, of course, nothing that remarkable; it is simply a specification of a conceptualization. That is, an ontology is a description (like a formal specification of a program) of the concepts and relationships that can exist for an agent or a community of agents. It is different from the way the word is used in philosophy. What is important is what the ontology is for.

Users, devices, servers, clients, network nodes—all these are objects. If they are regarded as such, they can be described in terms of their interfaces. Defining the programatical interfaces is not the issue here; it has been the object of much research and study in the past. The capabilities, preferences, and properties of an object can be described in terms of the functionalities that result from an action involving them (this is what is done in interface definition languages, like IDL). Or they can be described in a higher-level description format, the meaning of which is shared between the interacting objects: an ontology. To decide to use an ontology is to form an ontological commitment. It is an agreement to use a certain vocabulary (for instance, when asking queries and making assertions) in a certain way.

Any body of formally represented knowledge is based on a conceptualization: the objects, concepts, and other entities that are assumed to exist in some area of interest, as well as the relationships that hold among them. A conceptualization is an abstract, simplified view of the world that we wish to represent for some purpose. Every knowledge base, knowledge-based system, or knowledge-level agent is committed to some conceptualization, explicitly or implicitly. Using RDF, you commit to a specific set of conceptualizations, because you base your models on XML and graph theory (think of it like committing to use Chinese characters to write your language). An ontology is an explicit specification of a conceptualization. The term is borrowed from philosophy, where an ontology is a systematic account of Existence (with a capital E). For AI systems, what "exists" is that which can be represented.

Just defining the ontology in RDF is not enough, however. When an active object (e.g., an intelligent agent) wants to conduct an operation on a set of data (e.g., a Web page), it is always done within a context. The context on the Web is static and minimal, consisting of HTML, HTTP, and the TCP/IP standards. It is possible for an agent to have a much richer context to work in, such as the preferences of the user, his geographical location, the time of day, and his surroundings (e.g., whether there are several other devices in his close vicinity—which could imply that he is in a meeting). An intelligent agent acts on this context to personalize the management of information retrieval and message-passing.

So much for the theory. You already know how to create ontologies, which is what you do when you build RDF schemas. But what are they for?

In principle, any information retrieval that includes preconditions is subject to a contract between the sender and receiver. This applies whether this contract covers the privacy policies that one party promises to apply, or whether it covers the content adaptation capabilities and abilities of either party. Expressing these contracts is what you do with ontologies. So, ontologies are about languages for expressing contracts between entities. Ontologies provide a way of capturing a shared understanding of terms that can be used by humans and programs to aid in information exchange. They give you a method of providing a specification of a controlled vocabulary. Simple knowledge organizations such as Yahoo's taxonomy provide notions of generality and term relations, but classical ontologies attempt to capture precise meanings of terms. In order to specify meanings, an ontology language must be used. Agent-based systems to support the next generation of Internet commerce must adopt common ontologies if they are to interact without misunderstanding. By going down to the simplest core of the system, content can be defined that enables both application interoperation and information synthesis. This is a much larger problem than a simple agreement on tag names or mappings between roughly equivalent sets of tags in related standards.

Context becomes especially important in systems that go beyond the traditional client-server environment. In a client-server environment, the client implicitly accepts the context of the server. In peer-to-peer systems, the peers must exchange context to be able to communicate.

Now, a special case of the communication of a context between two active objects is agent communication, and Knowledge Query and Manipulation Language (KQML) is a language for knowledge transfer between intelligent agents. While powerful, it is also slow, and it mixes information and action. It also suffers from the fact that almost all research projects that use it find a need to extend it in some way. Abstracting the transport and expressing the content functionalities in RDF would make it fit into a simpler framework.

When you build a schema, you essentially create an ontology. But it has very few of the formalisms an ontology requires. RDF Schema is actually only a small piece of what is needed to develop a system that can reason about statements independently of human involvement, which, after all, was the goal for the AI work and the very intention of intelligent agent technology. However, that is frequently not what is needed. It is quite sufficient to have a system that enables you to make formal statements within a limited framework. That is what RDF schemas do.

You can understand that even if there is a very large number of RDF descriptions, it is simply not possible to describe everything to everybody's satisfaction. There will always be occasions when you feel you have a vocabulary that describes a topic better than someone else does. It may even be that you are part of a standards group that has designed a specific vocabulary for your area.

In that case, you can easily create and publish your own RDF Schema. All it takes is a URI to publish it at. That needs to be persistent, and you need to make sure the schema is accessible from the Internet at that address. Apart from that, it requires only a bit of sweat and a reasonably good XML editor.

The XML data model is a tree, and that structure is the key to creating your own schemas. You can create a tree structure that describes your site, placing the elements in the leaves and branches. If you remove the specific elements, and instead put in descriptions of them, you have the schema for the XML application you are using. RDF schemas work the same way. The property values and resources you are using are specific to the assertion you are currently making, but which type they are and the other characteristics they have are general. By creating a new vocabulary, you create a new application, and as you have seen, a vocabulary does not have to be very large. It may even be desirable that it not be very large, because that would make it harder to identify the subgraphs you may desire to match.

When you create a new vocabulary in RDF, you do not have to rewrite the entire specification. New vocabularies are introduced through XML namespaces. New RDF schema statements can define their relationship to other vocabulary items.

This goes even for the creation of totally new properties of RDF. New relationships can be introduced through new vocabulary items, although their introduction needs a great deal of care to ensure the semantics are adequately and consistently defined. A general principle is that application-neutral RDF processors should be able to understand and manipulate relationships without necessarily understanding the attributes to which they refer. In essence, you enable the drawing of inferences by matching two property values from different instances of a graph. Imagine, if you will, that the graph you are working with has only one arc. If the resources are the same, and the property value is the same, you can conclude that they are identical. This can be expanded to larger graphs, allowing you to identify which parts of the two graphs are identical.

The problem, of course, becomes what to do when you have identified the non-identical pieces of the graphs. What you really want is a rule language for expressing heuristics (a Greek word meaning rules of thumb). You want a rules markup language. And to reason formally about objects, and especially to let intelligent agents do it, you need something more than the schema: You need an ontology language. As luck would have it, there is such a language that is based on RDF Schema.

The Ontology Interchange Language (OIL) is layered on top of RDF Schema, with the addition of a separate set of elements for reification (statements about statements). Even a simple RDF processor (that only knows the RDF specifications) should be able to get most of the meaning out of an OIL ontology. The layering is done by adding functions to RDF Schema, known as Core OIL. The next level, Standard OIL, contains modeling primitives that are necessary both to provide what the AI world perceives as adequate power of expression (derived from frame-based languages), and to be well understood by existing parsers. This means that semantics can be very precisely specified, and complete inferences are viable. The next level, Instance OIL, allows for database capabilities.

To some extent, OIL and any other ontology language is overkill. When you can describe the domain of your inferences in RDF Schema, it is not necessary to have an ontology layered on top. It is when you want to start doing database-type operations that it becomes necessary. Then, you need to know which datatypes are which. Ontologies are about describing relationships between entities, and that is precisely what RDF does.

OIL adds a formal logic to RDF (even to the extent of expressing it using the symbols usually associated with formal logic). However, although formal logic is fine for analyzing statements by humans, it is overkill in the context of representing machine-understandable statements, at least in my opinion. While you might think the reverse applies, you have to remember that computers are stupid—but, of course, if you work in AI, you assume they are intelligent. Because they are stupid, they are not able to do advanced processing of information, and any logic that is done in a computer is essentially added to it by humans. Subtracting as much as possible of the framework for the representation of knowledge means enabling the computer to perform faster, even if it may not be possible to speak to it. The computer will not know that a rose is a subclass of flower unless you tell it, anyway. And if the processing you want to do can be expressed in a way that fits better into the machine format, the more efficient it becomes.

Hence, it is as efficient to express things in an RDF Schema as adding formal logic to them. It is only when comparing two schemas that a logic framework becomes useful. Much of what ontologies add can be performed as operations in the computer, for instance, grouping objects into classes. RDF Schema provides a more cost-efficient intermediary: The processor may be less complex, and there is less work to create the schemas once the vocabularies are decided on. That is the hard part in ontologies, too.

Intelligent Agents: Communicating Objects

Intelligent agents are a generic name for software programs that can enact instructions independently. They do not have built into them, as software programs usually do, all the logic for what they are supposed to do with a piece of data. Instead, the data can carry with it the instructions for what is to happen with that data.

Intelligent agents have been a buzzword in the computer industry ever since the 1950s, when computers that could reason for themselves were predicted to come into existence (and, by some, to supersede humanity) within a few years. This did not happen, but it gave rise to a large research field which also has influenced psychology and affected our understanding of ourselves to a significant degree (although one thing it has done is disprove its own hypothesis, that humans can be described in the same terms as machines).

Intelligent agents have a number of problems, the first being the name, because, of course, they are not really intelligent. Creating ontologies has been one of the biggest problems for the development of intelligent agents. Often the problem is that the creators of the ontology start from scratch, so everything has to be reinvented. That is fine if your ultimate goal is to produce an infinite series of research papers, but it does not work if your goal is to create a commercial product. And it definitely does not work if your intent is to create a vocabulary that enables reasoning about the content you are providing.

Intelligent agents should be called rule-based systems, because a piece of software cannot, by any definition, achieve intelligence—it is just a series of words. Saying that software can be intelligent is like saying that the book you are reading is intelligent. (Whether a computer can become intelligent is another matter, but we will not enter that discussion now.) Programmers tend to underappreciate their own efforts grossly: In reality, their input to a computer in the form of software is vastly larger than they appreciate, considering how much you give the computer to work with. This is especially true for traditional software. In agent technologies, it is highlighted through the technology used to input information.

The idea behind expert systems (which also should really be called rule-based systems) is that decisions are made according to a procedure that can be documented, formalized, and automated. The description of the objects to be acted upon is the ontology. This means that the goal is to create mathematically formal descriptions of the objects so that they can interact according to the predetermined procedures.

Metadata describes information in terms of different vocabularies; the vocabulary is then described in a schema to define its precise meaning. Having a precise meaning for the vocabulary entry is necessary if a computer is to be able to match it with another vocabulary item. RDF uses the namespace mechanism (essentially, the URI) to make sure each name is unique. So, once you define the properties of the vocabulary item precisely, the attributes of that item will be defined in the same way for all instances of it; the different instances can be matched and the intersection of the two sets can be determined.

KQML: The Agent Communication Language

KQML is a language and protocol for exchanging information and knowledge. It was part of a larger effort, the ARPA Knowledge Sharing Effort, aimed at developing the techniques and methodology for building large-scale knowledge bases that are sharable and reusable. (It has subsequently been replaced by a DARPA project with largely the same goals.) KQML is both a message format and a message-handling protocol to support run-time knowledge sharing among agents. It can be used as a language for an application program to interact with an intelligent system or for two or more intelligent systems to share knowledge in support of cooperative problem-solving.

KQML focuses on an extensible set of performatives, which define the permissible operations that agents may attempt on each other's knowledge and goal stores. The performatives comprise a substrate on which to develop higher-level models of inter-agent interaction, such as contract nets and negotiation. In addition, KQML provides a basic architecture for knowledge sharing through a special class of agents, called communication facilitators, that coordinate the interactions of other agents. The ideas underlying the evolving design of KQML are currently being explored through experimental prototype systems that support several testbeds, in areas such as concurrent engineering, intelligent design, and intelligent planning and scheduling.

KQML messages are designed as strings of ASCII characters (like most other message formats), but this is complicated by the fact that it is restricted by the Common LISP Polish prefix-notation. It is readable to humans, but it is not easy to understand. The messages are called performatives, and performatives take parameters identified by keywords.

Messages require a sender and a receiver, but how they are identified is not specified. The messages are labeled to identify them. The representation language, the ontology used, and the content are the other parts of the messages. The content is the object of the message (in the grammatical sense). It is not possible to define the language using RDF as it currently is encoded, at least not if you want to encode it in XML, because XML cannot be expressed in the LISP syntax used in KQML. However, given a LISP-like syntax for KQML, it would be possible.

KQML is one reason why agent technology is perceived to be so complicated. While this chapter is intended more to give you an orientation in the technologies, you can probably relatively easily see that the functions of KQML map easily onto RDF over HTTP.

Another problem with KQML, which of course was an advantage in the view of the designers, is that it has only a limited number of messages. It is, of course, possible to define additional messages, but not as easily as in RDF. It also forces you to a certain limited number of assumptions about the behavior of the agent that receives the message. This makes it harder to program the system for other behaviors, and it enforces assumptions about the system. But it also tells you how the traditional AI theory assumes that an agent system will work.

The discourse parameters of KQML (see Table 8.1) are intended for "speech acts," utterances stating intent. This is somewhat doubtful from a linguistic

Table 8.1 The KQML Discourse Category Parameters

NAME	PROPERTY	CONTENT	COMMUNICATION	PROCESSING AGENT
ask-if	response required	expression	advertise, subscribe, forward broadcast, facilitation performatives	All
ask-all	response required	expression	advertise, subscribe, forward broadcast, facilitation performatives	All
ask-one	response required	expression	advertise, subscribe, standby, forward broadcast, facilitation performatives	All
stream-all	response required	expression	advertise, subscribe, standby, forward broadcast, facilitation performatives	All
eos	response only	empty	standby, forward broadcast	All
tell	response only	expression	standby, forward broadcast	All
untell	response only	expression	forward broadcast	All
deny	response only	expression	forward broadcast	All
insert	no response	expression	advertise, forward broadcast, facilitation performatives	All
uninsert	no response	expression	forward broadcast	All
delete-one	no response	expression	advertise, forward broadcast, facilitation performatives	All
delete-all	no response	expression	advertise, forward broadcast, facilitation performatives	All
undelete	no response	expression	forward broadcast	All
achieve	no response	expression	advertise, forward broadcast, facilitation performatives	All
unachieve	no response	expression	forward broadcast	All
advertise	no response	performative	forward broadcast	All
unadvertise	no response	performative	forward broadcast	All
subscribe	response required	performative	advertise, forward broadcast, facilitation performatives	All

perspective, of course, because the parties in the discussion are not human, but merely computer software instances expressing the result of their encoding. This goes back to the AI assumption that agents could actually be designed to be intelligent, which, as I have explained in other places in this book, is rubbish.

The idea of the properties listed in Table 8.1 is that the sender queries for or requests information that the receiver has (or does not have). The responses correspond to this. On top of that, there is an advertise-subscribe function, which is actually a different kind of query.

The intervention and mechanics messages, as shown in Table 8.2, are intended to interrupt and handle the mechanics of a conversation. The intention is that you should consider these in the same way as communication between humans, allowing the agents to interrupt a communication, and to apologize for not being able to say more. The assumption is also that the agents are participating in a dialogue with each other.

The idea is that these messages should be replies to a query from the other agent, yet, for instance, enable waiting for a response. Whether a client has to wait before it answers could depend on its having to process another message, for instance.

KQML agents can be facilitators, which means that they assist in the communication between other agents (for instance, sending messages on to other agents and registering agents). Other agents can also request information from facilitators, getting a list of agents who are willing or able to respond to a message.

KQML assumes that all agents are peers, even if the communications system does not (e-mail, for instance, assumes clients and servers). This means that all systems have the same functions, although it would be easy to assume that facilitators, for instance, would be servers. The functions in Table 8.3 allow agents to have a story about other agents and functions they can perform.

Many of a KQML agent's functions are general and could (and maybe should) be realized by a general communications protocol. The fact that you can use filtering on the transport of information just strengthens the thesis I present in this book, however. Agents should not be intelligent, they should be stupid, and you should separate the work so you can optimize it depending on which entities perform the requested function best.

You will have also noticed in the short walkthroughs of the preceding tables that all the properties are either statements that the sender makes about itself or that the receiver makes about the message. This means that it is relatively easy to recast KQML as RDF and enable the agents to use RDF to communicate. Because KQML messages are supposed to be carried in the message body of a protocol anyway, and because the filtering mechanisms based on RDF are

Table 8.2 The KQML Intervention and Mechanics Category Parameters

NAME	PROPERTY	CONTENT	COMMUNICATION	PROCESSING AGENT	PURPOSE
error	response only	empty	forward broadcast	All	
sorry	response only	empty	forward broadcast	All	
standby	N/A	performative	forward broadcast	All	
ready	N/A	empty	forward broadcast	All	
next	N/A	empty	forward broadcast	All	
rest	N/A	empty	forward broadcast	All	
discard	N/A	empty	forward broadcast	All	

Table 8.3 The KQML Facilitation and Networking Category Parameters

NAME	PROPERTY	CONTENT	COMMUNICATION	PROCESSING AGENT	PURPOSE
register	no response	expression		facilitators only	
unregister	no response	empty		facilitators only	
forward	:content	performative		all	
broadcast	:content	performative		all	
Transport-address	no response	expression		facilitators only	
Broker-one	:content	performative	forward broadcast	facilitators only, only if advertised	
Broker-all	:content	performative	forward broadcast	facilitators only, only if advertised	
Recommend-one	response required	performative	subscribe, standby, forward broadcast	facilitators only, only if advertised	
Recommend-all	response required	performative	subscribe, standby, forward broadcast	facilitators only, only if advertised	
Recruit-one	:content	performative	forward broadcast	facilitators only, only if advertised	
Recruit-all	:content	performative	forward broadcast	facilitators only, only if advertised	

simpler to implement than a LISP filtering function, this would be a solution that enables the system to work better than traditional agents. Many of the functions in KQML, for instance, returning a message and stating that it is not well-formed, will be taken care of by XML in the RDF context.

Rule Markup Languages

When you have a policy for how an entity (such as an intelligent agent or a system to safeguard privacy) should behave, you express this by describing the facts which are to be the base of the behavior of the entity, and the rules for its behavior. RDF describes the facts in a way that can be used by an engine which draws conclusions, based on the rules which are fed into it.

This can be extended to a generalized way of describing any program (as consisting of facts, most often expressed as variables, and rules, expressed in programs as if-then statements). The W3C actually has several such rules languages, for instance XSLT, the PICS rules language, and the P3P rules language (which is called APPEL, A P3P Preference Exchange Language), and the XML Query Language, which is still a work in progress.. All of which are actually specialized rules languages. But it is questionable whether you need several different rules languages, in the same way as it is questionable whether you need more than one language to describe relations. All rules can be generalized to the form IF *condition* THEN *action*. The reason the specialized rules languages exist is because they have domain-dependent ways of describing the conditions and actions, but these could be easily expressed in a generalized rules language.

To describe what will happen to an object, it is not enough only to declare the properties of the object. You need to declare which rules apply to the processing of that property (in effect, this is what ontologies often do, by the way). In principle, there are two types of declarations: profiles and rule sets. A profile declares a set of properties, but does not describe actions. A rule set contains the rules for the interaction. They are written in the different rules languages, and they express what action will be taken if a precondition (or set of preconditions) occur.

Context Dependency: A Rule-Based Application

When the declaration meets the rule, processing happens. This can be done entirely automatically, as in context-dependent computing. The computer monitors, and responds to, various aspects of the user's environment, both physical and logical. Apart from the position, physical criteria could include date and time as measured by the computer's internal clock, and temperature or ambient light level measured by attached sensors. Logical criteria include the author of note, date of creation, subject keywords, and the historical period to which the note refers. Typically, the user can specify a set of criteria to describe contexts of interest and these act as search filters, defining which information is made active (or triggered) as the user moves through the environment.

When the user's present context matches the context on a document in the system, an event is triggered. Triggering can cause various actions, depending on the application; for instance, presentation of information to the user (such as the layout of information), running a program, or some other action. The information attached to a context is a program or a script. In most context-aware applications triggering is automatic, which means it is pushed rather than client (user) pulled. The user will still want to retain some control.

Context-aware applications have existed since the beginning of the 1990s. The first applications were based on the PARCTab, a PDA-like device that is really a dumb display terminal with an infrared link to a central server.

The model for a context-dependent application is that the author creates documents and aggregates of documents (for instance, WML cards and decks). One or more compound documents (decks) are loaded into the triggering engine. The triggering engine continually checks all its documents against the user's present context and triggers those that match. This can also be done when the user requests a document, a deck, or a resource in protocols such as HTTP, which is stateless (where essentially no communication takes place between the client and the server between requests).

The communication of parameterizations of the client request is a separate problem that has been addressed by the W3C, and is being discussed in the IETF. The protocol allows you to send user data along with the request, and to cache them. Note that it should also be possible to send data that does not relate to the present location, but rather some location where the user may be in the future. If the future location can be inserted as an override over sensor data, the user will be able to take virtual tours of tourist attractions without going there, for instance. It also becomes possible to use the context-dependent technique to create games.

When a document is triggered, the triggering engine sends the triggered document to the client's user agent, which interfaces with the user. The only programming that is needed in the client is to create the user agent application, with its user interface, and to set up a mechanism so that sensors can continually update the present context; once this infrastructure is in place, any author can create documents without programming effort.

Whether the user agent should be a specialized piece of software or an application on a platform, such as an HTML or a WML browser, has been debated among academics for some time. On the one hand there are advantages to generality, and on the other there are good things to be said of tailoring the user interface to a particular purpose. In practice, however, the customizability of the browser is sufficient that no special-purpose user agent is needed. Indeed, companies like Oracle and IBM have decided not to develop special-purpose client software any more, but trust that the Web can provide ample user interface functions. As long as we are talking about text, the variability of the user interaction is fairly low, anyway.

The basic task of a general-purpose triggering mechanism is to match the user's present context with the contexts and associated information supplied by the author. The trick in providing this customization is to design a matching algorithm which gives the user just the information he wants, with no surprises and no overloading, and makes the authorship of context-aware information straightforward. It is also an advantage if users do not need to understand the mechanism by which triggering is done: to them triggering is something that just happens. For simple applications, even authors should need only a minimal understanding, being able to define just the rules and facts that need to go into the application.

Another feature is that it is easy to make a system based on profiles and rules extensible. If the user adds a new sensor to augment the present context, then information that is not concerned with the output from that sensor should be triggered exactly as before. Information that is concerned with the output of the sensor should be triggered more precisely than before. If the author discovers that the user has a new form of sensor that was not allowed for in the original context-aware document, the amount of change required to cater for this should be minimal. In particular, no existing card in the deck should require changing, though the author might choose to refine some of the cards by adding a field that gives more focused triggering. The author can also choose to add extra cards to cater to the new sensor; this should not, however, adversely affect users who did not have the sensor.

Context-aware documents should not be tied to users who have a particular set of sensors. Instead it should be straightforward to write a document that is suitable for a diverse set of users, having a diverse set of sensors. Essentially, this would amount to constructing a document that consists of a tree structure, where rules are triggered by a combination of facts to create an output document. There may, however, be minimal requirements: many documents would be virtually useless in the field without some sort of location sensing. Minimal requirements should be determined in the document profile. If one of the user's sensors fails, the triggering behavior should continue in as reasonable a way as possible, and the author should be able to give special information to be triggered in such cases.

The University of Kent team designed their own algorithm for matching events with triggers, and which they see as central to triggering. Context-aware retrieval is different from ordinary retrieval: In addition to the matching algorithm, a key part of the model is the way data is represented. The method used to represent data is simple, each document (note) consisting of a set of fields, each of which is a name/value pair. The meanings of the fields (whether they are context or information) are not fixed, but can be determined by the application. The same situation would, of course, apply in an RDF-based solution, where the tags would tell us whether data was context or information.

During the work done at the University of Kent, it soon became clear that users want to trigger context-aware material using all sorts of criteria, just as they use all sorts of criteria for normal information retrieval. The users want filtering on the total information set, not just on the context information. For example, they may want any note whose `<body>` field contains the word *snake* to be triggered automatically when its location is matched, irrespective of any other fields. The rule is that the `<body>` field is a criterion for triggering, as well as the information triggered. This triggering method is reminiscent of the way search engines work, and could conceivably be seen as a search engine with a context filter.

Users and applications, not authors, control how information is triggered. Often this is done in ways the author never dreamed of. The author can, however, make suggestions on how their work may be used. Constructing a set of rules which apply to the facts of the document would enable the author to have more control. This is also true if the author provides a basic set of criteria, for instance in the document profile, for how the facts in the documents are to be handled.

When a match has occurred, triggering often consists of bringing to the user's attention those fields that were not part of the matching process. One problem is which values take precedence: Should a document be triggered if it has a temperature value as well as a position value, and only one of those match? This decision should be regulated in the schema used for the matching.

Rule-Based Content Management: Retrieval and Filtering

I mentioned before that you could filter based on the properties of your site's metadata. It is of course only one of many selection processes that could be done based on the semantic markup you have provided. Filtering is a process of excluding (blocking) things which have certain properties; constructing a set of rules for a set of facts on which the filtering is based. The key to filtering is understanding what to filter and how to filter. This applies equally well for filtering on a document level (e.g., removing words which may be contentious) as for filtering on a network level (e.g., blocking access to sites which may be perceived to be sensitive). Filtering on the network level is the foundation for the W3C PICS standard, a way to create labels and semantics for those labels.

What to filter is a question of selection: specifically, the problem is determining the criteria for filtering. In the case of network-based filtering, they could be determined "upstream" by governments or "downstream" by users of the information. Alternatively, they could be determined by the intermediaries, notably the Internet service providers, in the context of Internet content filtering. Concerns about filtering generally relate to censorship. In contrast, downstream filtering by the user, or at the user's request by a service provider, gives the user total control over the choice of information that he (or those in his care) wishes to access. Note, however, that if the user who exercises control over information access is different than the end-user of the information, there is censorship involved (e.g., for children, censorship by parents or teachers).

In the network-based filtering case, the site can be labeled using the W3C PICS system. A PICS label consists of a service identifier, label options, and a rating. The service identifier is the URI that the rating service has selected for itself, the options give additional information about the document and the rating, and the rating is an attribute-value pair that describes the document along one or more dimensions. A label can be a generic label (identified by the use of the `generic` option), and then it applies to any document whose URI begins with a specific string of characters (specified using the `for` option). This means it can apply to a site or a catalog, but it is not a default label. It can be complemented, but not necessarily overridden, by more specific labels.

The labels can have options defining the date on which they were given, a checksum, who issued the rating (person or rating institute), the URI of the item for which this rating applies, an option that determines whether it is a generic label or not, the date it was issued and the checksum, and a date when the label ceases to apply. There can also be a URI for more information.

These labels are general and do not apply a special filtering action; that depends on the service provider. The same model can be applied to documents. You do not have to mark up every element with every action that you want to apply to it. Instead, you can use generalized markup to provide a marker for an action, and then define the action in a separate rules document, or in the document profile. It is possible to include the PICS label in the head of the document (as you can see the W3C did), and there is also a mapping of the labels into RDF.

It is possible for a third party to rate a resource (just as, by the way, it is possible for a third party to point metadata to a site without the involvement of the site owner). A label bureau is an HTTP server that understands a particular query syntax, as defined in the following code sample. It can provide labels for documents that reside on other servers, and, indeed, for documents available through protocols other than HTTP. Rating services can also be encouraged to act as label bureaus, providing online access to their own labels. By default, the URI that identifies a rating service also identifies its label bureau.

A rating label in the Good Clean Fun system would, for instance, look like this:

```
(PICS-1.1 "http://www.gcf.org/v2.5"
       by "John Doe"
       labels on "1994.11.05T08:15-0500"
              until "1995.12.31T23:59-0000"
              for "http://w3.org/PICS/Overview.html"
              ratings (suds 0.5 density 0 color/hue 1)
              for "http://w3.org/PICS/Underview.html"
              by "Jane Doe"
              ratings (subject 2 density 1 color/hue 1))
```

The label sets ratings in terms of suds, density, and color/hue. These have to be interpreted by the server that receives the label, which has to be translated into action in some way.

Filtering does not happen by itself. The filtering agent, which may be a browser, a separate piece of software, or a proxy, needs input about what to keep and remove. When it comes to defining the rules, however, the question of what to filter is closely related to how to filter. In the network-based case, this extends to where in the information transfer chain the control (the blocking) should take place. PICS includes a specification for creating a rules system that defines how a service should act when receiving a label. It contains some simple verbs (`RejectByURL`, `AcceptByURL`, `RejectIf`, `RejectUnless`, `AcceptIf`, `AcceptUnless`) and mechanisms for constructing rule sets (setting policies). These rules are specific to PICS and they are not mapped into RDF. Mapping the rules into RDF would create a rules language, which would be useful, as we saw in Chapter 7, "Device Descriptions and User Profiles."

Filtering can be carried out in a variety of ways: by blacklisting, where the program checks a list of banned Internet sites and denies users access to a site on the banned list; by whitelisting, where the program checks a list of allowed Internet sites (e.g., "portals" for children) and denies users access to a site not on the allowed list; by using keywords, where the program checks a list of banned words or phrases, and denies users access to a site containing the banned text); and by rating, where the program looks up a rating attached to a particular Web page and denies users access to the page if the rating does not match the parameters set up by the user.

Filtering of text is, of course, nothing new. It was available long before the Web. The interesting thing about filtering based on XML is that the markup is in a text format, but the content of the elements does not have to be. This means that it is possible to filter multimedia, for instance, something not easily done unless the content is marked up in a way that the software can comprehend. This is exactly the reason for the filtering based on labels used in many rating systems: the Web can be used to transfer vast quantities of images, which at present can be filtered only via labeling. However, there is a more important reason, as well: Filtering based on labels allows for different heuristics (rules of thumb, in normal English) to be used on the same content.

Inserting filtering labels in the document is relatively easy. HTML 4.0 defines a couple of attributes that are particularly useful for this. The easiest to use in this context is `div`, because it introduces a hidden division of content. This can then be used to label the information, and the label in turn can be tied to filtering.

Another useful element is `link`, which defines an external link to a document. This could be used instead of the `profile` attribute in the head element. The advantage is that you could have a number of `link` elements, whereas it would be hard to have more than one `profile` attribute.

The `link` element can be used to link to a style sheet, as well as the `style` element. Using the `alternate` and `stylesheet` attributes on the `link` element, you can declare that there are a number of style sheets to select from. Based on the device profile, the system can then select the appropriate style sheet for the current content. The real trick, however, is content selection based on the profile. This could mean not only content selection based on presentation, but on other parameters as well, including the position of the user, the humidity and light levels, the user agenda, and other information. (Actually, that is precisely what this book is about, if you had not understood that yet. Either that, or the generation of content from a database using templates, which of course have to be selected in some way.) Retrieval and filtering are two extremes of a continuum. In information retrieval, user queries may vary significantly during a single session, while the collection of information to be searched is relatively static. In information filtering, user interests are relatively static, but those interests are matched against a dynamic information stream, such as stock quotes. Context-aware retrieval is similar to information filtering in that the present context, and the changing values of the fields within it, represent the dynamic information stream; while the documents are equivalent to a set of different user interests (actually they are the interests, as the author sees them, of the same user in different contexts). However, what is retrieved (i.e., shown to the user) is the document, not the retrieval-awareness, which is the opposite way to approach information-filtering.

A general lesson from the information retrieval field is that there is no single approach that covers all needs, and a combination of approaches is often needed. This idea applies strongly to context-aware retrieval. It is also possible to retrieve not just one, but a number of documents that match the context of the user. One concern is to not trigger too many documents: If the user is flooded with documents as a result of the sensor input changing, we have not solved the problem of information overload. More fine-grained rules and contexts will allow the application to determine if a piece of information is not desirable to the user, even though it falls within the parameters given. (For example, I am probably uninterested in the location of an ice-cream store in winter, even if I am passing by it.) However, one thing that we should have learned from the Internet is, "When in doubt, deliver it." The user can then make his own judgment regarding information relevance.

Context awareness and position relevance are not available on the Web and in WAP today. But the hooks for service providers to start building information systems that increase convenience for the user are already in the standard. And while the networks of today will allow you to build only text-based information systems, the bandwidths that will enable multimedia are not far off. As a matter of fact, the next-generation technologies are already being installed in Japan. Personalization is, in many ways, a special case of contextualization, because the profile that governs the adaptations is tailored to the specific user.

Of course, you could define your own RDF vocabulary for rule markup. After all, that is what RDF is for: You create a set of statements that lead to actions. However, it becomes somewhat problematic if you do it all yourself, at least if you are the only one doing it, and nobody else subscribes to the rules language you have defined. Not to speak of the rules.

Rules are very simple things. "IF you read the previous paragraph THEN read the next paragraph" is a very simple rule. Of course, it would be totally incomprehensible to a computer. On the other hand, as any military officer will tell you, it is quite easy to create very elaborate rule sets in natural language, enabling whole sequences of actions. But now we are giving orders to computers, so we had better do it in a way they understand.

The formal way of expressing rules is unfortunately easier for computers, but harder for humans. It allows you to create the rules upon which the computer should act if it is confronted with a property value from a profile. Creating the rules means creating a sequence of conditions on which instructions are to be enacted. It is very similar to actually programming the system. As a matter of fact, at this stage of the technology, it is doubtful whether it is easier to create the rules than it is to actually do the programming. The declarative approach may be more elegant and efficient in the end, but the rules language is too complicated for an ordinary mortal as of now.

On top of it all, there are actually several different ways of creating rule sets today. You can do it in XSLT, the language used for transformation of one XML variant into another. You can use APPEL if you are creating rules for P3P filtering. And you can do it in a generalized rule language. Because one of the most frequent uses for rules will be to determine how content will be filtered and presented when you are sending it to different terminals, it is very likely that you will use combinations of these technologies, for instance using XSLT to create the conditions, Xpath to address and combine the transformation sheet dynamically, and XHTML as input and output language.

When working with content through XSLT there are basically two ways you can process content: Remove it, or transform it. Transformations do not have to be limited to presentation transformation, but you might want to change the wording of a document when you are displaying it on a very small screen. This has actually been thoroughly researched by the AI community, but the results from natural language processing have taken a long time to filter down into applications.

Filtering, on the other hand, means removal of some material. It can depend on the device capabilities (in which case the material may simply not fit on the screen), or it can depend on the user's profile, for instance age (e.g., pornographic pictures are filtered away if you are under 18).

How much of the filtering is under the user's control varies between vendors in the existing PICS-based systems (which may be intentional, because parents may not want nosy teenagers sidestepping the filtering too easily). Some use ratings from third parties without publishing them, others provide detailed criteria descriptions of their filtering and rating systems. There is also the possibility that the user can fill out a list, either locally or on a server, with sites to be added to or removed from the filtering.

From the user point of view, filtering software management could usually be improved. Generally, there is a tradeoff between customization and ease of configuration (something that goes for all personalization systems, by the way). There is also a tradeoff between flexibility and ease of use.

One application of filtering that we touched on in the scenarios in Chapter 1, "Metadata, Resources, and the Resource Description Framework," is searches based on metadata. Presenting only those sites that have labels conforming to a certain set of criteria is a way of filtering out all other sites. Better searching mechanisms (for example by more widespread implementation of a common set of metadata) would improve the accuracy as well as efficiency of filtering, as well as any search. Searching could also impact the adoption of metadata in that a search engine listing entries according to the metadata descriptions would greatly enhance the usage of metadata. Any search engine can be configured to do searches this way, but at present, the amount of metadata is too small for it to be cost-efficient: a chicken-and-egg problem, as it were.

XSLT and Transformations

Once you have described a document (or rather, information object) using metadata, the description needs to be used for something. It can be matched with other descriptions. If these are in RDF, the matching becomes relatively simple. You can use them to match the properties of other objects with current objects, and you can match it with the properties of your client device.

If we assume for a moment the existence of a RuleML engine that takes profiles and rules as its input and gives XSLT transformation sheets as its output, you will need to define the rules for generation of content. You will also need to define the transformation rules, as we observed in the previous section.

XSLT was developed from XSL, the eXtensible Style Language, because the first step in XSL formatting is a tree transformation. The second step is the formatting itself, but this step is really optional (and can be skipped in XSLT transformations). XSL was designed as a formatting language, but because XML is also an object-oriented system, formatting can mean transformation, reorganizing the content from one source into a structure that can be used in another source. A transformation expressed in XSLT is called a stylesheet. When XSLT is transforming into the XSL formatting vocabulary, the transformation functions as a stylesheet, but it is simpler (and I believe more correct) to think about them as transformation sheets. Another side of transformation is interpreting formatting semantics to suit the presentation in different media. This variable media need generated the XSLT work.

XSL is designed using a declarative approach; XML is used to specify both the "pattern" and the "action" of the rules for rendering items. There is also an escape to an expression language similar to JavaScript if computation is required.

There are many books that do a much better job of describing what XSLT is and what it does than this one. *XSLT:Professional Developer's Guide*, by Johan Hjelm and Peter Stark (Wiley, 2001), for instance. However, a short introduction is probably needed for you to understand what the technologies mean to you. XSLT enables you to create a rule sheet for transformations (a transformation sheet) and apply it to a processor that takes the markup and, by using the rules, transforms it. It is actually possible to transform content using XSLT, too.

A transformation expressed in XSLT describes rules for transforming a source tree into a result tree. The transformation is achieved by associating patterns with templates. Patterns are matched against the elements in the source tree, and the result tree is created by creating instances of templates with content from the source tree. Result and source trees are separate, and the structure of the result tree can be completely different from the structure of the source tree. In constructing the result tree, elements from the source tree can be filtered and reordered and arbitrary structure can be added. For the transformations to work, both the input document and the transformation sheet have to be well-formed XML.

XSLT applies the transformation sheets recursively, but you can apply different transformation sheets to different elements in the document you start with. Instructions can select the elements they should process. There are also conflict resolution rules in XSLT, as there may be patterns that match more than one instruction. The most specific pattern wins.

Transformation sheets drive XSLT. They are a set of template rules made to match the source tree. This is a simple pattern-matching of the regular expression. The template is a piece of a result tree or an instruction of how to create a result tree that is associated with a place in the result tree. You can match against text, content, elements, attributes, and even to some extent count them (although it should be stressed that XSLT is not a programming language—for anything beyond transformations, you probably want to use something more powerful).

A precondition for the transformations to work is that the input document be well-formed. This means that it has a tree structure (it can have a tree structure even when not well-formed, but that structure might not be as readily usable). The instructions for creating patterns depend on where in the document tree things appear. The transformation sheets are also XML documents, so they can be transformed themselves if necessary. They must also be well-formed.

XSLT allows for general transformations: You can move things around, add parameters, "any transformation you can dream of," according to Henry Thompson, one of its authors. You can filter things out, copy duplicate parts, add things, and generate content, context, elements, and attributes.

The transformation sheet is basically a set of rules that explains how to go from source to result. You can stop before the actual formatting step, which means that the result of a transformation of an XML document can be HTML, or another XML document, or something completely different (for instance, a database format). You could create an HTML document containing only DIV and SPAN, and associate a stylesheet with those, if you want to generate only the empty template. XSLT can also transform HTML to XML.

For example, the following creates an HTML paragraph from an element `<person>` with the attributes `given-name` and `family-name`. The generated paragraph will contain the value of the `given-name` attribute of the current node followed by a space and the value of the `family-name` attribute of the current node.

```
<xsl:template match="person">
  <p>
   <xsl:value-of select="@given-name"/>
   <xsl:text> </xsl:text>
   <xsl:value-of select="@family-name"/>
  </p>
</xsl:template>
```

The transformation sheet and the original document are fed to the XSLT transformation engine, and the result is the output. All you need to do to transform XML to another XML format using XSLT is to pass through the XML elements within the transformation sheet, filling those elements with the values from the original XML document as you go. In many ways, it is similar to a database operation.

The output of the transformation is totally independent from the source. The tree structure can be walked through in any predictable order, not necessarily in the order that a parser would handle it. The resulting tree, however, is created as if it were a product of parsing. It can use any vocabulary specified—which is why it can translate from one XML application to another.

You can use XSLT to filter data, too, using the select attribute. The following expression will filter out all items that have names that are smaller than M (the less-than sign, <, is <, which also has to be escaped as in the following example, when used inside text).

```
<xsl:for-each order-by="+ type" select="item[name$lt$'M']"
xmlns:xsl="http://www.w3.org/TR/WD-xsl">
```

Patterns can extend to children and descendants of the target element, using the same element types (element, target-element, and attribute but not any). The example that follows will match employee elements, provided they have at least one salary child.

```
<target-element type='employee'>
 <element type='salary'/>
</target-element>
```

One thing this example demonstrates, by the way, is that whether you use attribute or subelement in the content model is fairly arbitrary.

Because you are now defining patterns for the transformations, there is always the risk that two rules may match and the patterns may collide. To avoid this, there is a set of precedence rules, which basically says that the richer pattern has precedence. If the precedence rule is not sufficient, you can apply importance and priority attributes to set the precedence for which rule should guide the transformation.

The results of XSLT transformations are still independent of presentation. The same results of one single transformation sheet can be rendered on different types of presentation devices: An XSLT processor is to interpret the result tree according to the semantics defined in XSL. It is quite possible to express the result of a transformation as a printer file, for instance; this was the original impetus for the design of the language.

When you transform XML documents using XSLT, the result is expressed using the vocabulary that you specify in the transformation sheet. The content is not touched. This means that the XSLT process can produce non-XML output, which can then be interpreted in other formats, so you could use XSLT to transform XML into HTML or SQL (Standard Query Language, the language used in most relational databases), then send it into a database directly.

An XSLT transformation sheet is an XML document, and as such, it must identify the namespace prefix that is used for the XSLT vocabulary. It has to use the standard XSLT vocabulary, specified at www.w3.org/XSL/Transform/1.0, as the transformation vocabulary URI. It is, of course, possible to use extensions to the XSLT recommendation, but these must then be specified by another URI. The common prefix for names in stylesheets is `xsl`, but it is not mandatory. You are, however, required to use the `<xsl:stylesheet>` or `<xsl:transform>` element from the vocabulary as the XML document element. The resulting vocabulary must be identified with the prefix `result-ns="prefix"` (where `"prefix"` can be any name) to identify the resulting vocabulary to the XSLT transformation engine.

As a transformation sheet writer, you can also use `<xsl:message>` to communicate with the user. This element contains an unstructured message that is communicated to the user by the transformation engine.

You have to create a new transformation sheet for each XML application you want to transform, but once created, the transformation sheets are general and can be used to transform any document in that language into any other language.

The P3P Rules Language: APPEL

When a user gets a policy that he cannot accept, there must be a set of rules to describe what he can do about it. This is what the W3C P3P working group has created with APPEL (see Table 8.5). The rules enable a rather limited set of behaviors: accept (the evidence is acceptable, provide the information requested), reject (do not provide information based on this policy), inform (show the information to the user and ask if the information is to be provided), and warn (show the information to the user and ask if the information should be provided, even though there is an automated policy for this). There are no provisions for rules where one set of data is collected only if another set is collected (e.g., zip code is requested if address is supplied). It is also limited to P3P policies matched with metadata sets.

Users can either provide rules themselves, or they can reuse rules created by others. The idea of the working group is that rules should be published by service providers and applied as each occasion arises. Rules apply within the opening and closing elements of `<APPEL:RULE>`.

Rules have to pass a separate application, an evaluator. The evaluator returns the behavior (as specified in its behavior attribute) of the rule. Rules trigger based on inferences made from the user's policy and the policy presented by the site. The rule evaluator may also return an explanation string (which can be displayed to the user) containing the name of the persona and/or the rule that was triggered. All rules in APPEL are evaluated strictly in the order they occur in the file.

There are three basic types of expressions: the expression, which uses attribute- and contained-expressions to match a full XML element; the attribute expression, which matches a single attribute and its value in an XML element; and the contained expression, which recursively matches contained subelements of an XML element.

An expression always consists of an element identifier (XML element name), an attribute expression (not necessary), a contained expression (not necessary), and a connective (which is optional). A connective is an attribute of an expression that determines how any contained expressions will be matched. By default, attribute expressions within an expression are implicitly ANDed together, if there is no connective. There are four connectives: or (one or more of the contained expressions are matched), and (matches if all the contained expressions can be found), or-exact (matches if one or more of the contained expressions can be found; if there are more expressions, it fails), and and-exact (matches if one or more of the contained expressions can be found; if there are elements not listed in the rule, matching fails). The last is the default matching semantics, if there is no connective.

Rules contain behaviors, an optional persona (a persona is a repository where user data can be stored), an optional explanation, and a number of expressions. If there are no expressions they will automatically evaluate to false. Expressions can only be `<POLICY>` or `<APPEL:REQUEST>` elements, or the degenerate expression, `<APPEL:OTHERWISE>`. Instead of matching it against the policy, the rule evaluator must always evaluate this expression to true. The attributes of the rules are always treated as strings by the application. If there is more than one expression, they will always be evaluated against one single policy (evidence in the APPEL parlance, which also contains URI and XML elements). There is a wildcard character, *, which can be used in attribute expressions to match ranges of values such as `<DATA name="User.*">`, which evaluates to all users.

The APPEL elements are combined with the P3P elements to create rules, as in the following example:

```
<POLICY entity="W3C">
  <STATEMENT APPEL:connective="and">
  <PURPOSE APPEL:connective="or-exact">
         <current/>
```

```
    </PURPOSE>
    </STATEMENT>
  </POLICY>
```

The following is an example of an APPEL rule set containing five rules that will trigger in order.

1. A "reject" rule (i.e., a rule with the string "reject" in its behavior attribute) will reject any policies asking for identifiable data that is distributed to 3rd parties.
2. Using an explicit match for the request URL, an "accept" rule then accepts a policy if, when connecting to www.my-bank.com, the requested data is only distributed to the bank and its agents.
3. An "accept" rule checks to see if only non-identifiable clickstream data and/or user agent information (such as browser version, operating system, etc.) is collected, and accepts if dispute information is available.
4. An "inform" rule matches any requests for the user's name for non-marketing purposes and initiates a user prompt informing the user that a site wants to collect her name under acceptable circumstances.
5. If none of the other rules matches, a "warn" rule encapsulating the degenerate expression `APPEL:OTHERWISE` will trigger, warning the user to (cautiously) decide on any policy that has not been covered by any of the preceding rules.

```
<APPEL:RULESET xmlns:APPEL="http://www.w3.org/2000/APPEL"
                crtdby="W3C" crtdon="13-Nov-1999 09:12:32 GMT">
   <APPEL:RULE behavior="reject"
      description="Service collects personal data for 3rd parties">
     <POLICY APPEL:connective="and">
       <STATEMENT APPEL:connective="and">
         <DATA-GROUP APPEL:connective="or">
             <DATA category="physical"/>
             <DATA category="demographic"/>
             <DATA category="uniqueid"/>
         </DATA-GROUP>
         <RECIPIENT APPEL:connective="or">
           <same/><other/><public/><delivery/><unrelated/>
         <RECIPIENT/>
       </STATEMENT>
     </POLICY>
   </APPEL:RULE>
   <APPEL:RULE behavior="accept"
      description="My Bank collects data only for itself and its
agents">
     <APPEL:REQUEST-GROUP>
       <APPEL:REQUEST uri="http://www.my-bank.com/*"/>
```

```
      </APPEL:REQUEST-GROUP>
      <POLICY APPEL:connective="and">
        <STATEMENT  APPEL:connective="and">
          <RECIPIENT APPEL:connective="or-exact">
            <ours/>
          <RECIPIENT/>
        </STATEMENT>
      </POLICY>
    </APPEL:RULE>
    <APPEL:RULE behavior="accept"
       description="Service only collects clickstream data">
      <POLICY APPEL:connective="and">
        <STATEMENT APPEL:connective="and">
          <DATA-GROUP APPEL:connective="or-exact">
            <DATA name="Dynamic.HTTP.UserAgent"/>
            <DATA name="Dynamic.ClickStream.Server"/>
          </DATA-GROUP>
        </STATEMENT>
        <DISPUTES-GROUP>
          < DISPUTES service="*"/>
        </DISPUTES-GROUP>
      </POLICY>
    </APPEL:RULE>
    <APPEL:RULE behavior="inform"
       description="Service only collects your name for non-marketing
purposes (assurance from PrivacyProtect and TrustUs)">
      <POLICY APPEL:connective="and">
        <STATEMENT APPEL:connective="and">
          <PURPOSE APPEL:connective="or-exact">
               <current/><admin/><custom/><develop/>
          </PURPOSE>
          <DATA-GROUP APPEL:connective="or-exact">
              <DATA name="User.Name.*"/>
          </DATA-GROUP>
        </STATEMENT>
        <DISPUTES-GROUP APPEL:connective="and">
          <DISPUTES service="http://www.privacyprotect.com"/>
          <DISPUTES service="http://www.trustus.org"/>
        </DISPUTES -GROUP>
      </POLICY>
    </APPEL:RULE>
    <APPEL:RULE behavior="warn" description="Suspicious Policy. Beware!">
      <APPEL:OTHERWISE/>
    </APPEL:RULE>
  </APPEL:RULESET>
```

In APPEL, the elements of the language can have attributes, which give information about the elements (for instance, their origin). Different elements have different attributes, as Table 8.5 demonstrates.

Table 8.5 The Elements of APPEL

ELEMENT	EXPLANATION	ATTRIBUTE	EXPLANATION
<APPEL:RULESET>	Denotes the beginning of an APPEL rule set	persona	Identifies which of multiple user data repositories should be used.
		crtby	Name or ID of the rule author
		crton	Time and date of rule set creation
		description	Short text explanation that can be displayed to the user
<APPEL:RULE>	Conditions under which a certain behavior should be carried out by the calling program	behavior	Behavior that should be carried out by the calling program if the expressions match
		persona	See under RULESET above
		crtby	See under RULESET above
		crton	See under RULESET above
<APPEL:OTHERWISE>			
<APPEL:REQUEST>	Allows creation of rules that apply to a specific domain	uri	The URI of the domain

XML Query Language

The first public drafts of the XML query language were published as I was working on this book, so what is said here may have been surpassed by a new, more refined, and hopefully better version by the time this book comes out.

The idea behind the XML query language is to create a language to make queries into large XML data sets and get a result—much the same way that SQL allows queries into large data sets in a relational database. Queries are based on the concept of XML as a tree, and the data model used borders on the RDF model. It is not a graph model (only nodes are first-class objects, not edges—arcs in RDF are edges), but it has a concept of nodes that can include identities. Nodes can be one of eight node types: document, element, value, attribute, namespace (NS), processing instruction (PI), comment, or information item. There can be fourteen types of attributes: String values, Boolean values, floating-point values, double values, decimal values, time duration values, recurring duration values, binary values, URI reference values, ID values, IDREF values, Qname (Qualified name) values, ENTITY values, and NOTATION values.

In the database world, it is common to translate a query language into an algebra: there are algebras for SQL and several other query languages. Having an algebra gives the semantics for the query language, meaning the algebra has to be well-defined in order for the operations of the query language to be well-defined. The algebra is also used to support query optimization. The laws in the XML Query language include analogues of most of the laws of relational algebra.

Types can be used to detect errors at compilation of queries, and to support query optimization. DTDs and XML Schema provide type systems (although not formal type systems) for XML. The XML Query algebra type system is based on the datatypes in XML Schema to represent the datatypes in the XML document. The type system is static, which means that it can be used to check the output type of a query on documents conforming to an input type when queries are being compiled, rather than when they are being run (note, though, that this assumes that the XML query processor will be similar in construction to query processors for SQL).

The algebra looks for all instances of an element and returns its contents, conditional on other expressions included in the algebra. The simplest operation is Projection, which returns all elements that correspond to the selection contained in the specified elements contained in the data set (document). The Selection operator (Where) selects values that satisfy a given predicate. The queries can also be used to restructure data, reorder, sort, count, and remove data, much as operations can be done on data in XSLT. Like SQL, it is also possible to join data sets using queries.

Queries can be grouped into functions, which take one set of data as input, and return a second set of data. (e.g., *for b in bib0/book do where notauthor("Buneman"; b) do b*). In general, an expression in the XML Query Language of the form

```
where e1 do e2
```

is converted to the form

```
if e1 then e2 else ()
```

where e1 and e2 are expressions (e.g., patterns and actions), and () is an empty data set, that is, no data will be returned. Clearly this, too, is a rules language.

Web of Trust and Digital Signatures

Agent systems have an enormous problem: How do I know that the other guy is who he says he is, and that he will do what he says he will do? For persons as users, this has been addressed by P3P, but authentication is not part of that specification. Using digital signatures, it is possible to validate the signature by verifying that the certificate used to create the signature belongs to the entity who claims to have sent it (because there is a central certification agency in the public key infrastructure, which guarantees that all certificates are unique). Of course, you have to trust that entity to really provide unique certificates, and trust that it provides certificates in such a way that nobody can steal them and misuse them. You then extend that trust to anyone using a certificate to sign messages directed at you.

In practice, though, our trust threshold is much lower than this. We will trust a brand, for instance travelocity.com, to provide a service and not misrepresent itself. If we are suspicious, we might check that the brand is using encryption, for instance TLS, to make sure that the data does not get intercepted and manipulated in transport.

This is because as humans, we can make a judgment call when we are interacting with a service. We can decide not to send a hundred dollars to mafia.com, even if it presents itself as a benevolent association for persons of Sicilian extraction. We can decide not to give our personal details when we think something looks suspicious. Of course, we are not always aware of the consequences, which is what P3P attempts to highlight.

Say you are in the habit of giving a hundred dollars to a charity each month. You do not care to handle this yourself, however, so you decide to automate the process using a piece of software that acts on your behalf—an intelligent agent. Intelligent agents come in many flavors and sizes; the only thing they have in common is an assumption of acting more independently than other software programs. In this case, it may be enabled to perform a set of actions when an event occurs. Say your calendar program shifts to a new month: It will then log into your bank account and order the payment of a sum of money to a charity you have chosen.

But what if you do not want to give the money to the same charity every time? You could give the agent a list of charities, but new ones appear all the time. Or you could give the agent a set of rules by which to look at the metadescriptions of charities, and then let it select which charity you want to donate money to yourself.

Let us assume, for instance, that you want to assist people with Italian ancestry. The agent would have to compare the description of the charity against a dictionary that broke down the terms used into smaller elements (e.g., Palermian is a subset of Sicilian, which is a subset of South Italian, which is a subset of Italian). It would then use the rules to decide which description came closest to the goal and act on that, authorizing the payment. You would check it once per quarter, maybe, if you were prudent. An agent, however, does not have any inhibitions. If we create a policy to donate a sum of money to a charity each month, it will gladly allow transfers to mafia.com. They said they were a benevolent association, didn't they?

Who somebody represents themself as is a different problem from making sure the data gets to them. The representation is a matter of policy, defining a set of rules for enabling the agent to act in a manner that is consistent with the way you wish it to act. This is more complicated than it may seem, because agents are unforgiving—there is no margin for error.

As humans, we tend to trust each other, and we trust someone else to recommend someone for us. This also goes for languages, even if we may discover that we have been grievously misunderstanding the other party. Here, using RDF and other knowledge-representation languages actually has an advantage, because it enables us to verify the stated meaning against the schema.

Trusting people whom other people we trust have recommended to us creates a web of trust. The recommendations are a social service and do not have to be part of any technical system. The trust may depend on the circumstances, however. We may trust the drugstore clerk to provide us with AA batteries, but we would not trust him to sell us a new car. The role a person assumes determines the level of trust we extend to them. It can be the same with agents, even though this has not been formalized in any agent communication language. For instance, I could create a policy for my agent that says "trust any agent that comes from an insurance company more than any other agent when it comes to buying insurance." This would suggest, of course, that the agent had a way of representing itself officially. Digitally signing its communications with both its own certificate and the certificate of the insurance company is one such way.

In the abstract architecture of the Foundation for Intelligent Physical Agents (FIPA), there is only a simple form of security: message validity and message encryption. In message validity, messages can be sent so that it's possible to determine the message has not been modified during transmission (e.g., by signing the message digitally). In message encryption, a message is sent in such a way that the message itself is encrypted, so that the message content cannot be read by others (e.g., using TLS). This is shown in the FIPA abstract architecture using attributes in the envelope; in HTTP, this would mean having additional header fields. Message validation and encryption is treated like any other type of message transformation.

The W3C has also worked out a technology for digital signatures, making it possible to sign documents electronically. However, like all the prevalent encryption schemes, it is based on the public key infrastructure (PKI), where certificates are allocated to individuals or companies based on identification. This takes place entirely offline. When you apply for an electronic certificate, it is granted to you based on verification of your identity by submission of a copy of your passport, for instance.

There is much to say about PKI, and the security and authentication systems that would be required for the semantic web to work would require a book of their own. There are already several good books on this topic, so I will not go into it further here.

CHAPTER 

Implementation Advice: When Intelligent Agents Meet RDF

There is a lot to learn from the knowledge representation industry if you want to implement a system using RDF. After all, they have already had a lot of the problems you will encounter, but they have often created their own specialized formats for representing the knowledge in their domain, and not used a general format. Sometimes, however, the knowledge representation formats are strikingly similar to RDF. This chapter summarizes some experiences from the RDF Interest Group mailing list, and from experience with knowledge representation systems such as the CommonKADS model.

In principle, a system using RDF can be implemented in two ways (actually in quite a number of ways, but there are two which are more likely): as a database system, or as a distributed system. They can be combined, databases being local components of distributed systems. But the principle is centralized versus decentralized. A database management system is usually run in a central server, with clients communicating with it. A distributed system can consist of peers who exchange information. This model is more likely in an agent system where there is not a central authority such as a bank or corporate database to update. It is also more likely in a model where users will be contributing to the content, because contributions can be exchanged only between concerned peers.

This is something new, but societies of agents have actually been around for quite a while—in universities. The MIT Media Lab has made them famous, but there are a large number in existence at other universities. They are not very difficult to implement, but they require a different mindset than the centralized database system. Even such a system will probably have to have some peer component, because it is becoming more and more frequent for database systems to exchange information, for instance in e-commerce systems where the catalog system needs to exchange information with the logistics and payment system, which in turn needs to talk to the bank and the ordering system, and so on.

In peer-to-peer systems, the unit of interchange is the transaction. HTTP, the protocol used on the World Wide Web, is actually a transactional system, even if we do not often think about it as such.

Separating content and action enables you to send an instruction to an agent and then get back a result, treating it as a black box and not caring about what the agent actually does. After all, if it gives you the result you expected, why should you care? As a matter of fact, while this way of thinking may sound strange, it is exactly the reason high-level computer languages were invented in the first place. It used to be that programmers had to write assembly code (itself an enormous advance over punched cards or, even worse, setting switches on the front panel of the computer).

This also implies that you could separate the reasoning engine from the user agent. This is a different architecture than systems have today, but in line with the emerging architecture of the Internet where proxies fulfill a capability server role (expressed, for instance, in the architecture of the WAP Forum).

In traditional software design, you would use the communications and knowledge models as requirements for the design of the software, creating, as it were, an architecture—a description of how the different pieces are combined. Now, I am assuming the architecture is different. Instead of creating an entirely new program from scratch every time, I assume that we create a set of agents once, and then send them assertions that they act upon. The closest comparison may be with routers and gateways in the networking world. A gateway acts in a specific way upon every packet it receives, depending on the protocol. A router just forwards it to the appropriate address. Consider the agents we are building to be like routers, but they not only forward single packages, they can also copy them and send them to inference engines (which may be part of the same agent, to be sure), which then create other assertions that can be acted upon by either forwarding them to the appropriate receiving agent or to a specialized interface agent.

If it made your head spin, it is not because it is complicated, it's just because it is different. But then, I remember how hard it was for the computer world to get its head around client-server architectures. This is very similar (although, of course, entirely different!). But you will note that this, also, constitutes an architecture, albeit an architecture where your house is composed of prefabricated elements, not one where you have to do everything from sawing the lumber to painting the windows.

A software architecture describes the structure of the software in terms of subsystems and modules, as well as the control mechanisms through which the models and subsystems interact. What I sketched out above is a reference architecture for a generalized agent system acting on assertions, and it should be seen as such. As with all reference architectures, it is a skeleton that can be instantiated for specific systems by selecting the appropriate modules and functions.

I will develop some specific aspects a little later in this chapter, but because this is an area where research is ongoing, the advice I can give you is fairly general. After all, I am in the process of implementing the stuff myself (to license it, contact your nearest Ericsson office).

Preserving Structure at the Cost of the Software

Generally, building a system will be much easier if you do not have to deviate from the reference architecture, but can use it as a blueprint for the system you are building. That you may have perfectly good reasons to deviate from it, for instance because you found a method of improving performance of the system as a whole, is a different matter. As long as you do not change the interfaces—which in this case are the assertions and the functionality interfaces—your implementation should be interoperable with other implementations. This is essentially a black box approach that enables you to ignore the specifics of the system. It is as if I were giving you a blueprint for a house, and then you were free to build the walls from wood, stone, brick, or whatever you liked. Of course, there is necessarily an interaction between the design and the implementation that may not be entirely simple to address. For instance, it is quite likely that if you, for some strange reason, want to implement your system in COBOL (you may be the last surviving COBOL programmer, what do I know?), you will have to make design choices that direct what input your system can accept. Now, that is the traditional way, but it is clearly not acceptable in the architecture I am proposing. If your software requires the assertions to look a certain way, how am I supposed to know that? It is far easier to specify a general format for the assertions, and if your system cannot handle it, then that is what has to be changed (for instance, by providing it with an interface agent).

This means that we preserve the structure of the assertions at the cost of the software. Of course, as a self-respecting programmer, you know that you are a master of the universe and the users should grovel before you. However, if you look around your cubicle, you will see that the situation in reality may be somewhat different, and by giving them the standardized interfaces you can create something worthwhile and still ignore what they think. The structural preservation is of the interfaces, not the software architecture.

The preservation of the structure of information content and the structure presented in the analysis models should be present in the finished artifact. This is a relatively new design principle, but it allows you to design your system by adding detail. It also allows you to start with scenarios, as I did in the beginning of this book, and then add assertions to those scenarios. What I am asking you to do now is add implementation detail to those assertions. It all makes perfect sense for your project manager, because this is a much more efficient way of designing a total system, so you might as well get used to it.

Apart from making your project manager happy, this design principle also ensures that you can meet a number of quality criteria for good software design. These include the following:

The reusability of code. One of the primary tenets of object-oriented design is the ability to reuse individual code fragments. This becomes impossible if you design your system as a monolith, where all the components are intermingled (another name for this design philosophy is component design). Reusability does not happen on one level alone, but can be done at many different levels of systems. It also reverberates through the design of the semantic Web, for instance by enabling you to reuse style sheets instead of composing the style in each document every time.

Maintainability and adaptability. Because the model keeps adding implementation detail to a very general scenario, you can go back and trace inconsistencies—and analyze the way they will affect the services provided. This implies that a scenario-based design model is not finished, but that it will continue to evolve until the software is done, when it also contains its own documentation.

Explanation. Because you started out by describing scenarios, breaking them down into assertions, expressing the assertions as interfaces, and the interfaces as software, you have a documentation of your system as well as an explanation for the rationale for it, all wrapped up into one. This, by the way, also gives you the knowledge-elicitation support that many traditional knowledge systems have such a hard time expressing (i.e., telling why you apply something in a certain way in terms of the universe of discourse of that domain).

Let me demonstrate how to use this method. First, let us take one of the scenarios we created in Chapter 1. Say, the one where Lara is trying to find a decent stylist. Here it is again:

Lara Mann is looking for a grooming service for her poodles. As a Los Angeles stylist, she realizes the importance of her dogs' image for her own image. She does not have the time to take care of them herself, however, so she needs to find a dog stylist close to her home. She takes a look in the yellow pages.

Under "Dog Care" there are a number of stylists, including three on the street where Lara lives. It does not say when they are open, however, nor whether they are any good. Two of them have very nice advertisements, but Lara had a horrendous experience with a hairdresser once, and she knows better than to trust advertisements. She is a member of the Poodle Owners Club of San Joaquin Valley, however, so she sends out an email to her friends and asks whether they have had any experience with the stylists near her.

While she is online, she also finds a couple of Web sites with poodle information, featuring consumer reviews of stylists. After reading a few of them (although they are all anonymous), she gets a really bad feeling about one of the stylists (who had the biggest advertisement). But when she gets the answers to her e-mails, the other ladies are overwhelmingly positive.

Poor Lara does not know what she should think. How is that stylist really? Whom should she trust? She ends up taking her poodles to one of the others, who colors the dogs bright red instead of cool pink, and cuts Soviet flags into their coats as well as Stalin mustaches. She regrets not choosing the stylist she was doubtful about, who meanwhile has given her neighbor's poodle an incredibly tasteful treatment.

We start by analyzing the information flows, structuring the information that the transactions will contain (this, of course, has to be done as generalized transactions). This means modeling the application as rules and profiles describing the facts that are being asserted about the objects of the transactions. Another aspect of designing the structure of the application as facts and rules is to design the presentation formats, how it will be presented to the user.

To create the structure of facts, we need to add the assertions. First, formalize the descriptions; create a schema for the vocabulary we are going to use; then apply the vocabulary to create the assertions. After having created the facts, we can see which rules we need to apply to the facts to create the desired output. Both these steps can be done in a traditional systems development tool, such as Rational Rose. However, because the output is not code, but data structures, you have to create "stereotypes" (as they are called in Rational Rose) to describe the facts and rules. These are the real output of the system. It is no longer necessary to output code.

The next step is to combine the facts and rules with interface agents and inference engines. The information will be input to an inference engine, which will create a template for the output based on the input heuristics and generate the output. Finally, put the protocols in place.

By the way, if you worry about this not being scalable, that is a very valid concern. Most agent societies work fine as long as you keep them below a hundred users and inside the same local area network. Well, there is a simple way of avoiding any concerns. Let's use the same mechanisms that we use on the Web for addressing and transport. After all, the Web scaled from one computer to millions (if not billions) in a little more than five years. It's hard to think about anything that scales the same way, actually.

Interestingly enough, because the information primitives we discussed in Chapter 6 are all request-response type transactions, they map well onto HTTP. Of course, messages are not hypertext as such, but this does not matter. They can either be transported in headers (such as the proposed `accept-feature` header of HTTP) or in the body of the message. HTTP has all the functions you need to exchange information, even if it is a bit clumsy when you try to return a message from a server to a client (you have to use HTTP POST or HEAD, and in that case you must create a new header). If the entities interacting are peers, as agents would be, the client-server–oriented method clearly does not work well (of course, a workaround is to make the client a server as well, but this is just a hack and does not solve the problem of bidirectional interaction). There is work ongoing to solve this, both in the IETF and the W3C, but the scope of this book does not include it. And anyway, although there are results published, there is no clear consensus around a standard. There most likely will be, because, as you can see, this method is so much more efficient for designing distributed systems.

User Requirements for System Distribution

Why must the systems be distributed, you may ask. There are two simple reasons: The first is the privacy of information. In a system where the user selects which information to give out, he will be in control of what happens to his own information, as well.

The second is one of information sharing. If all agents can interact with a central database, well and good. But in real life, I will be shopping with someone who does not have all my information. (I do not even want them to have all my information!) And my friends may have their information with service providers other than the one I am using.

I am certainly not going to change friends just because they prefer another service provider. (It is more likely that I will change service providers.) So the information had better be interchangeable between service providers, otherwise the users will simply vote with their feet and go to the one where most of their friends are.

Interchangeability can be achieved using standards for information exchange, of course. SQL is one such, but it is almost hard to describe as a standard any more, because each vendor tends to add proprietary components to it. XML is a better choice, because the extensions are transparent, as we saw in Chapter 3. And of course, RDF is encoded in XML. So for assertions, RDF works well.

In the architecture I sketched here, you have three types of components: inference engines, handling agents, and interface agents. There are different implementation concerns for each of the three.

Inference engines have actually been implemented in a number of cases, but mostly as database systems. Often, they have been built in Prolog, the logic programming language. Inferences are about logic, after all, and ontologies are described in a format that is intended for inferencing.

Interface agents are a different matter again. Here, there is actually some experience from interfacing to older systems, where the agent masquerades as an input and output device toward the system. This experience comes from both corporate systems and the Web, where a lot of old database systems have been provided with a Web server interface (often interfacing through a transaction engine). This means a limited set of interactions, but of course these old systems are limited by definition.

The handling agents have not really been implemented before, because the functionality they represent typically has been combined with that of the inference engines in the case of intelligent agent systems (one reason they scale so badly).

Now, you might ask yourself why the world needs yet another method to develop software. After all, you have been doing fine without methods up to now, right?

And that is just the point. Methods so far have been designed to develop software, not systems. The entire chain from user to database needs to be taken into account. And it needs to include documentation. Anything that is added as an afterthought (such as user interface design and documentation in traditional methods) gets half done, if at all.

Of course, there is still a lot you have to think of as you implement software to use RDF. Some general pieces of advice that apply to sound software design anywhere are as follows:

Make the code reusable. By declaring the role of the code elements, it becomes possible to reuse them automatically. The code fragments can be very different, of different granularity and types.

Build in maintainability and adaptability from the start. Preserving the structure of the analysis model makes it possible to go back and retrace the implementation steps, back to a particular piece of the model. Because the objects are independent, you can change one object without changing all. Of course, you did this in your college classes in object orientation, but you may not have done it since, especially if you are working at a traditional software company.

Explain and document what you do. The method allows for much more documentation and explanation than other methods. It may take a little more time, but if you are building an experimental system, that is all for the good. You should be able to look at a piece of domain knowledge and ask yourself in which part of the problem solving process it is used, and which role it plays there (this also goes for fortware, of course). Because the model is documented in the schema, it becomes possible to read it and use the structure for explaining the processes.

Let users extend the knowledge. Because the model is human-readable, it is possible to use it as documentation, and even to let the users extend the knowledge in the model, given appropriate editors. It also becomes possible to locate errors and problems that constitute gaps in the knowledge, if you have a tool that allows you to visualize the schema.

Knowing what you want to do when you implement an application can also be a great help. And in doing so, a reference architecture can be useful. FIPA, the Foundation for Intelligent Physical Agents, has developed such an architecture. To some extent, the document overlaps the XML architecture that I have described in the previous chapters, either because the two sets of specifications try to describe the same concepts, or because they have converged.

The FIPA Reference Architecture

The FIPA reference architecture document describes an abstract architecture for creating intentional multiagent systems. The idea is to use it to ensure interoperability between different agent implementations, and to achieve that, the specifications for the agent systems are expected to build agent systems that conform to the FIPA specifications (as well as any other specifications they may be written to).

The reference architecture is based on a model for agent communication which assumes that agents pass semantically meaningful messages between them, in order to achieve whatever task is to be accomplished by the application. Initially, the focus was on a single protocol architecture, but it soon became clear that it would be useful to support variations in the messages. This included the message transport, the format (strings, objects, or XML), and message attributes such as encryption and authentication.

Very few systems can be implemented from scratch using a multiagent architecture. It became necessary to integrate it with existing software environments, like different distributed computing platforms and programming languages, different message passing platforms, different models and systems for security, directory services such as LDAP, and technologies that allow for intermittent connectivity—the latter especially important in a wireless environment, where it is not possible to guarantee a continuous connection between the agents. The world also changes continuously, and specifications will need to develop accordingly. To avoid having to produce a new version of the base specification every year, FIPA decided to create a reference architecture that could accommodate a wide range of commonly used mechanisms, such as various message transports, directory services and other commonly commercially available development platforms.

An abstract architecture does not only allow for interoperability, by specifying a set of abstract interfaces which the implementations should conform to. It also enables reusability of agents. To enable these two goals, the common elements of the architecture need to be specified. Instead of specifying them as dependent on a particular implementation, the commonalties between implementations are identified (i.e., when they use different technologies to achieve the same functionality), and a set of architectural abstractions can be specified. If an implementation conforms to these, it will be able to interoperate with other implementations of the same specifications, even though it does not use the same technology. It also becomes possible to discover the relationships between agents and agent systems. Interoperability also becomes easier if systems share a common design (even if it may mean a tradeoff in terms of performance). An analysis of how senders and receivers are identified—and how messages are encoded and transferred—leads to an architecture built of abstractions, involving messages, encodings, and addresses.

Interoperability at an abstract level is hard to describe, though. In the context of the FIPA architecture, it means semantically meaningful message exchanges between agents. The FIPA architecture specifies a minimum set of functions, but does not prohibit those that extend it. These minimum functions include mechanisms for agent registration, agent discovery, and interagent message transfer. They have to be described in terms of the corresponding elements in the FIPA abstract architecture. A designer, however, has considerable latitude in how the actual implementation realizes the abstract specification. A specification for an implementation can describe all the functional elements of the FIPA specification, or it can describe just one element (which can be reused in several implementations).

Not all features can be described in the abstract, and some must remain implementation-dependent. There is very little consistency in the mechanisms used in different systems or in how to address and use those mechanisms. Concrete specifications will have to address these issues, but it is not clear how to provide a unifying abstraction for these features. So the FIPA architecture simply deemed items like agent lifecycle management, agent mobility, and domain descriptions to be out of scope. The architecture also does not address application interoperability. In the abstract architecture, agents which communicate using a shared set of semantics (such as represented by an ontology) can potentially interoperate. That is the level where RDF comes in.

The FIPA architecture defines at an abstract level how two agents can locate and communicate with each other by registering themselves and exchanging messages. The messages represent speech acts, which are encoded in an agent-communication language (such as KQML). To enable communication, a set of support services for the agents is required. Services can be implemented as application programming interfaces (APIs), or as agents in themselves. In that case, their behavior will be more restricted than agent behavior traditionally is because they have to preserve the semantics of the messages they are passing. The current version of the abstract architecture defines two support services: directory services and message-transport services.

Directory services provide a place where (agents) register directory entries. Other agents can search the directory entries to find agents with which they wish to interact. The directory entry should contain three things: a unique agent name, a locator (that describes the transport type and the transport-specific address needed to communicate with the agent), and a set of optional descriptive attributes, such as what services the agent offers, cost associated with using the agent, restrictions on using the agent, and so forth. These are represented as keyword-value pairs.

If it were not for the requirement for keyword-value pairs, the agents could easily be represented in RDF (because a URI is both a unique name and a locator in a transport protocol). A search engine or a database could then be used as a directory service. Agent interactions would then be a matter of exchanging profiles describing the agent and the service requested.

When an agent wants to provide a service, it first binds itself to a transport. Depending on the transport implementation, this can be done differently. In the case of an e-mail service, the agent needs to start a message-receiving agent (POP, IMAP, or X.400), and a sending agent (SMTP or X.400). In practice, it could just interface to the regular e-mail software, using interfaces such as Microsoft's Mail Application Programming Interface (MAPI). In HTTP, it would need to start a server (to be able to receive messages via the HEAD or POST methods). It can also contact an ORB, register with an RMI registry, or establish itself as a listener on a message queue. The agent can then be addressed via one or more transports.

Now the agent can send and receive messages, but the rest of the world does not know this. When it has established one or more transport mechanisms, the agent must advertise itself. It does this by constructing a directory entry and registering it with the directory service. The directory entry includes the agent's name, its transport addressing information, and a set of properties that describe the service. A stock service might advertise itself as "agent-service com.dowjones.stockticker" and "ontology org.fipa.ontology.stockquote"—or, using RDF,

```
description about agent-service://stockticker.dowjones.com
fipa:ontology="stockquote"
```

Having registered itself with the directory service, other agents can look it up by searching the directory (in an implementation-specific way). If the search is done in a meta-search engine containing metadescriptions (instead of Web page indices), the agent which orders the search can then select the service which fits its needs from the metadescriptions, and contact it directly.

In FIPA agent systems, agents communicate with one another by sending messages. There are two aspects of the messages passed between agents: the structure of the message itself, and the message when it is being prepared to be sent over a particular transport. A FIPA-message is written in an agent communication language, such as FIPA ACL. The content of the FIPA-message is expressed in a content-language, such as KIF or SL. The content language can refer to an ontology as the basis for the concepts being discussed in the content. The FIPA-messages also contain the sender and receiver names, expressed as FIPA-entity-names, which are unique names for an agent.

If HTTP and RDF were to be used, the ontology would be expressed using the XML namespace (according to some definitions, it may even *be* the namespace). There would be no agent communication language, but there would be a content language—which would be RDF.

When a FIPA-message is sent it is transformed into a payload and included in a transport-message. A payload is the message-encoding representation appropriate for the transport. In HTTP, this has been abstracted away. It would correspond to WBXML (the binary XML tokenization in the WAP architecture), which is not part of the protocol. The transport-message is the payload plus the envelope. The envelope includes the sender and receiver transport-descriptions, which contain the information about how to send the message (via what transport, to what address, with details about how to utilize the transport). The envelope can also contain additional information, such as the message-encoding representation, data-related security, and other realization-specific data that needs be visible to the transport or recipient. There may be additional envelope data included as well. The combination of the payload and envelope is a transport-message. In terms of HTTP, the message body would be the payload, and the headers the envelope.

If there is more than one transport and the agent decides to switch transport in the middle of the communication (something that is not disallowed in the FIPA specification, even if it may be impractical), the agents will still be able to recognize each other because the names are unique; therefore the receiving agent may still continue to reason about the sending agent, providing services to it even though the message transport changes.

When designing the system itself, you start with the system architecture. As we described above, you can actually design the system using the assertions as a starting point. You can draw this as a block diagram, or of course you can use a Unified Modeling Language (UML) design tool. But at this level, the granularity should be low, consisting of the functions you need to implement.

Modeling Your Application: Using UML

Before you start designing a Web site, you probably create a number of diagrams that describe it. You do layouts and diagrams that describe how the different parts of the site link together. When you create the metadata statements about your site, you essentially create an information application. If there were an easy way to go from a well-defined modeling system to RDF, you could create your statements directly from the model.

As luck would have it, there have been several attempts to translate UML into RDF. UML is as close as you get today to a universal modeling language, and it was developed by merging a number of development methods created by some of the driving people in object-oriented analysis. UML is a framework for describing a set of models that capture the functional and structural semantics of any complex information system. There are six levels of models in UML, which go into progressively more detail about the application design.

- Use case model (states the user requirements)
- Class model (captures the static information structure of objects)
- State model (describes the dynamic behavior of objects)
- Activity implementation model (describes work unit actions)
- Interaction model (models scenarios and message flows)
- Deployment model (describes how software subsystems are allocated to hardware components)

UML is intended as a language to model applications before development (one reason being to break them down into objects that can be reused), and it follows a development method that is a synthesis of several object development methods. Because programming languages contain declarative constructs for declaring data (like statements in RDF) and procedural constructs for sequential, conditional, or repetitive logic (like rules), they can be seen as abstractions of the language and defined in a metamodel (the exact constructs used when you develop the application are described in the model, of course). Which programming language you use when you develop the application does not matter. The metamodel is the same.

The level above the programming, where you describe the concepts you will use, is the meta-metamodel. This maps into the highest level of UML, where the concept descriptions are formalized.

UML models are described in diagrams and, as such, it would be possible to map them into labeled directed graphs. Not all diagrams can be mapped into RDF, however. UML is a very rich language, and it has a number of constructs that do not map well into RDF. The RDF Schema model is equivalent to a subset of the class model in UML. RDF Schemas use labeled directed graphs to describe schemas. Class schemas expressed in UML can also be viewed as labeled directed graphs. The RDF Schema graph is isomorphic to a subgraph of the UML class schema graph, because RDF Schema elements map directly into UML class model elements.

Given that UML class models actually describe the static information structure of objects, they maps well into the static information structures of RDF (static, that is, in a metasense—they may change, of course). RDF class properties map to UML class attributes, and RDF properties and property cardinality constraints map to UML associations and association constraints. RDF Schema does not have any counterparts to the other UML modeling areas, but would have to be extended. There have been attempts to do so too, but as long as what you want to model are not the states, activities, interactions or deployment models of UML, but the classes and use cases, there is no need to extend RDF.

UML class diagrams are a part of the structural model view of UML, which contains the classes and associations used to describe the system. Classes are descriptions of sets of objects with common structural features, behaviors, relationships, and semantics. They can have properties and be of types, just like resources in RDF. It is possible to draw RDF graphs as UML class diagrams, but the other way around is hard, because the UML class diagrams have more properties and methods than the RDF graphs.

Modeling in UML begins with use cases, which map well into a simple agent-based development model. From use cases, a use case diagram can be created describing the user view of the system, of which the class structure is only a part. This makes it possible to go from the use case via the class diagram to the RDF description. However, there are many good books about designing UML models, so I will not go into it here.

When you have created the abstract UML model, you identify the implementation platform. Unfortunately, there is no such thing as operating-system independent code (no more than device-independent presentations), and other software which you select will affect your choice. For instance, if you use Apache you will have a totally different integration architecture than if you choose Microsoft IIS. However, using a platform abstraction like servlets allows you to implement with a relatively high degree of independence.

Then, specify the architectural components. Identify the subsystems and design the detail. One simple way of doing it (if you are not using UML) is to take the functional diagram and extend it. This means that you preserve the structure of your design, because, of course, you started with the information and worked your way down to the architecture.

Finally, specify the individual components within each functional block. Use the analysis model as a guide for which components the blocks consist of, and then see if there are reusable components, or if you have to build entirely new ones. If you do, you can make both a second and third level of granularity, because the components need to be implementable.

Most often, the architecture is created in three steps: decomposing the system into subsystems, building the control regimen, and breaking down the subsystems into software modules. These architectural steps are essentially performed in the following design steps, so you will not have to perform them unless you are implementing new components in the last design step.

We have been assuming you are going to build an object-oriented system, and this is partly dependent on the fact that object-oriented systems are much more efficient than traditional systems when it comes to redesign and modification. This is useful whether you are building an experimental system or a production system. One way of modeling the system is the model-view-controller (MVC) model that was used in Smalltalk, but it is an abstract model and not in any way tied to using an object-oriented environment, if you do not want to.

The model has three major subsystems: the application model, the views (external views on application functions and data), and the controller.

- The application model is the subsystem that specifies the functions and data that together serve to deliver the functionalities of the application. In RDF-based systems, the application models contain only the reasoning functions, not the data structures, which are separate.
- The views subsystem contains the external views on the application, such as visualizations of the objects in terms of the human-computer interactions, but also in terms of SQL queries and other external interface definitions. The views make the static and dynamic information of the application available to external agents, such as users or other software systems. Typically there are multiple visualizations of the same object.
- The controller subsystem is the central command-and-control unit of the entire system. In most applications, it is an event-driven system, allowing for both internal and external events. It defines its own view objects and implements the communication model for the system, in particular the control information specified in the communications plan and the transaction elements (when the system is modeled as a transaction system).

A control structure also involves the performance of tasks. Tasks are the performance of an action or a method when initialized, in this model by an event. Tying back to the previous discussion, tasks can be documented as assertions in RDF.

A task object needs to perform two things: It needs to be initialized, setting the values for the task at hand; and it needs to execute the task method. Using RDF as the control language simplifies the creation of the control structures, because you have already decided on the control language.

One of the most important tasks in a system like this is the inference, the drawing of conclusions based on the input data. Inferences can be done in many ways (this has been the main topic of much of the AI research for several years), but one of the simplest ways is if you view the RDF graphs as trees and compare the leaves of the trees, generating a resulting tree that is the compromise. The inference is of course determined by the policies—which can be seen as yet another graph in RDF.

This method is by far the simplest, but there are more intelligent ways of doing it. The functional block does not specify how the inference should be done. There is open-source software available, and as we stated previously, this has been documented in several years of AI research. How the inference should be done is a matter of cost and requirements. (Essentially, what is your target platform, and how much does it cost to implement?)

It does help, however, if you know there is a way to arrive at a conclusion before you start trying to conclude. In this case, it means structuring the assertions in such a way that they can be used to arrive at a conclusion. It does not really matter how complex it is in practice, as long as you know it can be done. This is called an automated deduction view in knowledge representation. In practice, it means structuring the schema in such a way that the properties can be matched.

The object which performs the inferences (in the discussions above, the inference engine) can use one single inference method (and actually, as in the case of many CC/PP systems, be limited to one single schema), or it can use several. In practice, it turns out that many applications do perfectly well with a simple rulechain and set selection to derive the result tree. This is entirely an implementation issue, and more is not always better, because some inferences may call for speed, but others may call for matching multiple schemas in complex ways.

The views you construct onto the system receive the input from, and present the output to, agents that are external to the system. In traditional design, you would have had to create an entire library of objects to perform these functions; in object-oriented design, you can call a set of input and output objects; but if you are building a system which is interacting with the external agents in text format (and most systems are in practice—very few systems can actually handle multimedia input), the easiest way is to create an interface to a Web server and use HTML forms or Xforms to receive the input and present the content. This does not imply that you should create the forms as part of the inference. Rather, you specify what input and output you want to receive, and specify the input and output formats in terms of templates.

When designing the architecture specification, you derive the functions from the assertions, first specifying them in terms of functional blocks. Then, you add system specifics, such as implementation-specific issues.

Using a Search Robot to Find RDF Files

Resource discovery is one of the biggest problems for intelligent agents. How do you know when things you need to know will show up? In principle, this is an unsolvable problem, as it is not possible to know about something without being alerted to it, either by checking constantly, or having a registry which either checks constantly or alerts you automatically.

A simple solution is to combine a registry with a search robot. You request that the resource register its URI with the registry, and when new entries occur, send out the search robot to retrieve the information and index it. Indices can be reused, of course, and made available to more than one client. Registration could also be done automatically by a proxy, for example, when the user first retrieves the page, the proxy could automatically download the metafile (if one existed), using the OPTIONS method in HTTP (because it is talking to a server), and cache it. In transcoding proxies, this could then be used to automate adaptations of pages depending on user wishes.

Most search engines commercially available on the Web do not index metafiles separately. There are, however, several search robots available for use. One of them is the W3C search robot. Like all search robots, it follows the links in a page to get to the next page it should index. It has only a command line interface so far (but it works under Windows, Windows NT, and Unix), and it is delivered as part of the Libwww demonstration library of Web applications. It can be run using commands from the command line, or a configuration file (which can reside on a Web server).

If you set the robot to find metafiles for documents, you essentially create a catalog for the domain you are indexing (e.g., your intranet). Because there is no registration procedure, the robot will have to rely on all sites being linked at the meta level (if that is how you restrict your search). In an intranet, there could of course be a central registry for all sites, which would enable you to send out the search robot and retrieve the metafile when the site registered itself.

The W3C Webbot does not have an option to only look for certain file types, but it does take regular expressions, so you would have to use those to include only files that contain configurations. No file types are designated for this as yet, but you could use the .rdf file type, because it is likely that it will be an rdf file.

However, rdf is also of the mime type text/xml, and so could be stored with the .xml file type. This may complicate finding it, however.

The W3C Webbot can not only log data to a log file, it can also log it to a database. It uses MySQL, and if it is combined with a file download (also part of the W3C library), the RDF data could be automatically downloaded into the MySQL database, and retrieved with the Algae mechanisms used for the annotation server. This is an excellent way of collecting remote annotations, too.

CHAPTER 10

RDF Tools: An Overview

These reference materials apply to the entire book. I have not included any footnotes in the text, nor have I divided the references by chapter. Instead, I have divided them into sections according to their content. This is intended to assist you in your reading, not be a listing of research topics. As such, you may find it to be too introductory. Well, good for you! You are already an RDF master.

As with all lists, this is a subjective selection. I doubt it is even possible to create a comprehensive bibliography of the area. Nor is it desirable, since that would be unreadable. Any omissions and errors are the fault of the author.

The Web sites referenced were available at the time of writing (February 2001), but neither the publisher nor the author can take any responsibility for their availablility at the time of the publication of the book. Sorry, that is how it is with best-effort information provisioning.

This chapter is both a references section and a tools listing. The Semantic Web is a dynamic field, and there are new things happening all the time. Even if I wanted to, it would not be possible to list everything. And the underlying philosophy would require a book of its own. I will probably provide some of the philosophy at the Web site that accompanies the book.

You may also wonder why there are no books listed here, only Web sites. The answer is simple: Most of the immediate information is only accessible online. This is actually the first book about the Semantic Web! I will list some books on the Web site, but they are only secondary sources, to read about the philosophy and the underlying technologies used.

A specification for a data format is not much use if there is no data. In a computer environment, it is also worthless if you have to do everything by hand. But RDF has been around for quite a while, and there are both schemata and tools available for you to use in working with your information. However, as this is a rapidly developing market, and one that is changing on a daily basis, this list will be outdated when you get it. See it as a help in finding out which tools are available.

Most of these tools are free. Most are also open source. Open source software makes the source code available so you can modify it and correct errors, but if you want to use it in commercial products, special terms often apply.

RDF Specifications and Additional Reading

- **Resource Description Framework (RDF) Model and Syntax Specification (www.w3.org/TR/REC-rdf-syntax/).** Ora Lassila and Ralph R. Swick; W3C Recommendation February 22, 1999.
- **Resource Description Framework (RDF) Schema Specification 1.0 (www.w3.org/TR/2000/CR-rdf-schema-20000327/).** Dan Brickley, R.V. Guha; W3C Candidate Recommendation March 27, 2000.
- A much more accessible description of the data model than is found in the specifications can be found in **Resource Description Framework: Data Model Summary (www.w3.org/2000/09/rdfmodel/).** Dan Brickley; RDF Interest Group Discussion Document, September 8, 2000.
- **W3C Resource Description Framework (RDF) Resource Page (www.w3.org/RDF/).** The official W3C Web page for RDF.
- **W3C RDF Interest Group (http://lists.w3.org/Archives/Public/www-rdf-interest/).** A discussion list that has been going since August 1999 and sometimes becomes very deep; however, if you are looking for information on specific aspects of RDF and their development, look here. The home page of the group also contains a lot of discussion items around the future development of RDF **(www.w3.org/RDF/Interest/).**
- **Dave Beckett's Resource Description Framework (RDF) Resource Guide (www.ilrt.bris.ac.uk/discovery/rdf/resources/).** Much more comprehensive (and easier to read) than the corresponding guide at the W3C pages.

Semantic Web Philosophy

The W3C has summarized a lot of information about what it intends to do in the following activity statements and documents:

- **Metadata Activity Statement (www.w3.org/Metadata/Activity.html).**
- **W3C Semantic Web activity statement (www.w3.org/2001/sw/Activity).**
- **W3C Collaboration and Annotations page (www.w3.org/Collaboration/).**
- **W3C Data Formats (www.w3.org/TR/NOTE-rdfarch).** Tim Berners-Lee; W3C Note October 29, 1997.
- **Semantic Web Road Map (www.w3.org/DesignIssues/Semantic).** Tim Berners-Lee; September 1998.
- **Web Architecture: Describing and Exchanging Data (www.w3.org/1999/04/WebData).** Tim Berners-Lee, Dan Connolly, Ralph R. Swick; W3C Note June 7, 1999.
- **Metadata Architecture (www.w3.org/DesignIssues/Metadata).** Tim Berners-Lee; January 6, 1997.
- **Distributed XML (www.xml.com/pub/a/2000/09/06/distributed.html).** The role played by XML in the next-generation Web; Edd Dumbill; September 6, 2000.
- **Java, RDF, and the "Virtual Web" (www.earthweb.com/dlink.resource-jhtml.72.1061.|repository||common|content|article|19990901|gm_rdf1|rdf1~xml.0.jhtml?cda=true).** Leon Shklar; September 1, 1999.
- **The CC/PP philosophy: "How Would You Like That Served?" (www.xml.com/pub/a/2001/01/31/ccpp.html).** Didier Martin, in XML.com, January 31, 2001.
- **European Commission workshop on the Semantic Web (www.cordis.lu/ist/ka3/iaf/swt_presentations/swt_presentations.htm)** (presentations) and **(ftp://ftp.cordis.lu/pub/ist/docs/ka3/sw_wsproc2.doc)** (report).
- **The Semantic Web community portal (www.semanticweb.org/).** Addresses a number of areas other than those strictly related to RDF, but which have to do with the Semantic Web.

RDF Parsers

Parsers take over after the XML processor, translating the XML representation into an abstract form of the RDF data model. A parser is necessary if the application on the next level is to make sense of the data. There are a number of free and/or open source parsers available.

- **PerlXmlParser (www.w3.org/1999/02/26-modules/).** A set of CPAN modules written by Eric Prud'Hommeaux of W3C. It implements an RDF SAX parser and a simple triple-database interface for PERL (which has been extended into the Algae SQL database interface). The perllib was born of a need to implement an RDF infrastructure at W3C. This is currently used for access control and annotations, but will be used for a more diverse group of applications as our needs evolve; poor documentation. Annotea, the W3C's project to demonstrate RDF annotations to documents, uses Eric's software, but it has been integrated into an annotation demonstration system; more information at http://annotest.w3.org/ (requires both a specific editor and a specific server).
- **The ICS-FORTH Validating RDF Parser (VRP) (www.ics.forth.gr/proj/isst/RDF/).** Parses RDF Statements and validates them against an RDF Schema. The parser analyzes syntactically the statements of a given RDF/XML document according to the RDF Model and Syntax specification. The validator checks whether both the RDF Schemata and related Metadata instances satisfy the semantic constraints implied by the RDF Schema Specification. Written in Java; well-documented; understands embedded RDF in HTML or XML; full Unicode support; semantic and syntax checking of both RDF Schemata and Metadata instances, Statement validation across several RDF/XML namespaces; based on standard compiler generator tools for Java CUP/JFlex; currently in alpha release.
- **DATAX (www.megginson.com/DATAX/).** DATAX is a new Java 1.2-based library intended to simplify the exchange of structured data records using XML written in any RDF-compliant format (it requires no built-in knowledge of specific document types). The current version of DATAX is 1.0 beta. DATAX is based on the Java2 Collections package. It is not designed as a general purpose RDF implementation. Some of the more obscure RDF features are not supported in this release.
- **RDF Filter (www.megginson.com/Software/rdffilter-1.0alpha.zip).** A streaming Java- and SAX2-based filter and handler interface for RDF processing. Unlike DATAX, this interface does not build an in-memory tree, and should be suitable for very large RDF documents. The beginnings of a general-purpose RDF test suite are included with the distribution. Implemented in Java.
- **XWMF (eXtensible Web Modeling Framework) (http://nestroy.wi-inf.uni-essen.de/xwmf/xwmf.html).** Provides a number of tools, including an RDF parser (a modified version of the XOTcl RDF parser). The XWMF tools consist of several parts:
  - An RDF parser for processing RDF data models according to the RDF Model and Syntax Specification (www.w3.org/TR/1999/

REC-rdf-syntax-19990222). Currently not all RDF constructs can be processed. The rdf_parser is a modified version of the xoRDF - Version 0.9 (beta) an XOTcl based RDF parsing system. It requires TCL and the XOTcl package. XOTcl (pronounced *exotickle*) is an object-oriented scripting language based on MIT's OTcl.

- The rdf_handle tool for processing and querying RDF data models. The results (RDF triples) generated by the rdf_parser can be read by the rdf_handle. It is able to store the data of RDF data models in a suitable way and builds up a base for further processing of this data. One of the features of the rdf_handle is a query language similar to SQL. By means of the rdf_handle query language it is possible to query the triples of an RDF data model using a query string. The result is a subset of triples fulfilling a query.

The source code is commented in English; however, documentation concerning the source code is not available.

There is also a library module, with (XO)Tcl-Scripts that are useful for more convenient programming, and a package containing the TclXML parser (Version 1.1.1) written by Steve Ball. The TclXML parser is also available at www.zveno.com/zm.cgi/in-tclxml/.

- **Libwww (www.w3.org/Library/).** Contains an integrated RDF parser. The Libwww is the W3C free demonstration library. This RDF parser is based on Janne Saarela's Java-based SiRPAC and James Clark's expat XML parser.
- **SiRPAC: a Simple RDF Parser and Compiler (www.w3.org/RDF/Implementations/SiRPAC/).** SiRPAC is a set of Java classes that can parse RDF/XML documents into the 3-tuples of the corresponding RDF data model. The documents can reside on local file system or at a URI on the Web. Also, the parser can be configured to automatically fetch corresponding RDF schemata from the declared namespaces. It can be used as an embedded system, as well as run from the command line. SiRPAC builds on top of Simple API for XML (SAX) documents. There is also an online service at the URI above, which can be used to visualize the RDF graphs.
- **RDF Graph, RDF Parser, and Promenade RDF Parser (www.pro-solutions.com/download/).** The RDF Graph PERL module provides graph-level access to the data model of RDF. An application can now import an RDF/XML document, make changes or query the data model, and finally write out XML-encoded transfer syntax, if necessary. The RDF Parser PERL module implements a translation process from the RDF/XML document into the corresponding 3-tuple (triple) representation of the underlying data model.

The Promenade RDF parser is written in Java and implements a translation process from the RDF/XML document into the corresponding 3-tuple (triple) representation of the underlying data model.

SWI-Prolog Parser (http://swi.psy.uva.nl/projects/SWI-Prolog/packages/sgml/online.html). The source code for this RDF parser is less than 700 lines. It parses about 400 Kbps on a Pentium-II/450, according to the authors. It is based on Prolog, which many people regard as a good vehicle to reason about RDF statements. The RDF parser itself is written in ISO Prolog. The XML parser is written in ANSI-C. There is no standard for interfacing Prolog and C, but the interface is relatively small.

repat (http://injektilo.org/rdf/repat.html). A callback-based RDF parser built on James Clark's expat. It's implemented in Standard C; open source.

Dan Connolly of the W3C has written an **RDF parser in XSLT**; highly experimental **(www.w3.org/XML/2000/04rdf-parse/).** Another XSLT RDF Parser was written by Jason Diamond; it includes support for containers, rdf:value, and rdf:parseType and an XSL template that parses RDF when run through an XSL processor (http://injektilo.org/rdf/rdf.xsl).

Demonstration Services and Online Resources

- **RDF Schema Explorer (http://wonkituck.wi-inf.uni-essen.de/rdfs.html).** An online demonstration by Wolfram Conen/Xonar and Reinhold Klapsing, University of Essen, Germany, based on the SWI-Prolog RDF parser by Jan Wielemaker.
- **FRODO RDFSViz (www.dfki.unikl.de/frodo/RDFSViz/).** A tool that provides a visualization service for ontologies represented in RDF Schema; can also be downloaded.
- Dan Connolly's **Dublin Core extraction service (www.w3.org/2000/06/dc-extract/form).** Takes HTML and XML data and generates an RDF encoding of Dublin Core metadata for the file.

The SiRPAC RDF parser is demonstrated on the W3C site, as shown in Figure 10.1. It allows you to paste an RDF document into a form and get a visualization of a graph, triples, and a validation of the RDF, as in Figure 10.2.

The RDF parser which Janne Saarela, the chief designer of SiRPAC, created when he quit the W3C is available as a demonstration online, as shown in Figure 10.3. Results are presented as subject, predicate, and object (see Figure 10.4), and not visualized, as in the W3C service.

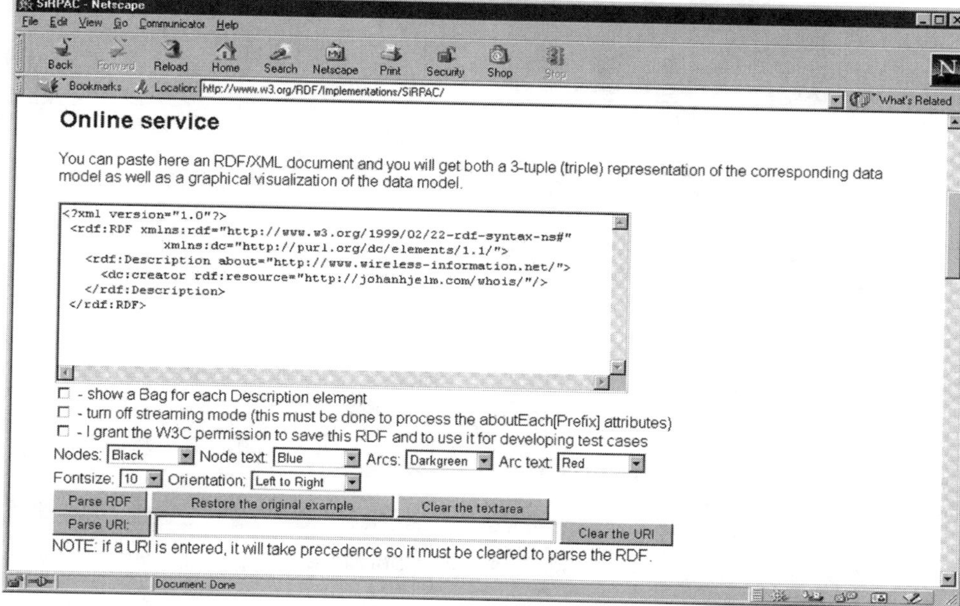

Figure 10.1 The SiRPAC demonstration online service input window.

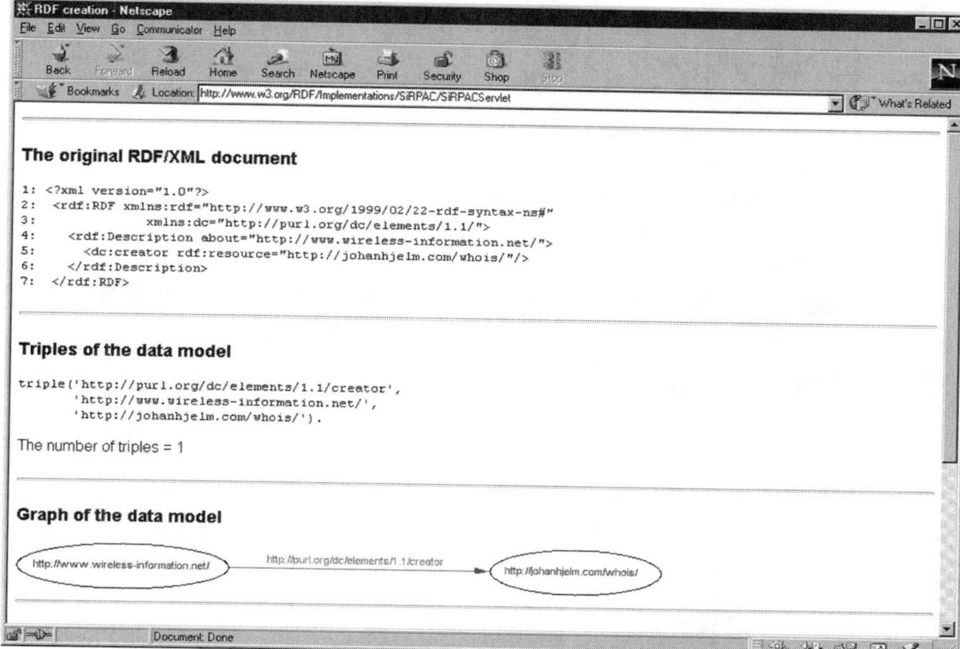

Figure 10.2 The resulting output from the SiRPAC demonstration online service.

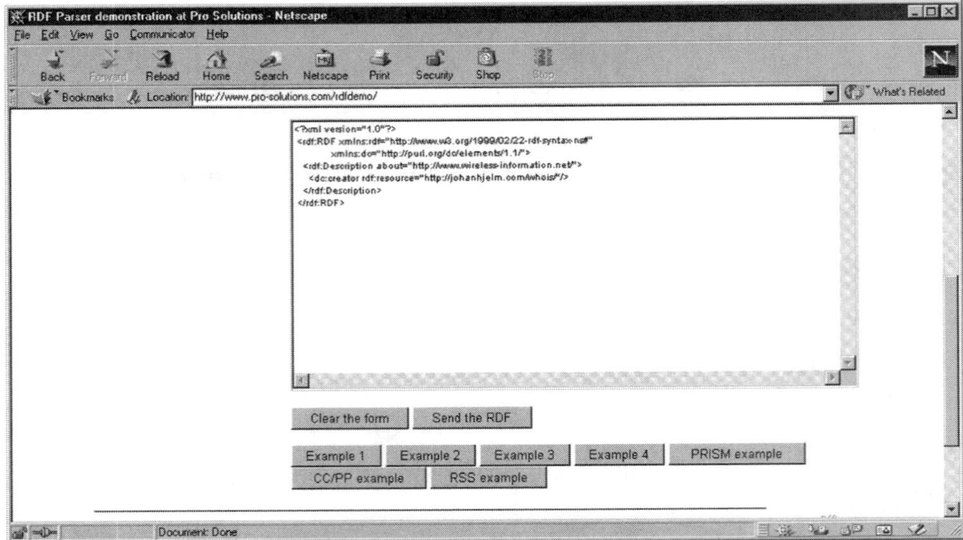

Figure 10.3 The input window of the ProSolutions RDF parser is very similar to that of SiRPAC.

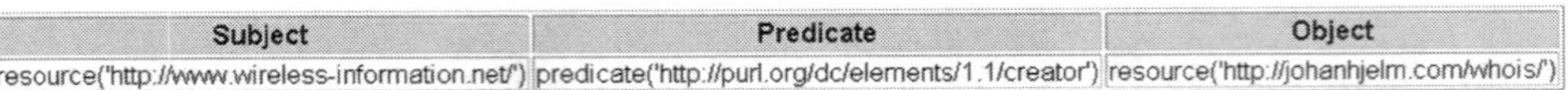

Subject	Predicate	Object
resource('http://www.wireless-information.net/')	predicate('http://purl.org/dc/elements/1.1/creator')	resource('http://johanhjelm.com/whois/')

Figure 10.4 The output from the ProSolutions demonstration system is divided into subject, predicate, and object.

The W3C RDF XSLT transformer is demonstrated online at www.w3.org/XML/2000/04rdf-parse/, as shown in Figure 10.5. It accepts only a URI as input. The service depends on an XSLT servlet that runs on an as-is, no-

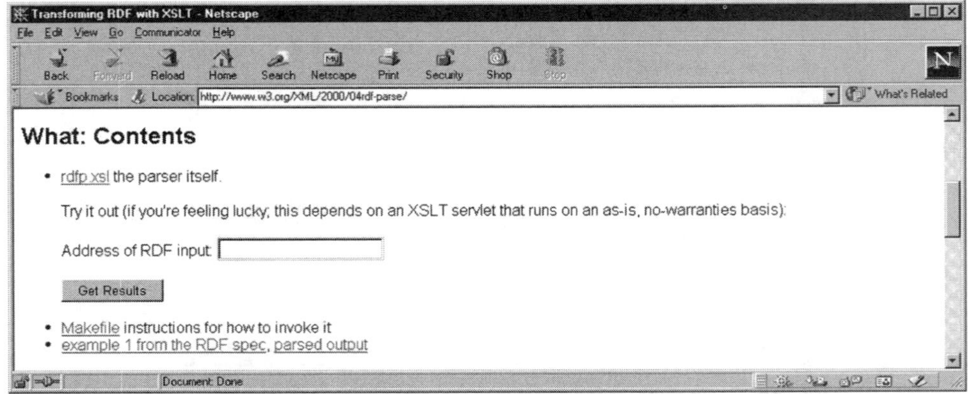

Figure 10.5 The input demonstration window for the XSLT RDF parser.

warranties basis. It currently has no support for collections, no support for quoted (reified) statements, and no support for parsetype="literal" nor parse-type= "resource."

RDF Database Interfaces

Database management systems are specialized at storing and retrieving (as a result of a query) data consisting of several fields that are interrelated in some way. This is a fair description of RDF triples, so it should come as no surprise that several systems attempt to harness database functionality for RDF data.

- **Algae (www.w3.org/1999/02/26-modules/).** *Algae* is a constraint-based query interface based on *algernon*. Aside from syntax, the principal difference between algae and algernon is that algae is not tied to an accessor (algernon assumes triples are accessed by subject only).

  The query consists of a series of constraints and a desired result set. It is used in the W3C Annotation server (as part of the database interface).
- **rdfDB (http://web1.guha.com/rdfdb/).** rdfDB Query Language is a database system for RDF that uses a SQL-like query language. The data is modeled as a directed labeled graph (RDF). Nodes in the graph can either be resources (written as URIs), integers, or strings. Other datatypes such as floats and dates will be implemented in later versions. All operations revolve around the concept of a "triple." A triple is intended to model the concept of a object with a property value. A collection of triples forms a database. There are no constraints on the set of triples that constitutes the database. (Some other RDF implementations refer to the concept of database as a "model"). It is also intended to be scalable, to handle millions of triples. A Java interface is available at http://4xt.org/downloads/JrdfDB/.
- **Redland RDF Application Framework (www.redland.opensource.ac.uk/).** Provides functions to store, query, and manipulate the data model; written in C; open source. Also contains the Rapier RDF parser **(www.redland.opensource.ac.uk/rapier/).**
- **The Web Resource Application Framework (WRAF) (http://uxn.nu/wraf/).** Uses RDF to describe all data in a Web fact system; reminiscent of a knowledge-management system.
- **RDF Schema editor (http://jonas.liljegren.org/perl/proj/rdf/schema_editor/).** A new version using PERL was produced as part of the WRAF project; open source.
- **Generic Interoperability Framework (GINF) (http://www-diglib.stanford.edu/diglib/ginf/).** From Stanford University; uses RDF as a

modeling language for the system. One use is interdataworking, a novel software structuring technique that facilitates data exchange between heterogeneous applications (www.interdataworking.com/converter/).

RDF APIs and Libraries

- **Jena (http://www-uk.hpl.hp.com/people/bwm/rdf/jena/index.htm).** An experimental Java API for manipulating RDF models. Its features include statement-centric methods for manipulating an RDF model as a set of RDF triples, resource-centric methods for manipulating an RDF model as a set of resources with properties, and cascading method calls for more convenient programming. It has built-in support for RDF containers and allows the application to extend the behavior of resources.
- **Redland (www.redland.opensource.ac.uk/).** A library that provides a high-level interface for RDF, allowing the model to be stored, queried, and manipulated. Redland implements each of the RDF model concepts in its own class, providing an object-based API for them. Some of the classes providing the parsers, storage mechanisms, and other elements are built as modules that can be added or removed as required. There is a modular object-based library written in C, as well as C, PERL, and Python interfaces for manipulating the RDF Model and parts: Statements, Resources and Literals. It includes parsers for reading RDF/XML and other syntaxes and handles storage for models in memory and on disk via Berkeley DB (SleepyCat). There are query APIs for the model by Statement (triples) or by Nodes and Arcs, and Statement Streams for construction, parsing, and de/serialization of models.
- **RDF Crawler (http://ontobroker.semanticweb.org/rdfcrawl/index.html).** A Java-based tool/API which downloads interconnected fragments of RDF from the Internet and builds a knowledge base from them; uses SiRPAC (W3C or Stanford version), GNU Java regex, Xerces/XML4J (all included).
- **RDFStore (http://xml.jrc.it/RDFStore/).** A PERL API for RDF Storage; PERL TIE seamless access to RDF triplet databases; supports either DB_File or BerkeleyDB support; automatic vocabulary generation and basic RDF Schema support.
- **XSLT extractor for RDF from Xlink (www.openhealth.org/RDF/rdfExtractify.xsl).** An XSL template that is run through an XSL processor to generate RDF from XML.
- **DataCraft (www.alphaworks.ibm.com/tech/DataCraft).** Creates XML/RDF views of databases and enables queries on those databases using

RDF Requires IBM's XML for Java libraries and a Web browser with Java and Swing (www.alphaworks.ibm.com/tech/xml).

- **CARA (http://cara.sourceforge.net/).** An RDF API written in PERL, based on the graph model of RDF; supports in-memory and persistent storage of RDF graphs. An RDF Parser is included in the API.

RDF Editors

- **Reggie: The Metadata Editor (http://metadata.net/dstc/).** Developed to enable the easy creation of various forms of metadata with one flexible program. As it stands, the Reggie applet can create metadata using the HTML 3.2 standard, the HTML 4.0 standard, the RDF format and the RDF Abbreviated format. The Reggie Metadata Editor uses a schema file (in its own format) to read in the details of all the elements in a set, their characteristics, and their descriptions. To create metadata based on a different element set or a different language, one simply needs to create a new schema file. The editor is an applet for the Web browser, Internet Explorer version 5 or Netscape version 6.
- **DC Dot (www.ukoln.ac.uk/metadata/dcdot/).** This service will retrieve a Web page and automatically generate Dublin Core metadata, either as HTML `<meta>` tags or as RDF/XML, suitable for embedding in the `<head>...</head>` section of the page. The generated metadata can be edited using the form provided and converted to various other formats (USMARC, SOIF, IAFA/ROADS, TEI headers, GILS, IMS, or RDF) if required. Optional, context-sensitive help is available while editing. DC Dot now extracts metadata from Microsoft Word and PowerPoint files as well as HTML Web pages.
- **S-Link-S Editor/Publisher (www.openly.com/SLinkS/Editor.html).** A Java application that publishers can use to author and publish metadata to facilitate journal hyperlinking using S-Link-S. The metadata is saved using RDF Syntax. You can use this application to publish your metadata into the S-Link-S Hyperlinking system.
- **RDF Schema editor (http://jonas.liljegren.org/perl/proj/rdf/schema_editor/).** An experimental prototype, written in PERL, for viewing, editing, and navigating in RDF data, based on RDF Schema. It has subsequently been integrated in the WRAF project. The Schema layer contains all logic and functions specific to the RDF Schema Specification. To get only the functions for the RDF Model andSyntax Specification, use the constructor in the `Simple::Model` class. The Schema and Simple layers are programmed to not know anything about the storage of the RDF

data. They use the methods in the Source layer, using the specified source class.

- **RDFPic (**http://jigsaw.w3.org/rdfpic/**).** The data-entry program has been implemented in Java; a specific Jigsaw frame has been used to retrieve the RDF from the image through HTTP. The RDF schema uses the Dublin Core schema as well as additional schemata for technical data projects for describing and retrieving (digitized) photos with (RDF) metadata. It describes the RDF schemata, a data-entry program for quickly entering metadata for large numbers of photos, a way to serve the photos and the metadata over HTTP, and some suggestions for search methods to retrieve photos based on their descriptions.
- **GraMToR (http://nestroy.wi-inf.uni-essen.de/xwmf/downloads/GraMToR-0.5-12.tar.gz).** A graphical editor for interactively constructing an RDF data model. The graphical representation can be serialized to XML-RDF syntax. Additionally, the data model can be serialized in triple notation. GraMToR is able to store an RDF data model in one of three ways: Files with the extension .rdf contain XML-RDF syntax, .fmr contain triple notation, and .brm contain triple notation with additional position information for the corresponding graphical RDF representation.
- **Protégé (www.smi.stanford.edu/projects/protege/).** From Stanford University; provides an integrated knowledge-base editing environment and an extensible architecture for the creation of customized knowledge-based tools; can generate RDF.
- **Mozilla (www.mozilla.org/releases/).** Probably the most widespread implementation of RDF, but very few people know this. Documentation of how Mozilla uses RDF can be found at www.mozilla.org/rdf/doc/.
- **Metabrowser (http://metabrowser.spirit.net.au/).** A Web browser with a metadata editor that lets you annotate pages with metadata and send them to a database.

Inference Engines and Logic Systems

- **Metalog (www.w3.org/RDF/Metalog/).** A next-generation query system for metadata based on RDF. It is composed of two major layers.

  The first layer consists of an enrichment of the RDF model. Metalog provides a way to express logical relationships like *and*, *or*, and so on, and to build up complex inference rules that encode logical reasoning. This "semantic layer" builds on top of RDF using RDF Schema.

  The second layer consists of a "logical interpretation" of RDF data (optionally enriched with the semantic schema) into logic. This way, the understood semantic of RDF is unwound into its logical components. This means that every reasoning on RDF data can be performed by acting upon the corresponding logical view, providing a neat and powerful way to reason about data. We call this level of reasoning the Metalog logic level.

The third layer is a language interface for writing structured data and reasoning rules. In principle, the first component already suffices: data and rules can be written directly in RDF, using RDF syntax and the Metalog schema. However, this is not convenient from the practical viewpoint. Indeed, RDF syntax aims to be more of an encoding language than a user-friendly language, and it is well recognized in the RDF community and among vendors that typical applications will provide more user-friendly interfaces between the "raw RDF" code and the user. The proposed language is innovative in that it tries to stress user-friendliness as much as possible: a program is a collection of natural language assertions.

- **Euler proof mechanism (ftp://windsor.agfa.be/outgoing/RCEI/NET/euler/index.html).** The facts and rules are acquired from the Web and translated into a kind of logic program. The proof engine follows only Euler paths (the concept Euler found several hundred years ago) so that endless deductions are avoided. That means that no special attention has to be paid to recursions or to graph merging.
- **Protégé (www.smi.stanford.edu/projects/protege/whatis.html).** A tool which allows the user to construct a domain ontology, customize knowledge-acquisition forms, and enter domain knowledge. It is a platform which can be extended with graphical widgets for tables, diagrams, and animation, and components to access other knowledge-based systems, as well as embedded applications; there is also a library which other applications can use to access and display knowledge bases.
- **SiLRI (Simple Logic-based RDF Interpreter) (www.ontoprise.de/download/silri.htm).** SiLRI is a main-memory logic-based inference engine implemented in Java. It implements a major part of Frame-Logic and has support for RDF. The implementation includes well-founded semantics and the rule language allows general logic programs, enabling specification-like modeling; based on SiRPAC.
- **Semantic Index System (SIS) (www.ics.forth.gr/proj/isst/).** A tool for describing and documenting large evolving varieties of highly interrelated data, concepts, and complex relationships, as opposed to large homogeneous populations in fixed formats (handled by traditional DBMSs).
- **OilEd (http://img.cs.man.ac.uk/oil/).** A simple ontology editor which allows the user to build ontologies using OIL. Not intended as a full ontology development environment, but rather the "NotePad" of ontology editors, offering just enough functionality to allow users to build

ontologies and to demonstrate the use of the FaCT reasoner to check those ontologies for consistency.

Vocabularies for Metainformation

Just as grammar alone does not make a language, so a metadata system does not work without vocabularies. RDF is an open format, and it is possible for basically anyone to create a schema and provide a vocabulary. Below are some of those I have found (not necessarily in RDF). The first three are resources, rather than vocabularies.

- **W3C Platform for Internet Content Selection (PICS) (www.w3.org/PICS/).**
- **Dublin Core home pages (http://purl.org/DC/).**
- **The Ontology Inference Layer (OIL) home pages with further links (www.ontoknowledge.org/oil/).**
- **PICS Rating Vocabularies in XML/RDF (www.w3.org/TR/rdf-pics).** Dan Brickley, Ralph R. Swick; W3C Note March 27, 2000.
- **RDF Site Summary (RSS) 1.0 (http://groups.yahoo.com/group/rss-dev/files/specification.html).** Gabe Beged-Dov, Dan Brickley, Rael Dornfest, Ian Davis, Leigh Dodds, Jonathan Eisenzopf, David Galbraith, R.V. Guha, Ken MacLeod, Eric Miller, Aaron Swartz, Eric van der Vlist; December 19, 2000.
- **Guidance on expressing the Dublin Core within the Resource Description Framework (RDF) (www.ukoln.ac.uk/metadata/resources/dc/datamodel/WD-dc-rdf/).** Eric Miller, Paul Miller, and Dan Brickley; July 1, 1999.
- **Document Content Description for XML (www.w3.org/TR/NOTE-dcd).** Tim Bray, Charles Frankston, Ashok Malhotra; submission to the World Wide Web Consortium, July 31, 1998.
- **CERES/NBII Thesaurus Partnership Project (http://ceres.ca.gov/thesaurus/).** For information on biological resources.
- **Representing PSL as XML (www.mel.nist.gov/psl/xml/).** The Process Specification Language (PSL) is a language to create descriptions of production processes. Josh Lutbell; September 1, 1999.
- **VCard in RDF (www.dstc.edu.au/Research/Projects/rdf/draft-iannella-vcard-rdf-00.txt).** Renato Ianella; January 1, 1999.
- The University of Essen gave a class in 1998 that modeled different aspects of a Web site in RDF. The documentation and information is all in German, but there are schemas (in a weird notation, but understandable) for the following:

  - **Access control (http://nestroy.wi-inf.uni-essen.de/xwmf/ps_ws9899/accesscontrol/accesscontrol.brm)**
  - **Maintenance (http://nestroy.wi-inf.uni-essen.de/xwmf/ps_ws9899/maintenance/maintenance.brm)**
  - **Layout (http://nestroy.wi-inf.uni-essen.de/xwmf/ps_ws9899/style/download/style.brm)**
  - **Navigation aspects (http://nestroy.wi-inf.uni-essen.de/xwmf/ps_ws9899/xlink/NCNew.brm)**
  - **Site structure (http://nestroy.wi-inf.uni-essen.de/xwmf/ps_ws9899/webpage_alt/webpage.brm)**
- **User Agent Profile (UAProf) (http://www1.wapforum.org/tech/documents/WAP-174-UAProf-19991110-a.pdf).** A vocabulary developed by the WAP Forum to describe a WAP terminal.
- **MusicBrainz Metadata initiative (http://musicbrainz.org/MM/).** A content description model for audio and video tracks on the Internet, designed to create a portable and flexible means of storing and exchanging metadata related to digital audio and video tracks.
- **WordNet in RDF (www.semanticweb.org/library/).** An online lexical reference system, where the nouns, verbs, adjectives and adverbs of English are organized into synonym sets, each representing one underlying lexical concept. Different relations link the synonym sets (since it is a number of large files, it is easier to select from there).
- The North American Electric Reliability Council (NERC) recommends that utilities use RDF together with schemata called EPRI CIM. The ontology used is available from cim-logic (www.cim-logic.com/cim-rdf/); more pointers from (www.langdale.com.au/XMLCIM.html).
- **Harvesting RDF Statements from Xlinks (www.w3.org/TR/2000/NOTE-xlink2rdf-20000929/).** Ron Daniel, Jr.; W3C Note September 29, 2000. Since both Xlink and RDF describe ways that resources are related (albeit for different purposes), data from one can be used in the other.
- **XMLtree (www.xmltree.com/).** A directory of who serves up XML content on the Web. As long as there are few enough to fit into the directory, it works.

Index

C

D

K

L

M

N

O

P

Q

R

CUSTOMER NOTE: IF THIS BOOK IS ACCOMPANIED BY SOFTWARE, PLEASE READ THE FOLLOWING BEFORE OPENING THE PACKAGE.

This software contains files to help you utilize the models described in the accompanying book. By opening the package, you are agreeing to be bound by the following agreement:

This software product is sold as is without warranty of any kind, either express or implied, including but not limited to the implied warranty of merchantability and fitness for a particular purpose. Neither Wiley nor its dealers or distributors assumes any liability for any alleged or actual damages arising from the use of or the inability to use this software. (Some states do not allow the exclusion of implied warranties, so the exclusion may not apply to you.)